T0389100

Medical Innovation and Disease Burden

Striking the right balance between public health priorities and medical innovation is a critical policy challenge for India, given their mutually conflicting nature and interests. On the one hand, the country has an expanding health industry with a strong presence of domestic and multinational private firms. The sector, with enormous state facilitation, could effectively position itself as the future engine of economic growth by rearranging itself to the new intellectual property and trade regimes. On the other hand, India has a huge burden of diseases implicated by a gamut of public health problems, including the uneven distribution of demographic and epidemiological transition, threat of new infectious diseases like COVID-19, increasing privatisation of healthcare, inadequately regulated pharmaceutical market, low affordability of life-saving medicines and, most importantly, escalating out-of-pocket healthcare expenditure coupled with poor financial risk protection. All these make the Indian healthscape not only diverse but also exceedingly complex. Given these, the central question that the book addresses is whether medical innovation in India is sensitive to public health needs and priorities. The book unearths a number of overriding issues related to responsiveness and equity in India's health innovation and highlights the need for a responsible innovation framework for India that balances the priorities of public health and industry goals.

Sobin George teaches at the Institute for Social and Economic Change, Bengaluru. His areas of research and writings are marginalities, social gradients of health, medical industry and labour rights.

Medical Innovation and Disease Burden

Conflicting Priorities and the Social Divide in India

Sobin George

CAMBRIDGE
UNIVERSITY PRESS

University Printing House, Cambridge CB2 8BS, United Kingdom

One Liberty Plaza, 20th Floor, New York, NY 10006, USA

477 Williamstown Road, Port Melbourne, vic 3207, Australia

314 to 321, 3rd Floor, Plot No.3, Splendor Forum, Jasola District Centre, New Delhi 110025, India

79 Anson Road, #06–04/06, Singapore 079906

Cambridge University Press is part of the University of Cambridge.

It furthers the University's mission by disseminating knowledge in the pursuit of education, learning and research at the highest international levels of excellence.

www.cambridge.org
Information on this title: www.cambridge.org/9781108832304

© Sobin George 2021

First published 2021

Printed in India by Thomson Press India Ltd.

A catalogue record for this publication is available from the British Library

Library of Congress Cataloging-in-Publication Data
Names: George, Sobin, author.
Title: Medical innovation and disease burden : conflicting priorities and the social divide in India / Sobin George.
Description: Cambridge, United Kingdom ; New York, NY : Cambridge University Press, 2021. | Includes bibliographical references and index.
Identifiers: LCCN 2020049872 (print) | LCCN 2020049873 (ebook) | ISBN 9781108832304 (hardback) | ISBN 9781108935838 (ebook)
Subjects: LCSH: Public health--India. | Medical care--India. | Equality--Health aspects--India. | Health services accessibility--India. | Medical innovations--India.
Classification: LCC RA529 .G46 2021 (print) | LCC RA529 (ebook) | DDC 362.10954--dc23
LC record available at https://lccn.loc.gov/2020049872
LC ebook record available at https://lccn.loc.gov/2020049873

ISBN 978-1-108-83230-4 Hardback

Contents

Tables

Figures

Acknowledgements

This research project is financially supported by the Indian Council of Social Science Research (ICSSR), New Delhi, and the Institute of Social and Economic Change (ISEC), Bengaluru. I received immense support from faculty members, library staff and administrative staff at ISEC to complete this study. I particularly thank Professor K. S. James, Professor M. G. Chandrakanth and Professor S. Madheswaran.

Apurva K. H. has helped to extract and compile the data on sales, export, income and research and development (R&D) of pharmaceutical firms from CMIE Prowess and the product focus of these firms from respective websites of the companies, which have been used in Chapters 1 and 2. I thank her for this valuable research support. I thank Ramya P. who helped to extract data from the WHO repository and from the database of the Central Drugs Standard Control Organisation, New Delhi. I also thank Arun B. Chandran for helping me organise the data on medical expenditure from the NSSO 71st round data. Discussions with Omkar Nadh helped me understand the medical technology ecosystem in India and the organisation of production in the sector. I have drawn from the works of Reji K. Joseph, and E. Differding on the pharmaceutical industry in India and drug discovery. I am grateful to Mohammed Saalim, Aditi Paranjpe and Abdul Raoof for their help in different stages of this work.

I thank B. B. Chand and Pradeep Hegde, librarians of ISEC, and Shailaja Prabhakar at the Centre for the Study of Social Change and Development, ISEC, Bengaluru, for their assistance with library materials and data management. Finally, I thank Anwesha Rana, Associate Commissioning

Editor of Cambridge University Press (CUP), and the publication team of CUP, especially Aniruddha De, Senior Production Editor, for their timely interventions, excellent copyediting and help all through this publication project.

Abbreviations

ABLE	Association of Biotechnology Led Enterprises
AIIMS	All India Institute of Medical Sciences
AYUSH	Ayurveda, yoga, naturopathy, Unani, Siddha and homoeopathy
BIRAC	Biotechnology Industry Research Assistance Council
CAGR	compound annual growth rates
CDC	Centre for Disease Control
CDs	communicable diseases
CDSCO	Central Drugs Standard Control Organisation
CMIE	Centre for Monitoring of Indian Economy
CRO	contract research organisations
CVD	cardiovascular diseases
DAH	development assistance for health
DNA	deoxyribonucleic acid
DSIR	Department of Scientific and Industrial Research
DST	Department of Science and Technology
DTaP	diphtheria, tetanus and pertussis
ETEC	enterotoxigenic *Escherichia coli*
ETL	epidemiological transition level
FDA	Food and Drug Administration
FICCI	Federation of Indian Chambers of Commerce and Industry
HPV	human pappiloma virus
ICMR	Indian Council of Medical Research
IFPMA	International Federation of Pharmaceutical Manufacturers and Associations
IHME	Institute for Health Metrics and Evaluation

IIFT	Indian Institute of Foreign Trade
IIL	Indian Immunologicals Limited
IIS	Indian Institute of Sciences
IPR	intellectual property rights
MMR	measles, mumps and rubella
MNCs	multinational corporations
MPCE	monthly per capita expenditure
MRI	magnetic resonance imaging
NCDs	non-communicable diseases
NCEs	new chemical entities
NIH	National Institute of Health
NLEM	National List of Essential Medicines
NPPA	National Pharmaceutical Pricing Authority
NSSO	National Sample Survey Organisation
OECD	Organisation for Economic Co-operation and Development
OOP	out-of-pocket
PHFI	Public Health Foundation of India
R&D	research and development
RPRC	Regional Plant Resource Centre
STI	Science, Technology and Innovation
TRIPS	Trade-related Aspects of Intellectual Property Rights
VBP	value-based pricing
VC	venture capital
VRV	vero rabies vaccine
WHO	World Health Organization
WTO	World Trade Organization
YLL	years of life lost

Introduction

The Coronavirus disease 2019 (COVID 19) pandemic has posed fresh challenges pertaining to the prevention, control and management of infectious diseases in the medical innovation landscape all over the world. Although the emergence and resurgence of communicable diseases have been serious health concerns, especially for poor regions and populations across the globe, these diseases did not receive adequate attention in medical innovations due to various political economy reasons and their confinement to limited (poor) regions. For instance, we have seen outbreaks of Ebola haemorrhagic fever in African countries, cholera in African and Asian countries, dengue haemorrhagic fever in India and other South Asian countries, Japanese encephalitis in India and Nepal, and influenza and malaria in African and South Asian countries in the recent past that perhaps did not receive sufficient attention of the vaccine, drug or medical equipment industry. Similarly, the worldwide severe acute respiratory syndrome (SARS) outbreak in 2002 and the Zika virus epidemic in 2016 also did not significantly change the priorities of medical innovations, which are mostly concerned with non-communicable diseases. However, the COVID 19 pandemic has exposed the lack of preparedness to emerging communicable disease problems across the world and compelled us to revisit the threat of communicable diseases in a globalised world since the infection changed the prevailing risk perceptions by crossing the binaries of rich and poor and exposing the entire humanity to infection. The COVID 19 pandemic thus poses certain questions on the epistemological base of the present organisation of medical innovation, which is built around the principles of techno-scientific capitalism and setting of priorities in medical innovation. This book attempts to discuss the mismatch between public health priorities and medical innovations which can have implications for the health of the global population in the future.

The last four decades have witnessed several path-breaking innovations in healthcare, particularly in drugs, vaccines and medical technologies. Advancements made in the research in health and life sciences across the world have played a conspicuous role in medical innovations. The proliferation of biotechnology and its associated streams of biomedicine, bioinformatics, genomics and advancements made in the field of synthetic biology have widened the scope of medical innovations to the next level. The competitive market regime, product patent protection and the facilitating policy environments in several countries for entrepreneurial research, especially for the patenting of publicly funded research outputs and the academia–industry collaborations, have indeed contributed to this new wave of biomedical research in many parts of the world. One of the major developments in the course of these changes and advancements in healthcare research and development (R&D) was the near complete dominance of the private sector and the emergence of venture capital as the most important players in health research funding. Along with these developments, there has been a sharp decline in the share of public funding in health R&D except for the research on neglected diseases, which is usually carried out through health departments, universities and research institutes.

Needless to say, innovations in healthcare have substantially contributed to the control, cure and management of diseases. Laal (2012: 471) listed out drugs including penicillin, aspirin, insulin, oral contraceptive, vaccination, statins, smart pill and Viagra in the group of innovative drugs; technologies including electrocardiography, X-ray, nano-healing, electric health records, laser surgery, MRI (magnetic resonance imaging), ultrasound, organ transplant; and devices including artificial hearts, robotic catheter, handheld medical scanner, bone injector drill, dialysis machine, lens implants, artificial joints and skin antennas as the major medical innovations. It is true that the human genome discoveries have opened up enormous possibilities in medical science. The human genome project has opened up what scholars noted as the 'post genomic era' that expanded the scope of medical innovation in personalised medicine, risk prediction and its management. Similarly, stem cell research, targeted therapies for cancer and combinational drug therapy for HIV (human immunodeficiency virus) survival were also significant innovations in healthcare. For instance, institutions such as the Harvard Medical School did pioneering research in the areas of cancer diagnosis and therapy, vaccines for diphtheria, causative features of Alzheimer's disease and its treatment, multiple organ replanting, identification of pathway linked to cartilage deterioration and bone attrition of rheumatoid arthritis, prediction of the chances of heart diseases, production of functional blood cells for the growth and regenerative therapy of skin and several internal organs, vaccines for herpes that stimulate the immune system from inside host cells, DNA-sequencing technologies for risk prediction of certain diseases, new cancer drugs targeting proteins that support survival of cancer cells, risk prediction of kidney failure in diabetic patients, RNA signature pathogens to determine best treatment options for infectious diseases, identification of a substance that thickens heart muscles often leading to heart failure, potential new therapies for osteoporosis, and vaccines to protect transmission of Zika virus from animals to humans, to list a major few.[1]

Such laboratory researches have contributed immensely to drug, vaccine and medical technology development through successful academia–industry collaborations. However, the increasing thrust of academia–industry collaborations in medical innovations and the rigorous commercialisation of innovations raise several crucial public health questions as well. Who decides the priorities of innovation and what are the considerations that go into the disease/health focus and target groups of these innovations? Do these innovations really add value to healthcare? Who are the beneficiaries of these innovations? Does it lead to social inequalities? Do such technologies lead to medicalisation/pharmaceuticalisation and, if so, who bears the burden more? What are the new discourses of health that these technologies bring in?

Fuchs and Sox (2001) identified thirty major innovations in the recent past from the original articles published in the *Journal of the American Medical Association* and the *New England Journal of Medicine* as part of their study on the views of practitioners on medical innovations. Practitioners who participated in the study considered MRI and computed tomographic (CT) scanning, ACE (angiotensin-converting enzyme) inhibitors, balloon angioplasty, statins and mammography as the major five innovations in terms of their usefulness. The least significant five innovations for them

---

1   Based on the 'timeline of discovery', available at https://hms.harvard.edu/about-hms/history-hms/timeline-discovery, accessed on 20 November 2019.

were bone marrow transplant, non-sedating antihistamines, sildenafil (Viagra), IV-conscious sedation and calcium channel blockers. These rankings may be questionable since they are conducted in a particular healthscape and are largely based on the experiences and perceptions of practitioners; however, the significance of the larger questions on the public-health relevance of medical innovations remains. Apart from the questions of their usefulness and probable contributions to population health, innovations in pharmaceutical and biopharmaceutical sectors across the world generated considerable scholarly attention for several reasons. Scholarly engagement on medical innovations dealt with a wide range of issues including their epistemological shifts, political economy, co-production and implications on access, affordability and the medicalisation of body and society (see Waldby 2002; Rose 2007; Clarke et al. 2009; Cooper 2011; Birch and Tyfield 2013). Among others, one of the compelling analyses was on the well-established interconnectedness of science and technology and capitalism (Levins and Lewontin 1985). Singer (1992) elaborated the observations of Levins and Lewontin (1985) on the interconnectedness between science and capitalism which is quoted here

> ... by the mid-point of the 20th century, science itself had become a commodity on a massive scale with the following characteristics: (1) research has become a business investment; (2) scientific discovery has become quantifiable (enabling an estimation of associated costs and benefits of investment and economically based investment decisions); (3) scientists have become 'scientific personnel' with associated proletarianization, loss of control and rational management; and (4) scientific labour must itself be produced, with the expectation that university training must be cost efficient. (Singer 1992: 400)

The *commodification* of science has also led to setting the priorities of research on a large scale as 'research itself has become a business investment' (Levins and Lewontin 1985). There is a growing literature on the political economy as well as bio-political economy of medical innovations in general and biomedical technology and life sciences in particular and the way through which such technologies can lead to patient–customer *subjectification* in advanced capitalistic societies. Waldby

(2002) by introducing the concept of *biovalue* attempted to understand the linkages between biotechnology, life science and capitalism, drawing from both Marxian notions of value and Michel Foucault's concept of *biopolitics*. The linkage of modern day capitalism and biomedical research and innovations in healthcare was extended by Rajan (2006) in his work on *biocapital and the constitution of post genomic life* by carefully invoking the Marxian political economy and Foucault's concepts of *biopower* and *biopolitics* together. He illustrated how the new knowledge base of medical innovations triggered by the advancements made in biomedical research and new technology develops a *technocapitalistic* paradigm of healthcare, which tends to shift the notions of health to risk management and simultaneously construct a new genre of patient–consumer subjects, which he called the 'patients-in-waiting'. He attributed it to the 'co-production of the market, state, and technology with their strategies, agents and policy institutions'. Birch and Tyfield (2013), however, did not view concepts such as *biovalue, biocapital* and *biopower* as something not entirely different from the Marxist framework of value of labour. They argued that *biovalue* is nothing but knowledge value, which is produced or co-produced, exchanged and circulated with several processes and institutions. Hence, for them 'there is nothing intrinsically valuable or capitalist about natural or biological materials without a number of supporting economic and extra economic processes and institutions' (Birch and Tyfield 2013: 313). Despite this disagreement on the formulations of 'bioconcepts' they also recognised the power of the (bio)knowledge economy to shift the social deterministic model of health and well-being to biomedical reductionism and individualised care.

Several studies attempted to understand the epistemic shift that the *technocapitalistic* biomedical paradigm brings about in the domain of health as well as the nature of capital and its strategies of circulation, co-production, accumulation and *subjectification* of patients/consumers (Jasanoff 2004; Rose 2007; Clarke et al. 2009; Cooper 2011; Birch and Tyfield 2013; Strasser 2014; Rajan 2017; Stevens and Newman 2019). Rose (2007), invoking the concept of *biopolitics*, elaborated how biomedical epistemologies project a 'molecular self', which ensembles body as a collection of several parts and micro cells that could be viewed and approached separately. He argues that the epistemological base of biomedicine is nothing but biomedical reductionism, which essentially endeavours to shift the 'corporeal self' to 'molecular self'. This molecular view of self opens possibilities for a wide landscape of innovations that can customise bodily appearances, redefine normalcy, medicalise body, predict risks and manage risks. Clarke et al. (2009) argued that the advancements in the 'technoscientific innovation', organisation and practice of biomedicine led to the 'biomedicalisation' of society in countries such as the United States (US). They explained the processes of biomedicalisation in the US and the epistemological shift that has come along with biomedicalisation and the processes through which it got consolidated, hegemonised and legitimised in the US. The increased focus on health risk and surveillance in the biomedical paradigm shifted the approach of healthcare to 'treatment of risk', which for them (Clarke et al. 2009) commodifies health and lifestyles. It also led to customisation of health with the focus on individualised medicines and technologies. The coming up of biomedical organisations, privatisation of research projects and the university–industry collaborations, technologies to zero in on to individualised traits and division of the population based on such attributes were also part of the processes of biomedicalisation (Clarke et al. 2009) that opened up the commercial frontiers of this discipline. They also explained the processes of 'technoscientisation of biomedicine' with the help of bioengineering, nanoscience, bioinformatics, genetic engineering, and so on. Another integral part of biomedicalisation is its normalisation and legitimisation with the proliferation of knowledge and information on the possibilities of biomedicine to the masses through various channels of communication. The latest contribution of medical sociology and anthropology, which attempted to expand our knowledge on the linkages of technology, capitalism and social control, is 'pharmaceuticalisation' (Abraham 2010; Williams et al. 2011). The concept of pharmaceuticalisation is invoked in medical sociology literature to explain the expansive efforts of pharmaceutical companies through the network of state, private institutions, media and other influential agencies. William et al. (2011) explained the major processes of pharmaceuticalisation such as 'reconfiguration of health problems as pharmaceutical solutions, mobilisation of patients or consumer groups around drugs, the use of drugs for non-medical purposes and the creation of new consumer markets and drug innovation and colonisation of health futures', among others.

For Cooper (2011) the epistemological shift that biomedicine and *biocapitalism* strive to bring in the notions of health is its technological innateness which sees 'life as a technological creation'. Using a Marxist political economy framework, she discussed the knowledge base, processes and actors behind the emergence of *biocapitalism* with the biotechnology revolution, its nature, reproduction and accumulative powers. She has illustrated how value creation and circulation happen in the life sciences with the integration of the latter into speculative markets and translation into marketable commodities.

In short, there is a general agreement that global health research views health as a technical response to disease instead of contextualising health within a social context. Thus global health research is involved in biomedical research that focuses on technological innovation rather than always directing research and policies towards the health needs of the population. This emphasis highlights the change in social relations and the behaviour of the state, business and people at large.

Medical innovations and public health priorities

Public health priorities of medical innovations have been a critical question in the scholarship of science and technology. It is already illustrated that infectious diseases are less prioritised in health R&D worldwide (Viergever 2013; George et al. 2018). The Global Observatory on Health R&D of the World Health Organization (WHO) provides the recent trend in global health R&D and innovation. The WHO Global Observatory data show that only 13 per cent of the global ongoing clinical trials are for communicable diseases (see Figure I.1). Data on R&D funding for neglected diseases provided by G-Finder (https://www.policycuresresearch.org) show that the major part of the funding for infectious diseases comes from the public sector, bilateral institutions and philanthropies. As per these data, the private sector contributed only 16 per cent of the global funding for neglected diseases of which the major part of the investments was from multinational companies. The data further show that HIV/AIDS (human immunodeficiency virus/acquired immunodeficiency syndrome) received nearly 35 per cent of global funding for neglected diseases in 2017. Within that 56 per cent was for the research on developing preventive vaccines of HIV.

Malaria and tuberculosis received 17 per cent and diarrhoeal diseases received 5 per cent of the total funds.

Nearly 72 per cent of the ongoing clinical trials are for non-communicable diseases (NCDs) (see Figure I.1). Within NCDs there is an added focus on oncology R&D worldwide which does not match the public health need of many countries including India where cardiovascular diseases (CVDs) were the major causes of morbidity and mortality among NCDs (Dandona et al. 2017; Milne and Katin 2019). For instance, the data on registered clinical trials across the world available on the WHO Global Observatory show that out of the 175,848 registered clinical trials as of January 2019, nearly 37 per cent were for oncology (see data for different types of cancers given in Figure I.2). CVDs, on the other hand, constituted only 9 per cent of the global clinical trial. The WHO data also show that the preventive focus of global healthcare R&D is too little. For instance, the data show that nearly 92 per cent of the ongoing global R&D was for drug development whereas the share of vaccines was nearly 6 per cent (see Figure I.3). The regional distribution of global healthcare R&D is also important in this context to understand the priorities of healthcare R&D. As it is clear from Figure I.4, Europe and North America together dominate the R&D innovations in healthcare with a share of nearly 59 per cent. Across countries, the US dominates with a share of nearly 23 per cent of the global ongoing R&D, followed by Japan (7.8 per cent), China (6.6 per cent), Germany (6.5 per cent) and United Kingdom (UK) (6.1 per cent).

Figure I.1   Number of products in pipeline by health category

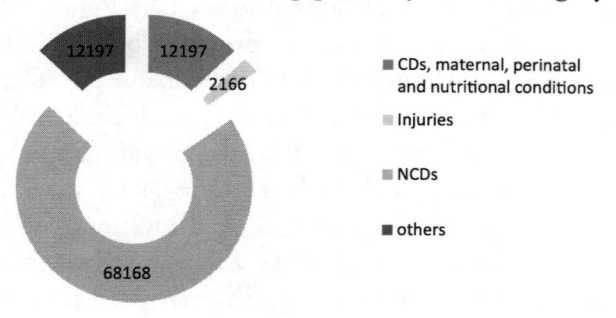

Source: WHO Global Observatory on Health R&D (data as of January 2019).

Figure I.2   Global clinical trial by disease or condition

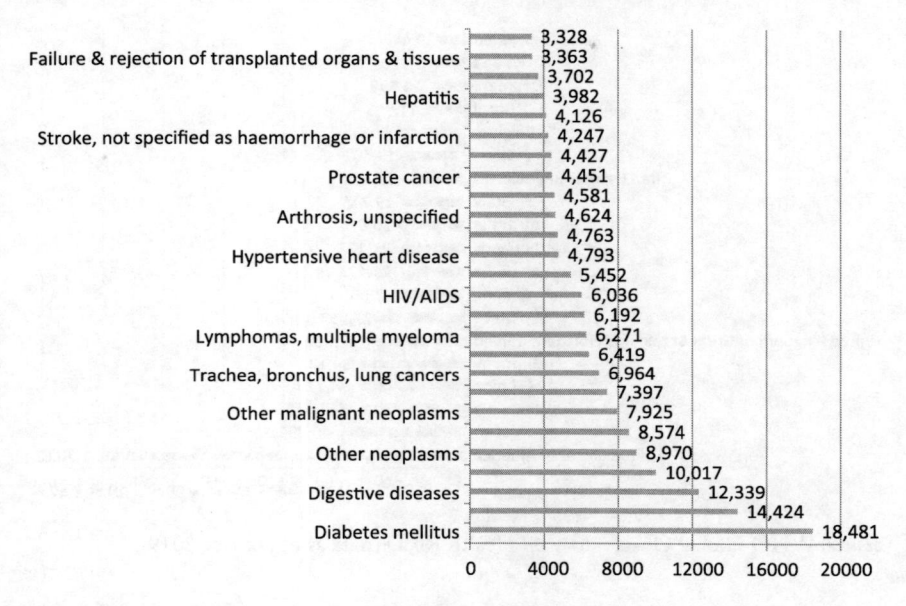

Source: WHO Global Observatory on Health R&D (data as of January 2019).

Figure I.3   Type of health products in the pipeline from discovery to market launch for all diseases

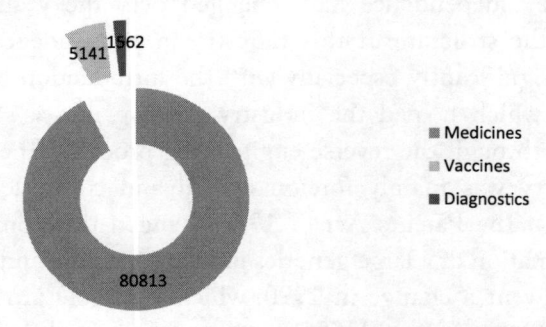

Source: WHO Global Observatory on Health R&D (data as of January 2019).

Figure I.4   Clinical trials by major country as of 2018

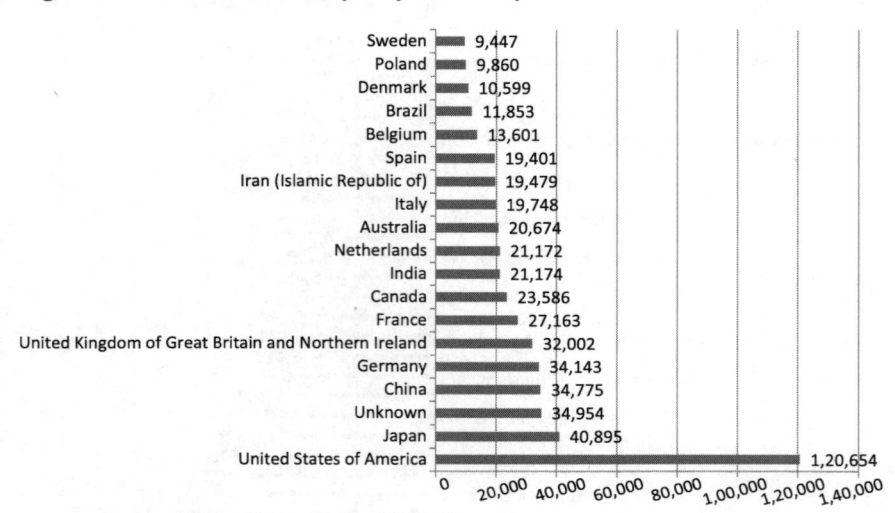

Source: WHO Global Observatory on Health R&D (data as of January 2019).

Health R&D in India

The pharmaceutical/biopharmaceutical sector is one of the fastest growing industrial segments in India. The structure and the composition of the industry since independence have changed over the years. As already well known, the structure of this industry in post-independence India has changed significantly, especially with the introduction of the Patents Act of 1970 which helped the industry develop into a strong generic manufacturer through the reverse engineering process.[2] The composition of the industry was mainly foreign owned and controlled until 1970 (Joseph 2016). The Patents Act of 1970 changed this composition and led to the formation of a large generics industry in India and the structure further underwent a change in 1990, which is largely attributed to the World Trade Organization (WTO) agreement on Trade-related Aspects of Intellectual Property Rights (TRIPs) (Joseph 2012). The post-product intellectual property rights (IPR) regime, however, has taken away this significant advantage that India had. The policy reforms placed the Indian

---

[2]   For a discussion, see Grace (2004), Dhar and Gopakumar (2011) and Mondal and Pingali (2017).

pharmaceutical industry in the open general license category by removing restrictions on foreign players (Joseph 2016). The country's patent laws had to comply with the standards of TRIPS. Though it is claimed to have a positive impact on innovation in the country's industry, the TRIPs regime also raises uncertainties over issues of availability, accessibility and affordability. We have a growing body of literature that focuses on the effect of the TRIPs regime on the performance of the industry on varied aspects such as the structure and composition, production and export, market access and accessibility, to list a few in the TRIPS era.

The current structure of the industry is constituted mostly of a 'small number of large firms and large number of small firms' (Danzon 2006). These large firms represent 80 per cent of the net-worth of the whole pharmaceutical industry (Schuhmacher et al. 2016). The evidence shows that in the TRIPs era, the production of drugs in value terms has seen a four-fold increase with industry being more export-oriented due to the cost advantage that India possesses (Schuhmacher et al. 2016). Indian firms fare relatively better in market value and market penetration though it is the foreign firms that seem to do well in profitability, which is often attributed to the Indian firms' focus on generics. However, the sustenance of this advantage necessitated technology and innovation in the post-TRIPs regime. As Dhar and Gopakumar (2006) noted, R&D intensity has increased in generic drug firms post-TRIPs.

With the opening up of the economy collaborative alliances have begun to come up between foreign and domestic players mainly in two forms: contract research arrangements and contract manufacturing and outsourcing arrangements (Joseph 2011). The former includes clinical trials that are said to be cheaper and faster in India, whereas the second arrangement involves the medium and small firms that serve as suppliers to global players by dealing with dosage development and production (Dhar and Gopakumar 2006). Mergers and acquisitions are also a major development witnessed in the sector. In addition, the rise of off-patent drugs or blockbuster patent expiry in the recent times adds to the growth, especially in the sector of contract research services (ICRA 2011). India has become a preferred destination for outsourcing services (contract research) of such big firms, collaborative research and clinical research. Regulatory compliance with international standards along with the presence of a huge and varied patient population characteristics, highly skilled, technologically adapted and English-speaking personnel, world class infrastructure, low cost of production and, most importantly, conducive legal environment make India a preferred destination for international firms to undertake contract and collaborative research (Frew et al. 2008; Chowdhury 2011). This has resulted in the opening of branches of contract research organisations (CROs) by multinational companiess to pursue their research activity in India.

The biopharmaceutical industry in India is a leading sector with immense growth potential within the biotechnology sector. It is a highly innovative and knowledge-intensive industry. The growth of the biopharmaceutical industry is driven mainly by its growth of exports and the data show that the export revenue of Indian biopharmaceutical products is more than the domestic sales of biopharmaceutical products. For instance, as per the data given by the Department of Pharmaceuticals, Government of India, the export of biopharmaceutical products grew at an annual rate of 47 per cent as against the growth in domestic sales, which was 5 per cent in 2010. The biopharmaceutical sector grew as a subsector within the pharmaceutical industry rather than developing as an independent entity. Some scholars argue that this is mainly because the rise of biotechnology sectors, particularly genomics in the 1990s, coincided with the neoliberal policy reforms that, arguably, opened up entrepreneurism in healthcare (see McGillivray 2017). Moreover, as already discussed, India's pharmaceutical and biopharmaceutical sectors underwent a structural change in the post-liberalisation period that was induced by the TRIPS agreement with the change from process-driven manufacturing to product development, which required the industry to expand its R&D base to be relevant and competitive. The pharmaceutical industry paid attention to the biotechnology sector through investments in its R&D, alliances and collaborations, and also through mergers and acquisitions (see Joseph 2016). However, the structure and orientation of the biotechnology sector differ from that of the pharmaceutical industry. Unlike the pharmaceutical industry, biopharmaceutical products are specific, non-standardised and cater to smaller populations. Despite the specific focus and limited scalability, the biopharmaceutical industry has a growing presence in India (Otto et al. 2014). Its growth, however, is higher than the conventional pharmaceutical industry, which we will illustrate in the following chapters.

Biopharmaceutical products largely include vaccines, diagnostics and therapeutics. Vaccines account for the major share of the revenue of the biopharmaceutical industry in India. The Indian biopharmaceutical companies focus more on developing biogenerics by producing off-patent drugs and involving in contract research. This is mainly due to the cost, time and complexity of the development of new chemical entities (NCEs). For instance, drug development depends on complex scientific and technology foundations, and regulations affecting the production of these drugs are stringent in nature. However, Indian biopharmaceutical companies are also a part of the global R&D value chain that provides services based on high-end technology, drug discovery, contract manufacturing, clinical trials and contract research.[3]

Public health relevance of medical R&D

How is India's medical R&D performing? What is its population and disease focus? It is estimated that on an average, pharmaceutical firms spend nearly 15 per cent of their sales turnover on R&D (Joseph 2016). While the spending on R&D by Indian firms was relatively less, the recent past witnessed an increasing trend, especially from 2001–02 (Joseph 2016) due to the entry of multinational firms, mergers and large-scale clinical trials in India. Most importantly, the private sector accounted for this increase. R&D intensity in the public sector, however, remained as low as 2 per cent of their sales turnover (Joseph 2016: 93). The medical biotechnology sector, which focuses on promotive and preventive care, also undertakes large-scale R&D activities in India through contract and collaborative research. The mission document of the Biotechnology Industry Research Assistance Council (BIRAC) states unambiguously that one of its objectives is to develop affordable and public health relevant technologies and products in healthcare. It states:

---

[3] The biopharmaceutical value chain can be illustrated in the following way. It starts with the (a) research and drug discovery that involves universities and contract research organisations; (b) preclinical studies on animals; (c) phases I and II that constitute control study to determine safety and efficacy followed by phase III that involves open trials to earn Food and Drug Administration's approval; (d) manufacturing to increase scale of production that ensure bioequivalence; (e) market from synthesis to approval and finally (f) phase IV that involves post marketing surveillance when introduced to larger population. For a discussion on biopharmaceutical value chain, see Aitken (2016).

Development of affordable and accessible biopharmaceuticals (vaccines and biosimilars) and medical devices & diagnostics relevant to public health needs of India by supporting Public and Private institutions, researchers, start-ups, entrepreneurs and companies that have established proof of concept and are on the path of product development. Shortlisted products are – vaccines for dengue, HPV and pneumococcal & a new and complex vaccine for emerging disease; biosimilars for cancer, rheumatoid arthritis, diabetes and critical technologies to develop medical devices. Additionally, novel product development for complex, emerging, high priority infections will also be considered.[4]

With state facilitation and investment from Indian and global manufacturers, seed/angel firms and venture capital initiating R&D in the biotech industry has been growing in India. The major R&D initiatives of the biomedical technology sector in India include vaccines, non-vaccine therapeutics, diagnostics and contract services for clinical trials, research and manufacturing. India is also a manufacturing hub of vaccines for the world.[5]

R&D in drug, vaccine and diagnostic technology is well studied in India, covering its various facets, such as the implications of the new IPR regime after 1995 (Abrol et al. 2011), types of R&D investments (Joseph 2011), R&D innovation and growth of Indian companies (Abrol and Singh 2016) and therapeutic focus and status, and challenges of proprietary drug discovery in India (Chaudhuri 2010; Differding 2017). However, there is a dearth of studies on the linkages between R&D and the disease burden

---

[4] 'Industry–Academia Collaborative Mission for Accelerating Early Development for Biopharmaceuticals: "Innovate in India (i3) Empowering Biotech Entrepreneurs and Accelerating Inclusive Iinnovation"', National Biopharma Mission Document, 2017, p. 6, available at https://birac.nic.in/webcontent/National_Biopharma_Mission_Document.pdf, accessed on 9 October 2020.

[5] The priority areas of vaccine research in India include tuberculosis (TB), rotaviral diarrhoea, malaria, chikungunya, avian flu and human pappilomavirus (HPV). Indian companies are also involved in the manufacture of bio-therapeutics – recombinant human insulin and monoclonal antibody enzymes such as streptokinase, erythropoietin and interferon. Regenerative medicine, including stem cell research, is another area in which both government and private agencies are involved. For details, see Joseph (2016).

in the country as well as on the questions of equity and social divide due to medical innovations.

The R&D activities in the pharmaceutical and biopharmaceutical sectors assume importance in the context of the existing and emerging complex health problems in the country stemming from a wide range of issues, including the demographic and epidemiological transitions, resurgence and emergence of infectious diseases, burden of non-communicable diseases and growing out-of-pocket healthcare expenditure. It is not sufficiently known how the conflicting interests of the industry and public health priorities are dealt with. Are the state and the industry sensitive to these problems that have implications for the disease burden of the population? How are priorities set in medical innovations? What has been the disease focus of the R&D activities of pharmaceutical, biopharmaceutical and medical technology firms in India? Are medical innovation endeavours responsive to the complex disease burden? Are the questions of appropriateness, equity and affordability adequately addressed in medical innovations? What are the possible social divides in terms of accessibility and sharing of the benefits and burdens of medical innovations in India? Finally, how can India develop a responsive and responsible medical innovation framework? The book, drawing from diverse sets of available secondary data, discusses these questions in detail.

We begin by mapping the pharmaceutical and biopharmaceutical landscape of India. It analyses the structure and organisation of the pharmaceutical and biopharmaceutical/medical biotechnology industry in India by examining its production, market, export and R&D spending; the generics, biosimilars and new chemical entities developed and marketed in India from 2001 to 2017 and its therapeutic focus; and whether the R&D in drug development by pharmaceuticals and the medical biotechnology industry is responsive to public health priorities of the disease burden, availability and affordability of drugs in India. Data on production, market share, and share in R&D activities of the companies are obtained from the Centre for Monitoring of Indian Economy (CMIE) Prowess database. It should also be noted that the data from CMIE Prowess presented here have certain limitations. First, the database provides a single figure on the R&D expenditure of companies. It has no further classification as to how much is expended on either preventive or therapeutic care, on varied diseases, on chemical-based or biotech-based drugs, on infectious or chronic diseases, and so on. This is a major limitation for any meaningful analysis for the implications on public health. However, we tried to overcome this problem by juxtaposing the disease focus of the newly approved drugs with the disease burden, which is presented in Chapter 3. Second, the biotechnology sector has become deeply integrated into the pharmaceutical industry. Because of this, a separate classification of the R&D expenditure of the biopharmaceutical industry is lacking despite the biopharma industry being the one with the highest growth among varied biotechnology sectors. Thus an independent study of the biopharmaceutical industry may not be tenable with the Prowess database. We have attempted to overcome this problem by drawing data individually from the major biopharmaceuticals listed in the *Biospectrum Survey* of ABLE, for which Prowess also provides data. The rest of the information is collated directly from the annual reports of the biopharmaceutical companies. Details on the drugs approved in India from 2001 to 2017 are obtained from the database of the Central Drugs Standard Control Organisation (CDSCO), Government of India. These drugs are further organised according to their therapeutic areas. Data on NCEs up to 2016 were taken from Differding (2017). Further, R&D initiatives on NCE development are compiled from websites of the corresponding pharmaceutical and medical biotechnology companies and available published articles in journals. The data on disease-specific mortality are collected from the mortality database of health statistics and information systems of the WHO for the years 2000, 2005, 2010 and 2015. Data on prices of various brands of recently approved generics are compiled from the web portal of the National Pharmaceutical Pricing Authority, Ministry of Chemicals and Fertilizers, Government of India. Data on medical expenditure and morbidity patterns are estimated from the unit level observation of the National Sample Survey Organisation's (NSSO) round on social consumption – health. Data on funding of healthcare start-ups in India are collated from various web sources that are mentioned in the respective chapters. Data on clinical trials registered in India are compiled from the Clinical Trial Registry developed and managed by the Indian Council of Medical Research (ICMR).

The book is organised into five chapters. The first chapter discusses nature, structure, composition and the major drivers of the pharmaceutical, biopharmaceutical and medical technology (mostly medical devices) industry in India. It also examines the new organisation of the sector and the inter-linkages of big pharmaceuticals, hospitals, the public sector, universities and start-up companies. The chapter also discusses the specific indicators such as production, income, sales, export and R&D spending of these sectors as a whole and across public, Indian private companies and multinational companies over a period of time. The second chapter examines the institutional co-production of health R&D and the disease focus of the R&D in drugs, vaccines and medical technology. The third chapter discusses the mortality and morbidity burden of India across demographic groups and disease conditions in detail and examines the responsiveness of drug development, which constitutes the major share of medical innovation, to the disease burden. The fourth chapter discusses the issues of affordability and equity of medical innovations in India. The chapter offers a detailed analysis of the burden of medical care across regions, income groups, social groups and diseases, drawing from the 71st round of the NSSO data. Further, the chapter also sheds light on the issues in drug price regulation by examining the variations in prices of selected drugs across various brands for selected diseases. The fifth chapter presents a framework for responsive and responsible medical innovation in India that aims to balance the priorities of public health and industry goals.

1

Medical Innovation and Its Institutional Co-production in India

This chapter attempts to understand the medical innovation landscape of India in detail by specifically focussing on the pharmaceutical, biopharmaceutical and medical technology sectors. The first part of the chapter overviews the performance of these sectors with a special focus on research and development (R&D). The second part attempts to unearth the institutional co-production of medical R&D. This section of the chapter examines the formal and informal actors and processes in the network of production, the institutional network of funding and product development. The data presented in the chapter are drawn from secondary sources and published literature on medical innovations in India and other countries. The data on industry performance are obtained mainly from CMIE Prowess,[1] reports of the Association of Biotechnology Led Enterprises (ABLE) and the published reports of the Department of Science and Technology, the Department of Biotechnology and the Ministry of Chemicals and Fertilisers. The data on funding are compiled from various sources including CMIE Prowess for private and public Indian and foreign companies, the Department of Science and Technology, the Biotechnology Industry Research Assistance Council (BIRAC), Government of India (GOI), for funding of research institutions and websites of the companies

---

[1] Prowess, a database on the financial performance of India's Inc. released by the Centre for Monitoring Indian Economy Pvt Ltd (CMIE), is a principal source of data on various manufacturing and non-manufacturing industries, including data on the pharmaceutical industry and its performance. The data is mainly sourced from annual reports of these companies. The database provides data on indicators like sales, income, profits, R&D expenses, trade, and various receipts and expenditure categories.

and service aggregators for the funding of start-ups. The data on clinical trials across companies and disease and participating hospitals are compiled from the Clinical Trial Registry of the Indian Council of Medical Research (ICMR).

The Indian pharmaceutical industry: sales, export and R&D

Studies have already shown that the Agreement on Trade-Related Aspects of Intellectual Property Rights (TRIPs) regime provided an impetus for the industry to change its direction and destination and become more export oriented in its production activities (Dhar and Gopakumar 2006). Concerns were raised that imports would increase in the product patent regime and unfavourably affect the balance of trade. However, the Indian pharmaceutical industry could achieve a positive balance of trade mainly due to the export of formulations[2] (Joseph 2009). Studies further revealed that the compound annual growth rates (CAGR) of exports of formulations are greater than those of bulk drugs in the TRIPs era, a trend opposite to one observed in pre-TRIPs era.[3] These trends showed that imports also increased though the leading importers are multinational companies (MNCs), which was attributed to the removal of restrictions in the post-reform period.

The performance of the Indian pharmaceutical industry including public, private and the MNCs in terms of income, sales, export and R&D has been mixed from 2000 to 2016 (see Table 1.1). However, if we examine the trend between 2000 and 2016, there was an overall growth pertaining to sales, exports and R&D spending in the sector. For instance, total income and sales grew by nearly 9 per cent during this period. Export earnings grew by nearly 14 per cent. Most importantly, R&D expenditure in the pharmaceutical sector as a whole grew by nearly 18.5 per cent. Similarly, R&D as a percentage of sales grew by nearly 9.5 per cent. The data also show the target population of the sector. As it is clear from Table 1.1, these

---

[2] Formulations are medicines that contain the use of one or more bulk drugs with or without medical aids. Bulk drugs are chemical, pharmaceutical, and biological or plant products that are used as active ingredients in any formulation.

[3] For more information, see 'Study on Indian Pharmaceutical Industry', Working Paper No. 37, Export-Import Bank of India, available at https://www.eximbankindia.in/Assets/Dynamic/PDF/Publication-Resources/ResearchPapers/39file.pdf, accessed in September 2018.

Table 1.1   Income, sales, R&D, export and import in Indian pharmaceutical sector (all) (INR million)

Year	R&D expenses	Total income	Sales	Export earnings	Imports of finished goods	R&D % sales
2000	3478.2	281735.3	272947.6	58472.4	3428.8	1.27
2001	4742.2	309110.3	296796.2	72602.1	3757	1.60
2002	6584.5	363483.5	351362.6	99328.8	4681.3	1.87
2003	10338.1	428053	409661.2	125512.3	4084.9	2.52
2004	14692.9	469718.6	450846.2	143366.6	3892	3.26
2005	19391.3	561866.8	534577.3	171807.3	5189.4	3.63
2006	24278.7	689335.1	648227.8	232143.1	5592.8	3.75
2007	26578.1	823884.7	767958.1	279572.2	5156.1	3.46
2008	32105.2	951495.3	898435.2	347354.5	5559.3	3.57
2009	37574.2	1086673	1022029	389365	7301.3	3.68
2010	44315.4	1426216	1184036	454632.3	8668.1	3.74
2011	50203	1459782	1375040	568453.9	9669.2	3.65
2012	59694.2	1577047	1509930	657715.8	10742.2	3.95
2013	73471.8	1886714	1745326	799815.8	13921.8	4.21
2014	86084.9	1999903	1865598	861738.4	16974.1	4.61
2015	84942	1627795	1543086	733693.7	13693.7	5.50
2016	81036.1	1348528	1274465	653950.6	9703.9	6.36
CAGR (%)	18.52	9.21	9.06	14.20	6.12	9.46

Source: CMIE Prowess, estimated.

firms cater largely to the international market. For instance, the share of exports in total sales almost reached 50 per cent by 2016.

Public sector enterprises have a meagre share in the pharmaceutical sector. As evident from Table 1.2, the public sector showed a negative growth in income, sales and export. R&D investment was less than 1 per cent of sales revenue for public sector enterprises although it showed an increase over the years. Public sector R&D spending showed an increase from INR 5.9 million in 2000 to 77.6 million in 2014 with a CAGR of 17.18 per cent. It should, however, be mentioned that the R&D spending

Table 1.2   Income, sales, R&D, export and import, government enterprises (INR million)

Year	Total income	Government enterprises (INR million)			R&D % sales
		Sales	Export	R&D	
2000	3962.1	3916.7	684.4	5.9	0.15
2001	1857.8	1792.6	594.1	1.8	0.10
2002	5141	4566.8	801.3	14.3	0.31
2003	5215.7	3977.2	215.7	39.2	0.99
2004	4705.1	4479.6	276.6	49.7	1.11
2005	4710.8	4526.6	261.4	41.9	0.93
2006	8128.6	5582.9	488.4	62.2	1.11
2007	8108.3	7982.5	576.5	80.5	1.01
2008	8235.1	7920	432	107.4	1.36
2009	8395.7	8139.7	614.5	107.5	1.32
2010	7335.9	7264.4	653.4	113.9	1.57
2011	8174.3	7921.5	398.9	135.3	1.71
2012	10412.5	10163.6	659.3	140.2	1.38
2013	10848.9	10532.6	653.6	90.2	0.86
2014	9068.7	8950.7	691	77.6	0.87
2015	4590	4531	289.1	-	-
2016	327.8	326.4	-	-	-
CAGR (%)	-14.66	-14.62	-5.39	17.18	11.67

Source: CMIE Prowess, estimated.

mostly includes the cost for developing non-infringing generics and biosimilars. In short, the drug production in the public sector is mostly focussed around developing generics and biosimilars.

Table 1.3 highlights the overriding role of the Indian private sector in the pharmaceutical industry. The growth in sales and income for the private sector was more than the overall growth in the sector. For instance, while the income and sales of the Indian private sector companies together grew at CAGR 10.5 per cent and 10.3 per cent respectively between 2000 and 2016, the growth in income and sales for the sector as a whole for the same period was 9.2 per cent and 9 per cent respectively. R&D as a percentage

Table 1.3 Income, sales, R&D, export and import, Indian private enterprises

	All Indian private companies (INR million)					
Year	Total income	Sales	Export	R&D	Import	R&D % sales
2000	204095.9	199228.1	46839.5	2647.8	1615.6	1.3
2001	226391.7	218750.6	56518.9	3765.8	1784.5	1.7
2002	257072.2	249189.9	71150.1	4481.9	2367.7	1.8
2003	307638.9	295627	91400	7298	1832.7	2.5
2004	346423.8	333818.1	108947.5	10554	1757.8	3.2
2005	433330.9	414323.2	136939.1	13468.2	1490.7	3.3
2006	544583.5	514777.3	189062.6	18670.1	2397.5	3.6
2007	660205.8	622896.8	233692.9	20432.8	2826.1	3.3
2008	779569.2	739040.4	292533.3	25108.6	2248.7	3.4
2009	893717.2	844016.5	328162.6	29283.6	3567.5	3.5
2010	1178094	959253.2	375350	35309.6	3854	3.7
2011	1179090	1107344	456163.6	40908.2	4228.1	3.7
2012	1289710	1239572	551986.2	48869.5	4182	3.9
2013	1553041	1439713	678927.8	60716.8	6040.6	4.2
2014	1644471	1538705	738934.1	73140.7	7143.4	4.8
2015	1441247	1366678	700643.4	81081.9	4350.7	5.9
2016	1209698	1141871	631938.1	78603.3	1536.1	6.9
CAGR (%)	10.47	10.27	15.31	19.95	-0.30	9.67

Source: CMIE Prowess, estimated.

of sales of the Indian private sector has also shown an upward trajectory. Though in the initial years R&D as a percentage of sales remains more or less the same for both Indian private sector and foreign companies, one can see a gradual increase in the performance of Indian private companies. Nevertheless, the trend is not the same for the MNCs.

The structure of the industry, as it is well known, is oligarchic in nature where the large firms lead the market and the smaller ones follow. The preponderance of large private sector firms in the Indian pharmaceutical sector is evident and the private sector in fact drives the growth in the pharmaceutical industry (see Table 1.4). We have taken the data of the performance of 13 major private companies. These companies include Sun Pharmaceuticals, Cipla, Lupin, Dr Reddy's, Aurobindo Pharma, Cadila, Abbott, Torrent Pharma, Intas Pharmaceuticals, Biocon, Emami, Wockhardt, Glenmark and Ipca laboratories. They, together, accounted for nearly 50 per cent of the total Indian market in 2016. The performance in terms of income, sales, exports and the R&D of these companies also has been robust with a CAGR of nearly 14 per cent in income and sales, 18 per cent in export and nearly 21 per cent in R&D between 2000 and 2016. The share of R&D spending to sales also grew by 7.5 per cent during this period.

Table 1.4 Income, sales, R&D, export and import, major 13 Indian private companies (INR million)

Year	Total income	Sales	Export	R&D	R&D % sales	Import
2000	82508.2	81030.8	21688.6	1924.8	2.38	438
2001	94061.4	91362.9	29961.4	2733.7	3.0	347.9
2002	107663.5	105802	34986	3027.8	2.86	424.3
2003	129556.7	125105	46102	5443.8	4.35	258.3
2004	139505.1	133237.6	50087.3	7830.6	5.88	195.7
2005	172412.2	160746.6	63563.1	9242	5.75	145.7
2006	236327.9	219021.8	98936.8	12752	5.82	225.8
2007	273945.5	249590.7	112505	13380.7	5.36	288.7
2008	319090.2	295660.7	141714	15914.4	5.38	415.3
2009	349,318	325,129	160687.4	18473.2	5.68	487.3
2010	413546.3	383607.1	193956.2	23617.8	6.16	626.9
2011	481795.7	443744.9	238583.3	27060.9	6.10	1058.4
2012	549033.6	522656.4	294200.1	34195.7	6.54	924.3
2013	682928.6	652134.6	356512.7	43736.8	6.71	1204
2014	819811.3	786902.7	411466.1	57229.9	7.27	1082.7
2015	916871.4	877772.6	471221.7	70751.3	8.06	1169.9
2016	871072.5	834046.8	471095.1	70751.3	8.48	1169.9
CAGR (%)	13.86	13.71	18.11	21.20	7.49	5.78

Source: CMIE Prowess, estimated.

The contribution of foreign MNCs in drug production, sales, export and R&D is presented in Table 1.5. It shows that although the MNCs have a notable presence in the Indian pharmaceutical sector, their performance in terms of sales and exports is not as robust as that of the Indian private companies. For instance, while the income of the Indian companies together grew nearly by 14 per cent between 2000 and 2016, it was 4 per cent for the foreign MNCs. Similarly, domestic sales and exports of the foreign MNCs were less than that of the Indian private firms together. The R&D investment of the foreign MNCs as a percentage of sales was also noticeably less than that of the Indian

Table 1.5   Income, sales, R&D, export and import, all foreign MNCs in Indian pharmaceutical sector (INR million)

Year	Total income	Sales	Export	R&D	Import	R&D % sales
2000	73677.3	69802.8	10948.5	824.9	2150.7	1.2
2001	80860.8	76253	15489.1	975.2	2377.1	1.3
2002	101270.3	97605.9	27377.4	2089	3045.1	2.1
2003	115198.4	110057	33896.6	3012	2783.4	2.7
2004	118589.7	112548.5	34142.5	4100.8	2216.3	3.6
2005	123843.6	115746	34606.8	5882	3757.4	5.1
2006	136671.5	127916	42592.1	5558.2	3975.6	4.3
2007	155631.7	137139.4	45302.8	6065.2	2994	4.4
2008	163771.6	151553.8	54389.2	6900.7	4019.3	4.6
2009	184640.5	169952.2	60587.9	8183.1	5401.3	4.8
2010	240786.5	217518.7	78628.9	8892.1	6399.3	4.1
2011	272517.6	259775.4	111891.4	9175.3	7343.9	3.5
2012	276924	260195.2	105070.3	10697.1	8871.5	4.1
2013	322824.1	295080.8	120234.4	12677.4	11007.2	4.3
2014	346363	317942.8	122113.3	12866.6	14187.6	4.0
2015	181957.8	171877.2	32761.2	3860.1	12058.8	2.2
2016	138501.3	132267.4	22012.5	2432.8	8167.8	1.8
CAGR (%)	3.71	3.76	4.11	6.36	7.85	2.60

Source: CMIE Prowess, estimated.

private companies. While the share of R&D in total sales was nearly 8.5 per cent for Indian firms in 2016, it was 1.8 per cent for the foreign MNCs in 2016. Similarly, their growth rate in R&D spending was also considerably less than that of the Indian firms.

The data on the Indian pharmaceutical industry over a period of 16 years of the new intellectual property rights (IPR) regime revealed a gradual decline in the share of the public sector in the income of the industry as a whole, along with the emerging strong presence of Indian private firms, which showed a steady gradual increase in income, sales, export and R&D spending. The performance of government enterprises, Indian private companies and the MNCs in 2000, 2011 and 2016 is further illustrated in Figures 1.1, 1.2 and 1.3. While the Indian private firms showed a steady increase in income generation, the income of the MNCs not only was significantly lower than that of the Indian private firms but decreased by nearly 16 percentage points between 2000 and 2016 as well. The income of public sector pharmaceuticals has been negligible as compared to the private sector, and it stood as low as 0.02 per cent of the total in 2016.

Figure 1.1   Share of income of private, public and MNCs in the total income at major points in time

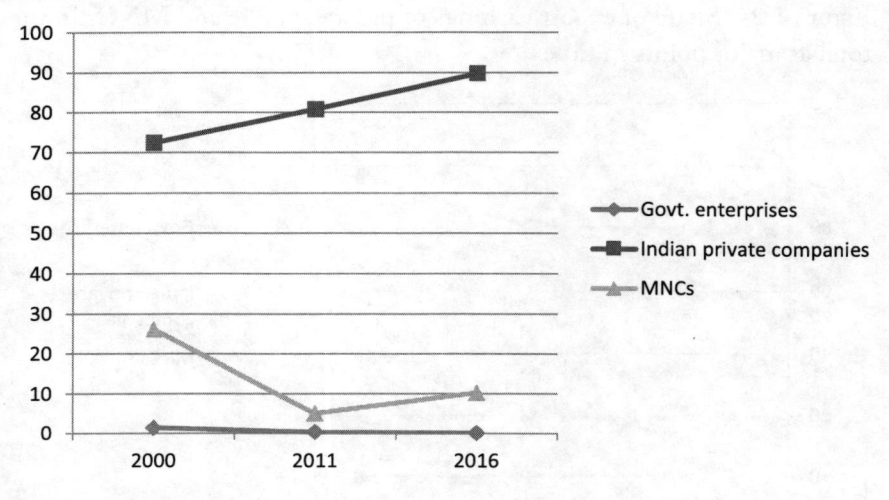

Source: CMIE Prowess, estimated.

Another noticeable trend is the increasing focus of the Indian private firms in pharmaceutical exports. As is evident from Figure 1.2, as much as 97 per cent of Indian pharmaceutical exports was from the Indian private sector companies. Most importantly, it increased by nearly 16 percentage points between 2011 and 2016, whereas the share of the foreign MNCs in India decreased by 16 percentage points during this period. The export from Indian public sector companies was negligible. Similarly, the Indian private sector companies together held the major share of R&D in the sector. The Indian private sector companies accounted for 76.1 per cent of the total R&D expenditure in the sector in 2000, which further grew to 97 per cent of the total R&D expenditure (see Figure 1.3). The share of the public sector has always been negligible in R&D. Although the MNCs together accounted for nearly 24 per cent of the total R&D in 2000, it declined considerably to 3 per cent in 2016. The nature of the R&D activities could be one of the reasons for the preponderance of the Indian private sector. It must be mentioned that much of the R&D activities by these companies are concentrated in developing non-fringing generics and biosimilars, and the development of new chemical entities (NCEs) has been negligible due to the higher cost and uncertainty of success involved in its development (see Differding 2017).

Figure 1.2   Share of export earnings of private, public and MNCs in the total at major points in time

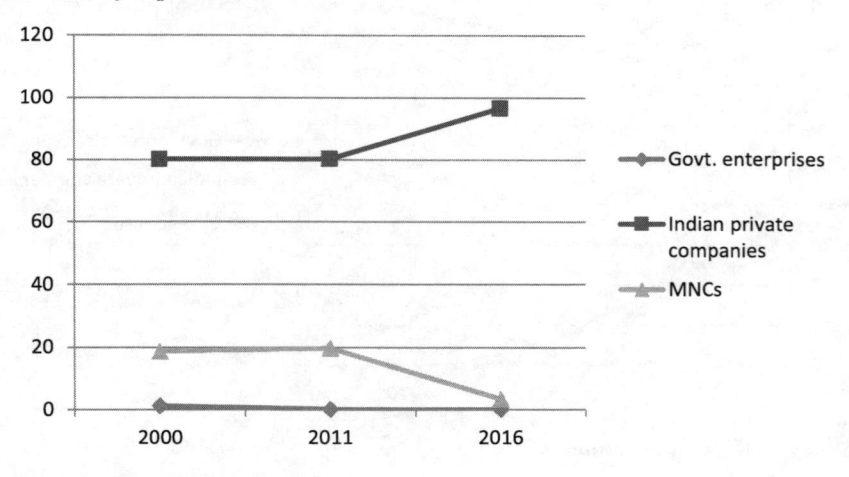

Source: CMIE Prowess, estimated.

Figure 1.3   Share of R&D expenditure of private, public and MNCs in the total at major points in time

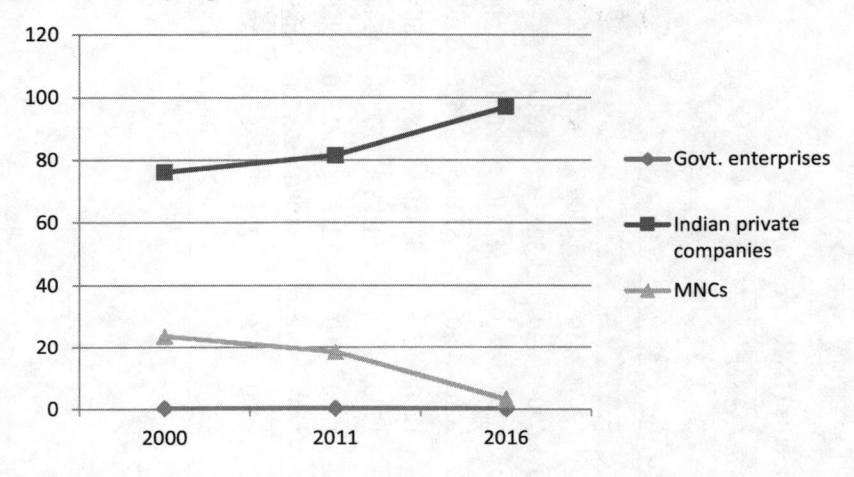

Source: CMIE Prowess, estimated.

Performance of the biopharmaceutical industry in India

The biotechnology sector in India has majorly been export intensive. The biopharmaceutical segment constitutes for more than 65 per cent of the total biotechnology exports of India, followed by bioservices, which constituted nearly 33 per cent of the biotechnology exports (see Table 1.6). These two sub-sectors together contribute more than 90 per cent of the total exports in biotechnology.

Table 1.7 illustrates the performance of the major biopharmaceutical companies in India.[4] The major biopharmaceutical companies are identified from the *BioSpectrum Survey* conducted by ABLE – an industry association of biotechnology firms in India. These include both Indian (private and public) and foreign entities. These firms develop/manufacture vaccines, biosimilars and diagnostic services. The data on the performance of these

---

4   The major companies considered here are Bharat Biotech International, Bharat Serums and Vaccines, Biocon, Biological E, Cadila Healthcare, Dr Reddy's, Intas, Lupin, Panacea Biotec, Serum Institute of India, Syngene International, Torrent, Wockhardt, Gennova, Sanofi India, Concord Biotech, Merck, GlaxoSmithKline, Novartis, Pfizer, Ranbaxy, Shantha Biotechnics, Virchow drugs, Bharat Immunologicals, Haffkine Biopharmceutical Corporation, and Indian Immunologicals.

Table 1.6　Indian biotechnology industry, revenue of various sub-segments (INR crore)

| | Total biotechnology revenue (INR crore) | | | | | | | | | | | | |
| Year | Bio-pharma | | Bio-services | | Bio-agri | | Bio-industrial | | Bio-informatics | | Total BT revenue | Total E | Total D |
	E	D	E	D	E	D	E	D	E	D			
2002–03	6630	6120	1150	200	100	1000	1230	1120	640	110	18300	9750	8550
2003–04	13900	10900	2500	250	200	1600	880	1620	690	110	32650	18170	14480
2004–05	14640	21060	3910	340	230	3070	510	2690	720	280	47450	20010	27440
2005–06	24950	22130	6840	360	360	5620	410	3340	1010	190	65210	33570	31630
2006–07	36730	23000	10520	500	470	8790	450	3500	1200	250	85410	49370	36040
2007–08	39990	29000	15020	700	520	11500	300	3800	1500	400	102730	57320	45400
2008–09	48680	30150	19640	980	610	14330	890	3890	1700	500	121370	71520	49850
2009–10	47680	40610	25070	1320	580	18780	1240	4400	740	1570	141990	75300	66680
2010–11	55350	51100	29860	2600	740	24060	1500	4760	1060	1460	172490	88520	83970
2011–12	62100	64670	32240	5250	1530	28980	1670	5290	850	1810	204390	98410	105980

Source: Biospectrum Survey (June 2012).
Note: E = Export, D = Domestic.
1 crore = 10 million.

Table 1.7 Income, sales, R&D, export and import, major biopharma companies (INR million)

Year	Total income	Sales	R&D expenses	OM jobs	OP jobs	Outs expenses	Imports	Exports	R&D per cent sales
2000	91708	88875.2	2048.8	612.4	497	1109.4	1621.4	2730.8	2.31
2001	104933.9	99471	3004.5	594.5	728.2	1322.7	2161.6	3484.3	3.02
2002	129730.9	125848.8	4728.2	905.3	1459.8	2365.1	3049.3	5414.4	3.76
2003	150435.5	143386.7	6881.6	1354.7	2163.3	3518	2327.1	5845.1	4.80
2004	164419.8	157392	9271.4	1692.5	2347.1	4039.6	2108.3	6147.9	5.89
2005	187388.4	175815.5	11565.2	2033.8	3311.7	5345.5	1931.9	7277.4	6.58
2006	235021.7	219809.2	13200.1	3064.7	3393.6	6458.3	2871.1	9329.4	6.01
2007	259435.6	232049.1	13929.9	2426.6	3972.8	6399.4	2355.2	8754.6	6.00
2008	280490.4	262463	15912.4	2453.2	5134	7587.2	2748.3	10335.5	6.06
2009	325372.9	298847.4	19056.3	2547.1	5792.7	8339.8	4394.2	12734	6.38
2010	383223.4	349354.9	23095.7	3524	6404.4	9928.4	4813.1	14741.5	6.61
2011	446875.2	420496	25810.4	4055.6	8383.6	12439.2	6490.4	18929.6	6.14
2012	508476.3	477156.5	30677.8	5272.3	10758.9	16031.2	7221.8	23253	6.43
2013	602293.4	555262.6	37462	5706.7	16381.4	22088.1	9424.8	31512.9	6.75
2014	643535.3	599333.8	41904.2	6091.9	16260	22351.9	13454.1	35806	6.99
2015	526408	493391.8	42848.3	4661.9	11866.3	16528.2	12110.9	28639.1	8.68
2016	489501.2	459761.5	42681.3	4314.5	11150.6	15465.1	8219.9	23685	9.28
CAGR %	9.85	9.67	17.86	11.48	18.30	15.50	9.55	12.71	8.19

Source: CMIE Prowess, estimated.

Note: OM jobs: outsourced manufacturing jobs; OP jobs: outsourced professional jobs; outs expenses: total outsourcing expenditure companies are extracted from the CMIE Prowess database. This dataset, however, does not provide information on certain biopharmaceutical companies mentioned in the *BioSpectrum Survey*. Also, no separate data on investments in biopharmaceuticals exclusively by firms is found in the CMIE database (see Table 1.1A for the firms included). Hence, it should be mentioned that the figures provided are subject to either over- or under-estimation. Despite these limitations, one can still make out certain general inferences on the overall performance of the Indian biopharmaceutical sector from the data provided here. First, sales, R&D expenditure and outsourcing expenditure show an increasing trend between 2000 and 2016, although a slight reversion was marked in 2015–16. The income of these major companies together showed a CAGR of nearly 10 per cent between 2000 and 2016. Similarly, sales grew at a rate of 9.7 per cent during this period. Interestingly, the highest growth was witnessed in the R&D expenses, which grew at a rate of nearly 18 per cent during this period. The R&D expenses as a percentage of sales also showed an increasing trend. Another interesting trend is that there has been a balance between imports and exports of goods and services for the period under study. India's pharmaceutical industry has always shown this trend since the inception of Patents Act, 1970, and has continued its position in the TRIPS era too. Table 1.8 also indicates the increasing outsourcing expenditure of the big biopharmaceutical industry in India with the emergence of a more connected value chain, which encompasses start-up manufacturing companies and clinical trial firms to high-end product development. For instance, the data show that the total outsourcing expenditure of these firms grew at a rate of 15.5 per cent annually between 2000 and 2016.

Table 1.8 provides data for only government biopharmaceutical enterprises that are into vaccine development. Major government enterprises that we examined include Bharat Immunologicals Ltd, Haffkine Biopharmaceuticals Ltd and the Indian Immunologicals Ltd. The role of government enterprises is relatively insignificant, resulting in dwindling public sector role in the health sector. The R&D expenses do not show a positive growth, implying the declining role of public institutions in the health sector. Most importantly, government enterprises have shown a negative trade balance, reflecting the possibility that Indian state (read public sector) has been spending more on imports than emphasising on domestic production.

Table 1.8 Income, sales, R&D, export and import, major biopharma government enterprises (INR million)

Year	Total income	Sales	R&D expenses	OM jobs	OP jobs	Outs expenses	Exports	Total forex spending	R&D % sales
2000	1570.4	1558	0	0	4.4	4.4	498.1	978.4	0
2001	1352.7	1333	1.2	0	4.4	4.4	566.5	836.6	0.09
2002	1723.7	1699.8	13.6	0	7.2	7.2	638.2	614.5	0.80
2003	1935.5	1182.4	28.1	0	9.6	9.6	51.5	373.9	2.38
2004	1717	1697.1	38	0	9.8	9.8	65.9	628.5	2.24
2005	1802.8	1739.8	41.1	0.1	9.6	9.7	68.9	582.8	2.36
2006	2062.9	1995.6	50.4	0.1	7.7	7.8	340.3	411.9	2.53
2007	3007.3	2979.1	79.9	6.4	12.8	19.2	470.8	870.3	2.68
2008	2654.3	2566.9	95.7	34	11.7	45.7	280.7	960	3.73
2009	3099.3	3018.2	106.3	40.6	27.2	67.8	446	344.3	3.52
2010	2891.8	2865	113.7	45.6	28.9	74.5	459	370.9	3.97
2011	3652.8	3592.1	119.5	41.3	35.3	76.6	178	963.6	3.33
2012	5851.5	5814.7	127.6	76.4	26.2	102.6	461.3	1717.4	2.19
2013	6581.8	6461.1	77.6	118.2	29.6	147.8	401.9	2446.2	1.20
2014	5960.7	5893.9	77.6	118.2	31.4	149.6	401.9	2024.2	1.32
2015	1469.7	1462.4	0	0	4.7	4.7	0	1137.1	NA
2016	NA	NA	NA	NA	NA	NA	NA	NA	NA
CAGR %	-0.41	-0.40	29.78	70.75	0.41	0.41	-1.43	0.94	19.16

Source: CMIE Prowess, estimated.

Notes: OM jobs: outsourced manufacturing jobs; OP jobs: outsourced professional jobs; outs expenses: total outsourcing expenditure. No data on imports available and thus total foreign exchange expenditure is used.

As is true for the pharmaceutical sector, the biopharmaceutical sector is also dominated by the Indian private firms. Table 1.9 shows the performance of major Indian private biopharmaceutical firms for the period 2000–15.[5] The Indian private firms performed relatively better in all indicators than the major MNCs operating in India in the biopharmaceutical sector. As the table shows, all indicators of performance, including income, sales, the R&D expenditure and export, showed a positive growth for the Indian private biopharmaceutical companies taken together. The Indian private companies appeared to have maintained their place in the market in the post-TRIPS era by increasing R&D investments. It grew at a rate of nearly 21 per cent annually between 2000 and 2016. The R&D expenses as a part of sales showed a stable growth. Around 10 per cent of the sales revenue was spent on research investments by Indian private companies as against less than 5 per cent by the MNCs during this period. Also, Indian firms were more export oriented than the MNCs and more than 50 per cent of the companies' sales revenue came from exports. Also, imports of the major Indian firms were less than that of the MNCs.

Table 1.10 illustrates the performance of the major biopharmaceutical MNCs in India, which include Sanofi, Concord Biotech, GlaxoSmithKline, Novartis, Pfizer, Ranbaxy, Shantha Biotechnics and Virchow Drugs. The role of Ranbaxy among the MNCs is significant because it contributed around 40 per cent of the total income of the MNCs in 2000 and this share has been maintained closely even after its acquisition by foreign players. The company is also a key contributor to R&D investments, accounting for more than 70 per cent of the total research expenditure. For instance, Ranbaxy solely contributed around 90 per cent to the total R&D in 2016. However, as a whole there has been a fall in the share of sales revenue spent on R&D of the foreign biopharmaceutical MNCs. Interestingly, the decline has been witnessed post 2005. As already discussed, the imports of the major MNCs were more than that of the major biopharmaceutical Indian private firms.

A comparison of government enterprises, Indian private companies and MNCs operating in the biopharmaceutical sector shows that the Indian private sector holds the major share of the income and R&D

---

[5]   Those major companies are Biocon, Dr Reddy's, Biological E, Cadila, Hester Biosciences, Intas Pharmaceuticals, Lupin, Panacea Biotec, Serum Institute of India, Syngene International, Torrent, Wockhardt, and Gennova Biopharmaceuticals.

Table 1.9 Income, sales, R&D, export and import, major Indian private sector biopharma (INR million)

Year	Total income	Sales	R&D expenses	OM jobs	OP jobs	Outs expenses	Exports	Imports	R&D per cent sales
2000	45286.5	44364.5	1345.9	307.2	232.9	540.1	10719.5	282.6	3.03
2001	50934.8	49021.2	2156.1	201.8	228.4	430.2	16299.6	284.5	4.40
2002	59184.2	58189.7	2756.7	332.1	404.3	736.4	19276.4	387.7	4.74
2003	70226.2	67904.4	4179.8	467.1	708.1	1175.2	24908.6	284.5	6.16
2004	79547.7	77016.3	5580.4	635.8	587.7	1223.5	30570.7	272	7.25
2005	102849.6	97997.1	6290	896.4	1055.4	1951.8	39042.7	220.7	6.42
2006	144607.6	135931.4	8834.8	1849.3	1467.1	3316.4	69891.8	341.5	6.50
2007	157404.7	145274.2	9246.5	1365.4	1674.9	3040.3	70166	376	6.36
2008	176285.2	168689.8	11163.8	1176.4	1952.6	3129	87581.9	472.3	6.62
2009	207217.1	193791.5	13580.9	1275.9	2492.1	3768	99300.4	632	7.01
2010	243758.9	230228.7	17775.9	1494.1	3606.2	5100.3	117892.9	654	7.72
2011	288707.5	273361.7	20671.9	1852.8	4612.8	6465.6	152762.5	970.2	7.56
2012	353622	335315.7	25449.4	2901.4	6001.4	8902.8	202727.6	861.3	7.59
2013	429762.8	403359.5	31180.4	3371.3	7767.1	11138.4	266848.7	1199.4	7.73
2014	453610.3	430141.7	35589.4	3573.5	7455.3	11028.8	274228.9	1043.1	8.27
2015	426550.9	401796.7	42455.9	3774.9	9890.3	13665.2	268518	1151.5	10.57
CAGR (%)	14.02	13.77	21.57	15.68	23.43	20.19	20.13	8.78	7.80

Source: CMIE Prowess, estimated.

Table 1.10 Income, sales, R&D, export and import, major biopharma MNCs (INR million)

Year	Total income	Sales	R&D expenses	OM jobs	OP jobs	Outs expenses	Imports	Exports	R&D % sales
2000	44851.1	42952.7	702.9	305.2	259.7	564.9	1338.8	9155.9	1.64
2001	52646.4	49116.8	847.2	392.7	495.4	888.1	1877.1	12619.5	1.72
2002	68823	65959.3	1957.9	573.2	1048.3	1621.5	2661.6	21374.4	2.97
2003	78273.8	74299.9	2673.7	887.6	1445.6	2333.2	2042.6	27052.3	3.60
2004	83155.1	78678.6	3653	1056.7	1749.6	2806.3	1836.3	27372.8	4.64
2005	82736	76078.6	5234.1	1137.3	2246.7	3384	1711.2	26411.1	6.88
2006	88351.2	81882.2	4314.9	1215.3	1918.8	3134.1	2529.6	30341.2	5.27
2007	99023.6	83795.8	4603.5	1054.8	2285.1	3339.9	1979.2	29502.1	5.49
2008	101550.9	91206.3	4652.9	1242.8	3169.7	4412.5	2276	33154.5	5.10
2009	115056.5	102037.7	5369.1	1230.6	3273.4	4504	3761.1	34888.9	5.26
2010	136572.7	116261.2	5206.1	1984.3	2769.3	4753.6	4150.9	39196.8	4.48
2011	154514.9	143542.2	5019	2161.5	3735.5	5897	5514.9	59609.3	3.50
2012	149002.8	136026.1	5100.8	2294.5	4731.3	7025.8	6360.5	43325.3	3.75
2013	165948.8	145,442	6204	2217.2	8584.7	10801.9	8225.4	44156	4.27
2014	183964.3	163298.2	6237.2	2400.2	8773.3	11173.5	12411	44967.6	3.82
2015	98387.4	90132.7	392.4	887	1971.3	2858.3	10959	6880.4	0.44
2016	62950.3	57964.8	225.4	539.6	1260.3	1799.9	7068.4	566.6	0.39
CAGR (%)	1.99	1.76	-6.69	3.35	9.29	6.82	9.79	-16.37	-8.45

Source: CMIE Prowess, estimated.

spending in the biopharmaceutical sector (see Figure 1.4). The sub-sector held as much as 87 per cent of the total income in 2016 by increasing nearly 22.5 percentage points from 2011. The Indian private sector accounted for nearly 100 per cent of the R&D spending in the sector (see Figure 1.5). While the role of the public sector in Indian biopharmaceutical has

Figure 1.4   Share of income of private, public and MNCs (biopharma) in the total at major points in time

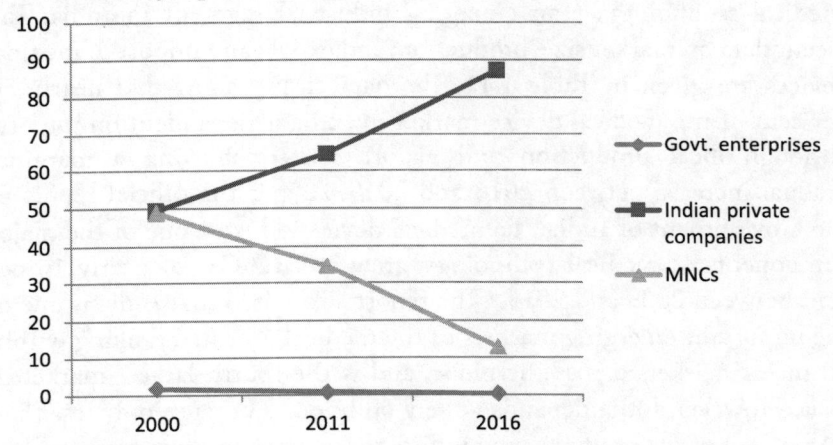

Source: CMIE Prowess, estimated.

Figure 1.5   Share of R&D expenditure of private, public and MNCs (biopharma) in the total at major points in time

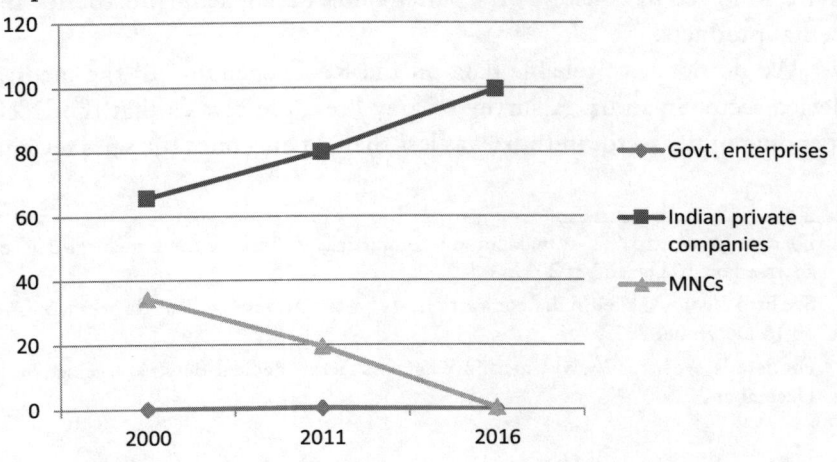

Source: CMIE Prowess, estimated.

always been negligible, one could also see a declining trend in income and R&D spending of the MNCs in India. While the share of the income of the MNCs in the total declined from 49 per cent to 13 per cent, R&D spending declined to nearly 0.5 per cent of the total in 2016 from 34 per cent in 2000.

The Indian medical device/technology sector

Medical technology is an emerging industrial segment in India. The recent data on market size, production, and export and import of medical devices are given in Table 1.11. The data clearly show that nearly 50 per cent of the medical device market in India is dependent on imports although local production and export started showing a marginal gradual increase between 2016 and 2019. As per the official report of the Government of India, the medical device industry, one of the major components of medical technology, grew at a CAGR of nearly 16 per cent between 2009 and 2015.[6] The report also noted that India is one of the important emerging markets of the medical industry, ranking within 20 major markets across the globe, and is the fourth largest market in Asia. However, India depends largely on imports because only less than 40 per cent of the products used in India are domestically manufactured.[7] Domestic manufacturing firms dominate the medical device sector in India with a share of nearly 65 per cent.[8] Within the medical device industry, the segment of diagnostic imaging holds the highest market share, followed by consumables, patient aids, orthopaedic prosthetics and dental products.

We do not have reliable data on the R&D spending of the medical device sector in India. A survey of grey literature reveals that the R&D spending of the sector in India was less than 2 per cent of the sales revenue

---

[6] For details, see http://www.makeinindia.com/article/-/v/sector-survey-medical-devices, accessed on 16 December 2019.

[7] See http://www.makeinindia.com/article/-/v/sector-survey-medical-devices, accessed on 16 December 2019.

[8] For details, see https://www.investindia.gov.in/sector/medical-devices, accessed on 16 December 2019.

Table 1.11 Market size, production, import and export of medical devices, India (USD million)

Medical devices and equipment	2016	2017	2018	2019 (estimated)
Total market size	7620	8929	9490 (est.)	10194
Total local production	3950	4542	4700 (est.)	4935
Total exports	160	192	210 (est.)	241
Total imports	3830	4579	5000	5500
Share of import in market size (%)	50.26	51.28	52.69	53.95

Source: www.export.gov (compiled from Global Trade Atlas, and unofficial estimates from trade sources and industry).

in 2014.[9] Studies also showed that the MNCs in India did not invest significantly in medical device R&D. For instance, Joseph et al. (2019) noted that the foreign direct investment (FDI) in R&D in India is as less as 0.7 per cent of the total R&D FDI inflow to India.

The institutional network of medical innovation

As we already discussed in the introductory chapter, the beginning of the biomedical technology paradigm was with an epistemic shift in the discourse of health from prevention, cure, promotion and rehabilitation to risk management since it started with the altering of the definition of 'diseases as risk' (Clarke et al. 2009). For instance, specialised knowledge domains including gene mapping and individual traits based medical solutions, which constitute the major part of biomedical innovation, also re-emphasise the biomedical model of health. It is, hence, important to understand the new knowledge paradigm and meanings that the research in biomedicine brings in through its formal and informal networks and formal institutional arrangements. In the following sections, we discuss the way in which the new medical research and innovation paradigm operates and reproduces its values through its institutional arrangements.

---

[9] For details, see 'The Medical Device Sector in India', September 2014, available at http://www.jjdinnovations.com/india/medical-device-industry-india/, accessed on 16 December 2019.

State, academia and industry linkages in India

The Indian innovation model of healthcare products in general and medical biotechnology in particular is somewhat similar to that of the Western countries, especially the United States (US) (see Nadh 2018). Biomedical research in India is also part of its global value chain and structure where funding comes from big Indian firms, global firms, research institutes, private equity funding, venture capital and Indian and foreign governments. Research experiments are either initiated in India or outsourced from Western countries. Clinical experiments involve public and private universities, research institutes, medical colleges and private hospitals. These are discussed in detail in the latter part of the chapter. What is more important here is the role of the state. Although public funding for R&D in medical innovations is negligible in India, the state plays a proactive facilitative role in the promotion of R&D, largely motivated by the potential of the sector to drive economic growth as it is expected in the Western countries with the emergence of the biotechnology sector.

The Department of Science and Technology (DST) has several focussed programmes, including the technology development board, which helps to commercialise technologies and adopt foreign technologies; technology system development programmes for the promotion of advanced technologies; national science and technology entrepreneurship development board; drug and pharmaceutical research programmes; start-up research grants; and policy research centres, among others (see Tiwari et al. 2017). BIRAC, established in 2012 under the Department of Biotechnology (DBT) of the Government of India, is a dedicated body to promote innovations in the sector and its commercialisation. The national biopharma mission document of BIRAC details its objectives, which include 'development of affordable products; development of affordable products; building and strengthening domain specific knowledge and management skills and creating and enhancing technology transfer capabilities in public and private sector including Intellectual Property Management'.[10] BIRAC supports biotechnology innovation start-ups in

---

[10] For details, see 'Industry–Academia Collaborative Mission for Accelerating Early Development for Biopharmaceuticals – Innovate in India (i3) Empowering Biotech Entrepreneurs and Accelerating Inclusive Innovation', available at http://www.birac.nic.in/webcontent/Biopharma_Vacancy_Mission_Document_I.pdf, accessed in October 2018.

India in several ways. It has provisions to grant seed money up to INR 20 million for the setting up of start-ups that have the potential to grow. It also arranges to obtain private equity investments, called ACE (Accelerating Entrepreneurs) funds, of up to INR 80 million for start-ups that have shown *positive* results. Other than this, BIRAC has programmes such as small business innovation research initiative, contract research and service scheme, university innovation cluster, regional innovation centres and bio-incubator support[11] for facilitating research and translation of research output into commercial products. As per the data provided by BIRAC, nearly 430 start-ups in human health received assistance from BIRAC as of January 2019. We have attempted to understand the product/service focus of these start-ups and obtained information on 344 firms from their respective websites. A broader classification that we attempted based on the information available on their websites shows that the majority of them were medical devices and diagnostic technology start-ups for diagnosis and management of non-communicable diseases (NCDs), followed by pharmaceuticals, biopharmaceuticals, capacity building and health data service firms and genomic R&D firms (see Figure 1.6). This pattern is in line with the global trend in health R&D, which showed an increased focus on NCDs and biomedicine as discussed in the introductory chapter.

Figure 1.6   Broader classification of areas of focus of start-ups that received assistance from BIRAC (as of January 2019)

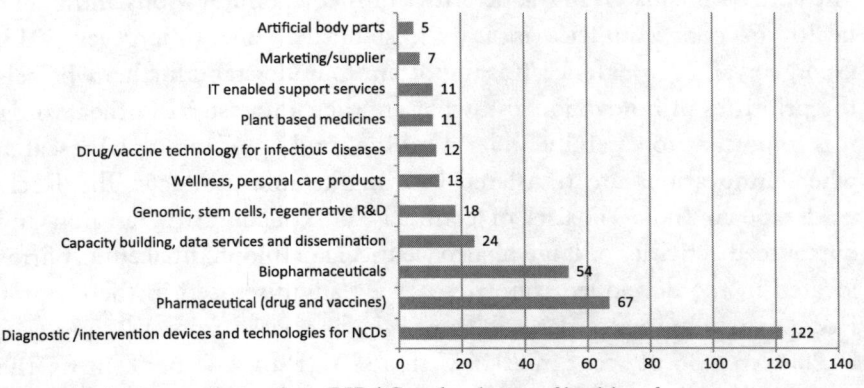

Source: Author's compilation from BIRAC and websites of health industry start-ups.

---

11   For details, see http://www.birac.nic.in/index.php, accessed in October 2018.

What is important to note is that although the objective of state facilitation and promotion is to support innovations that are useful and affordable (in principle), the emphasis on economic growth and commercialisation of research output overpowers the programmes and activities of DBT. The biotechnology policies in India have an inherent component of applied research that endeavour to commercialise and market the products that are developed. While product development, industrial growth and economic growth appear to be noble objectives, it is debatable whether the present organisation of innovations is capable of striking the right balance between the health needs of the country and the growth goals of the industry. This is perhaps due to the overall shift in the state's focus from regulation to promotion and facilitation of research and product development. Furthermore, the adoption of the US model of institutional arrangements where the funding for innovation comes largely from private firms and speculative capital could lead to a supply-driven market in which affordability may not be a priority. Arguably, the present structure and organisation of medical innovations in the pharmaceutical and biopharmaceutical sectors could dilute the noble objective of developing useful and affordable innovations as mentioned in the national biopharma mission document.

Funding agencies and priority areas in medical innovation

The general mismatch in the priorities of medical innovations and public health in poor countries is a well-established one (Viergever 2013; George et al. 2018). Hence, it is important to understand further who sets the priorities of innovation and what are their interests? In other words, it is important to carefully understand the funding of industrial research where innovations are translated into marketable products. The R&D landscape in India consists of contract and collaborative research and outsourced activities of large pharmaceutical and biopharmaceutical firms located in the developed countries. As already discussed in the chapter, R&D expenditure as a percentage of sales increased from 1.27 per cent in 2000 to 6.36 per cent in 2016 with a CAGR of 9.46 per cent for the pharmaceutical sector. The share of R&D in the total sales was more in the biopharmaceutical sector, which increased from 2.3 per cent in 2000 to 9.28 per cent in 2016 for the biopharmaceutical sector with a CAGR of 8.19 per cent. Although at a slower pace, innovations in the healthcare sector in India tend to pick up gradually with the concerted efforts of the government and the Indian pharmaceutical MNCs. R&D in the pharmaceutical sector in India is driven majorly by the Indian private firms and as per the data provided by CMIE, Indian private companies accounted for 96.6 per cent of the total R&D in the pharmaceutical sector in 2016. The share of the MNCs was nearly 3.4 per cent in 2016 whereas the public sector companies contributed only 0.1 per cent of the total R&D in the pharmaceutical sector (see Figure 1.3). Similarly, nearly 99 per cent of the R&D in the biopharmaceutical sector in 2016 was from Indian firms (see Figure 1.5). Drug development has been a very low priority for the public sector pharmaceutical companies. Sources other than public and private manufacturing companies for the funding of health R&D in India include the Council for Scientific and Industrial Research (CSIR), ICMR, DBT and DST in the public sector and USAID, the Bill & Melinda Gates Foundation and the Wellcome Trust in the non-profit non-public sector (Dandona et al. 2017). These funds are provided mostly for research studies conducted in public and private universities and specialised research centres. The global health R&D repository of the WHO regularly updates the number of grants for health research by funder, type of grant, duration, health category and recipients in its regions. As per these data, Indian institutions have so far received 435 external grants of which 191 were from the National Institute of Health (NIH) of the US, 89 were from the Canadian Institute of Health Research (CIHR), 67 were from the Medical Research Council (MRC), UK, and 21 each from the Wellcome Trust and the Bill & Melinda Gate Foundation. It should also be noted that out of the 22 ongoing externally supported collaborative research projects in Indian institutes as of May 2019, 17 are on NCDs and the remaining 5 are on infectious diseases. Within the NCDs, the majority (11) are on cardiovascular diseases.

Other sources of funding of medical innovations in India include angel investors and venture capital for start-ups in the pharmaceutical and biopharmaceutical sectors. A report the daily *The Mint* in November 2018 showed that investments in medical innovations increased from USD 163 million in 2016 to USD 343 million in 2017.[12] Venture capital investments

---

[12] For details, see Sriram (2018).

are also picking up in India. A report by KPMG (2016b), for instance, showed that venture capital investments in healthcare and the life sciences in India increased by 23 per cent between 2013 and 2015. It is extremely difficult to obtain the data on such investments; however, some grey literature on investments in start-ups between 2015 and 2018 have been gathered through a web search.[13] Most of these healthcare start-ups offer web-based booking and interaction services, diagnostic and treatment services, online pharmacy, health and wellness centres, development of therapeutics, home-based medical care, biomedical research and clinical trials (see Figure 1.7). It should be noted that the data presented here cover only those firms that publicised information on the source of funds, amount, type of investment and area of operation. BIRAC has provided a list of beneficiaries, including private companies, research institutions, entrepreneurs and start-ups financially supported through their various programmes. Some of the start-ups in the healthcare sector featuring in the BIRAC beneficiary list are not included in the data presented here due to lack of further information on funding. The data given, hence, are incomplete and merely indicative of the private funding that came to healthcare start-ups in India through seed/angel funding and venture capital.

The data show that venture capital investments are found more in start-ups that are already established and working in the areas of specialised care, online pharmacy, biomedical and genomics and health and wellness centres (see Figure 1.8). Venture capital has considerable presence in internet-based service platforms and diagnostic and intervention technologies as well. For instance, as per our data, out of the 105 funding deals in internet-based booking and interaction services in healthcare that included doctor booking, doctor–patient interaction, healthcare information, virtual health clinics, drug information and service aggregators, 57 per cent were seed/angel investments and remaining 43 per cent were venture capital investments. Similarly, out of the 39 funding deals between 2015 and 2018 in diagnostic, devices and intervention technologies, 54 per cent were seed/angel funding.

---

[13] Data presented here are compiled from https://trak.in/india-startup-funding-investment-2015/, accessed in January 2019.

Figure 1.7 Number of start-ups that received private funding in India by area of focus, 2015–2018

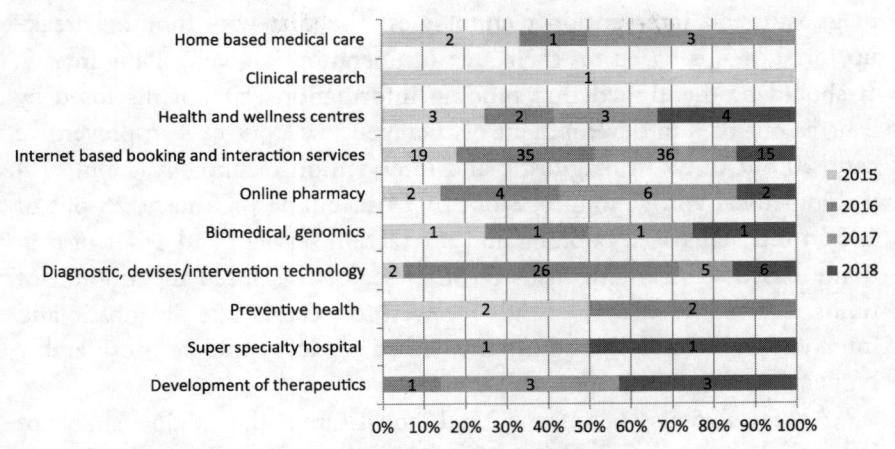

Source: Compiled from https://trak.in, accessed in January 2019.

Figure 1.8 Type of funds received by the start-ups by area of focus, 2015–2018 (number)

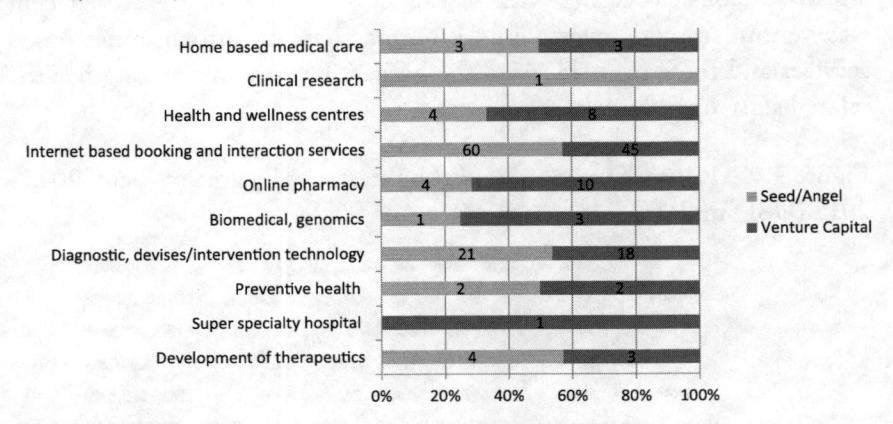

Source: Compiled from https://trak.in, accessed in January 2019.

Although not complete, the data on funding provide some information on the priority areas of private seed and venture capital funding for healthcare start-ups in India. Our data show that out of an investment of USD 12.54 billion between 2015 and 2018, 29 per cent was for internet-based services and interactions, 17 per cent was for super speciality hospitals, 15 per cent for health and wellness centres, 12 per cent for online pharmacy, 10 per cent for home-based care services and 8 per cent for diagnostic and intervention technologies. The year-wise funding break-up for start-ups based on their area of operation is given in Figure 1.9. It should be mentioned that funding information was not disclosed by 2 firms out of 7 in development of therapeutics, 1 out of 4 in preventive care, 20 out of 39 in diagnostic and intervention technology, 1 out of 4 in biomedical and genomics, 3 out of 14 in online pharmacy, 26 out of 105 in internet-based booking and interaction services and 1 out of 6 in home-based services. All firms in other sectors disclosed the amount of funds received. Hence, the funds received for sectors like diagnostic and intervention technology and internet-based services could be considerably higher than what is given.

As is obvious, venture capital constituted the major share of investments in terms of total amount (see Figure 1.10). Firms which have areas of specialisation such as super speciality hospitals, online pharmacy, biomedical genomics and preventive health were mostly supported by venture capital investments. These were also the start-ups that were already established earlier with seed/angel funding. Nearly 70 per cent was venture capital investments in firms that are into internet-based services and these firms received the highest investments among health-related start-ups.

Figure 1.9   Private funding received by start-ups by area of focus, 2015–2018 (USD million)

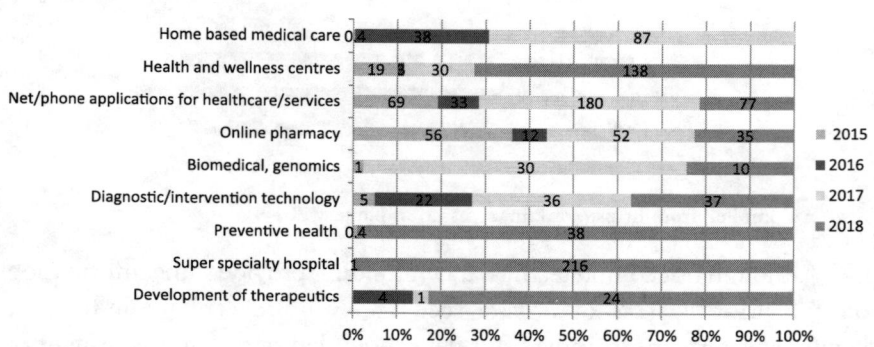

Source: Compiled from https://trak.in, accessed in January 2019.

Figure 1.10 Amount of funding received by start-ups by area of focus and type of fund, 2015–2018 (USD million)

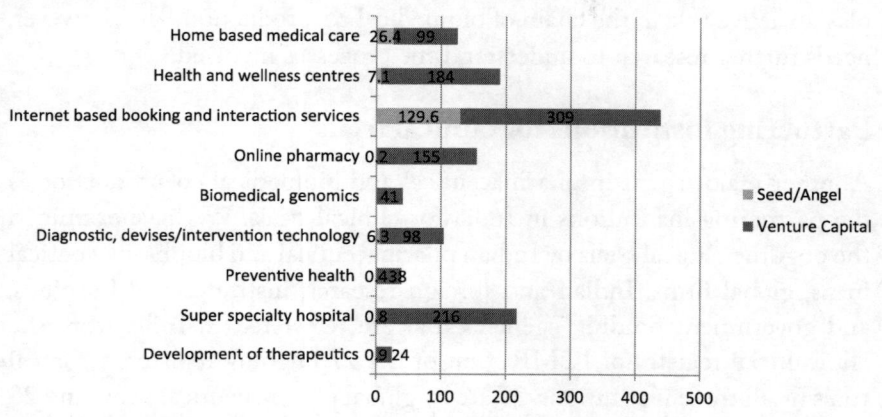

Source: Compiled from https://trak.in, accessed in January 2019.

Data on start-ups in the healthcare sector also allow us to understand the trajectories of commercialisation of medical innovations. As is clear from the data, most of these firms are internet-based information services and consumer service interfaces, online pharmacies, health and wellness centres, home-based care solutions and diagnostic services. Except for a few firms that are into biomedical development, most of these do not directly involve in product or technology development, but take an active role in knowledge dissemination and consumption. In most of the cases these technology-enabled platforms can replace the role of doctors and specialists, who otherwise possibly account for patients' social and biomedical environments for diagnosis and treatment. It is still a grey area how the virtual medical encounters contribute to the biomedicalisation of healthcare. Proliferation of unregulated medical encounters like telemedicine, over the counter purchase and purchase of drugs through online pharmacies with or without practitioner's prescription are typical examples. Similarly, online health and wellness centres, which provide preventive and therapeutic advice as well as guidance on selection of diagnostic technology, could also play a major role in the subtle legitimisation of biomedical knowledge. The direct advertisement of products to the patient (customer) through various channels such as advertisements in online health platforms, patient advocacy groups, social media, public sponsored events, festivals, national health programmes, free health camps, civil society and faith-based organisations and hospitals is also rampant in India. Arguably, such knowledge and service platforms play an active role in the chain of biomedical co-production. This, however, needs further research to understand the processes involved.

Partnering institutions for clinical trials

Another major agent in pharmaceutical and biomedical co-production is the partnering institutions in India for clinical trials. We have examined the ongoing clinical trials by Indian pharmaceutical and biopharmaceutical firms, global firms, Indian and foreign research institutes and hospitals, and government funding agencies that are registered in India from the clinical trial registry of ICMR. Out of the 77 ongoing registered clinical trials by all these institutions, 37 are by global pharmaceutical firms and 23 by Indian firms (see Figure 1.11). There are 7 ongoing registered clinical trials by Indian and foreign government funding agencies, and 6 by Indian and foreign research institutes. As is clear from Figure 1.11, cancer has the highest focus in clinical trials, followed by cardiovascular, diabetes and hypertension. Nearly 50 per cent of the clinical trials for cancer drugs were registered by the global firms. The disease focus of the clinical trials of global firms also included cardiovascular diseases, diabetes, hypertension, asthma, arthritis and acne. The focus of the Indian firms has predominantly been on cancer, followed by diabetes and hypertension.

The clinical trial data also give information on the participating hospitals, which are part of the complex chain of co-production of innovation. We have identified the private, charity and public sector hospitals from the clinical trial registry data. As is clear from Figure 1.12, private and charity hospitals together dominate the clinical trials of pharmaceutical and biomedical firms in all categories of diseases. Participation of public hospitals was limited to the trial of drugs and technologies for cancer, cardiovascular, diabetes, asthma and hypertension.

The firm-wise information of clinical trials, disease focus and participating hospitals is given in Tables 1A.1–1A.5 (see Appendix 1A). As already discussed, cancer received the highest focus of Indian firms. The major Indian firms that undertake clinical trials for cancer in India include Glenmark, Biocon, Reliance Life Sciences, Zydus Cadila Panacea Biotech, Dr Reddy's, Boehringer Ingelheim India, Cipla and Itas

Figure 1.11   Number of ongoing registered clinical trials in India by disease focus and type of institutions (as of March 2019)

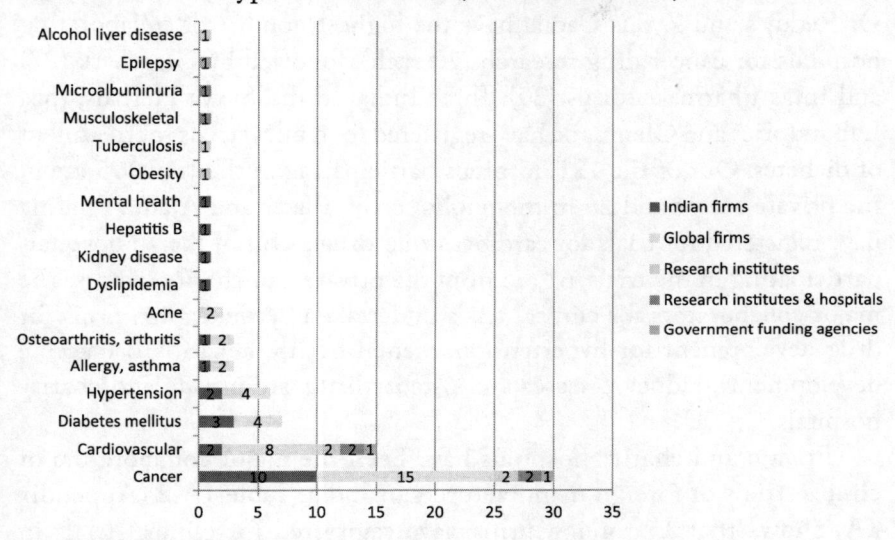

Source: Clinical Trial Registry, India, ICMR.

Figure 1.12   Number of participating hospitals in the ongoing clinical trials by sector and disease focus (as of March 2019)

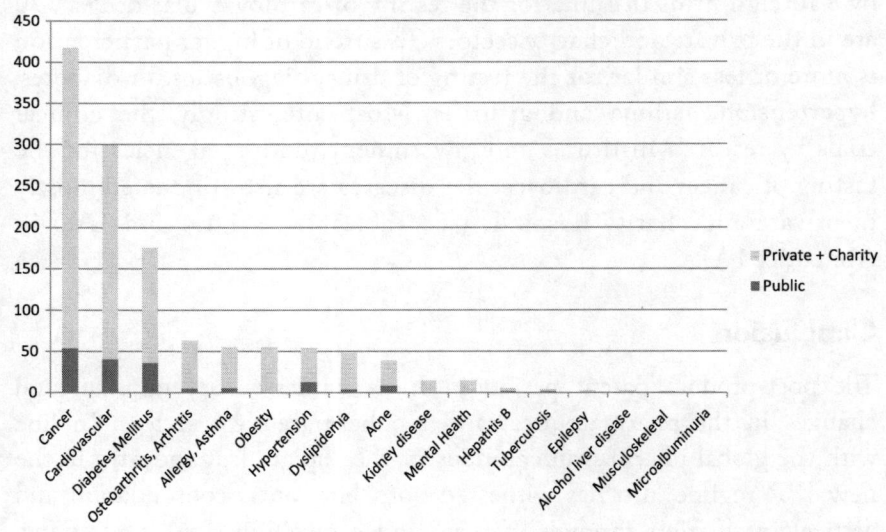

Source: Clinical Trial Registry, India, ICMR.

Pharmaceuticals. As is clear from Table 1A.5, out of 177 ongoing trials, 157 are in private and charity hospitals and 20 are in public hospitals. Dr Reddy's and Zydus Cadila have the highest number of collaborating hospitals for cancer drug research (29 each), followed by Glenmark (27) and Intas Pharmaceuticals (20). Three Indian firms, Surya Herbals, Ipca Laboratories and Glenmark, have registered for clinical trials for treatment of diabetes. Out of the 121 hospitals participating in the trials, 95 are in the private sector and 26 in the public sector. Pfizer and Ajanta Pharma have registered for trials for cardiovascular drugs. Out of the 73 hospitals participating in the trials, 61 are from the private and charity sectors. The major collaborators for clinical trials undertaken by the Indian firms for drug development for hypertension, mental health, hepatitis B (vaccine development), kidney diseases and osteoarthritis are private and charity hospitals.

Private and charity hospitals have been the major collaborators of clinical trials of foreign manufacturers in India. Table 1A.2 (Appendix 1A) shows that 15 foreign firms have registered for clinical trials in India for the testing of drugs and diagnostic for the treatment of cancer. Out of the 249 participating hospitals, 217 are in the private and charity sectors. Similarly, out of the 191 clinical trials conducted by 8 foreign firms in India for the testing of cardiovascular drugs, 170 are in the private and charity sectors. This trend of higher participation is more or less similar for the testing of drugs/diagnostics for diabetes, hypertension, asthma and arthritis. Most interestingly, the clinical trials by research institutes and government funding agencies for the testing of cancer and cardiovascular diseases are also conducted mostly in private and charity hospitals (see Tables 1A.3, 1A.4 and 1A.5 in Appendix 1A).

Conclusion

The post-product patent period in India witnessed several structural changes in the pharmaceutical and biopharmaceutical sectors. In line with the global pharmaceutical industry, the Indian drug industry in the new IPR regime also has witnessed both horizontal consolidation and vertical integration through mergers and acquisitions, out contracting, decentralising production and establishing linkages through global value chains. The emergence of the biomedical and biopharmaceutical firms in a big way in India also led to the establishment of several back-end small service providers in the sector. The expansion of research network and collaboration is another trend that we noted with the involvement of industry, state, government research institutions, public sector laboratories, universities, small, medium and large Indian companies, Indian MNCs, foreign MNCs and contract research organisations of big companies in the new product patent regime.

Another important finding is the dominance of Indian private sector companies in income, sales, export and R&D spending in both pharmaceutical and biopharmaceutical sectors. While the Indian private firms showed a steady increase in income generation in the pharmaceutical sector, income of the MNCs has been significantly lower than that of the Indian private firms. The Indian private sector also holds the major share of the income and R&D spending in the biopharmaceutical sector, and the role of the public sector in Indian biopharmaceutical has always been negligible. Also, R&D activities, especially NCE development, are undertaken mostly in the biopharmaceutical sector rather than the conventional pharmaceutical sector. It must also be noted that NCE development is at a very nascent stage in India. The production and R&D landscape of the pharmaceutical and biopharmaceutical sectors witnessed complete dominance and control by the private sector in the product patent period. The industry has also been led by a few companies that produce branded generics. Most importantly, as evident from their export volume and revenue, a significant part of the drug and vaccine development in India firms is aimed at fulfilling the requirement of the international market.

The Indian medical innovation landscape is also characterised by a complex institutional network for the commercialisation, co-production and value realisation of the knowledge. The direct partners of this network include Indian and foreign big pharmaceutical and biopharmaceutical companies, Indian contract research firms, private hospitals, Indian and foreign seed/angel investors, venture capitalists, state facilitating agencies such as DST and its dedicated wing of BIRAC for promotion, technology transfer, funding and commercialisation, state funding agencies for research such as CSIR, ICMR and universities, private and public research institutions and individual entrepreneurs. Media, virtual information and service providers, civil society groups facilitating clinical trials, patient discussion groups and forums, online pharmacies that advertise directly to patient-customers, health and wellness centres and an array of care, beauty, career and personality development institutions are indirect agents in this network of co-production as they disseminate the information and become part of the marketing strategies of the manufacturers. The direction and disease focus of medical innovation is also largely determined by the nature of funding. The overwhelming presence of private funding and the domination of global firms in R&D can lead to the development of products that will have better market returns and for the benefit of the population in the developed world. The venture capital investment in Indian medical innovation start-ups is an example – it showed the emphasis on merely the market success of the product.

Appendix 1A

Table 1A.1   Ongoing clinical trials by Indian pharmaceutical companies by disease focus by type of hospital

| | | Number of hospitals involved | | |
Disease	Firm	Public	Private	Total
Asthma	Glenmark Pharmaceuticals Ltd	2	25	27
	Biocon Ltd	2	8	10
	Reliance Life Sciences	0	12	12
Cancer	Reliance Life Sciences	1	11	12
	Panacea Biotec Ltd	1	3	4
	Zydus Cadila	6	23	29
	Dr Reddys Laboratories Ltd	2	27	29
	Boehringer Ingelheim India	3	14	17
	Cipla Ltd India	0	17	17
	Intas Pharmaceuticals	3	17	20

(Contd.)

Disease	Firm	Number of hospitals involved		
		Public	Private	Total
Cardiovascular	Pfizer	7	50	57
	Ajanta Pharma	5	11	16
Diabetes mellitus	Surya Herbal Ltd	0	1	1
	Ipca Laboratories	18	44	62
	Glenmark	8	50	58
Diagnosis of scabies	Zydus Worldwide	1	10	11
Dyslipidemia	Zydus Cadila	4	44	48
Hepatitis B	Cadila Healthcare	2	4	6
Hypertension	Ajanta Pharma	13	23	36
Kidney disease	Intas Biopharmaceuticals Ltd	0	15	15
Mental health	Mylan Laboratories	1	14	15
Osteoarthritis	Encube Ethicals	1	24	25
Postmenopausal atrophic vaginitis	Famy Care Ltd	0	10	10

Source: Clinical Trial Registry, India, compiled.

Table 1A.2 Ongoing clinical trials by global pharmaceutical companies operating in India by disease focus by type of hospital

Disease focus	Firm/primary sponsor	No. of trial hospitals		
		Public	Private + charity	Total
Acne	Morningside Healthcare	4	17	21
	Cadila Healthcare	5	13	18
Allergy	Hetero Labs Ltd	2	7	9
Asthma	Novartis	2	17	19

Disease focus	Firm/primary sponsor	No. of trial hospitals		
		Public	Private + charity	Total
Cancer	Boehringer Ingelheim Pharmaceuticals	2	17	19
	Hexal AG	5	29	34
	AstraZeneca AB	0	3	3
	Celltrion	2	10	12
	Mylan GmbH	1	25	26
	Roche Products	2	15	17
	Novartis	1	2	3
	Novartis	1	4	5
	Novartis	2	10	12
	Archigen Biotech	1	20	22
	Actavis Inc	1	26	27
	Bayer AG	1	9	10
	Teva Pharmaceuticals	2	18	20
	Eirgenix Inc	0	9	9
	Hetero Biopharma	10	20	30
	Bristol Myers Squibb	4	33	37
Cardiovascular	Boehringer Ingelheim	1	14	15
	LivaNova PLC	0	11	11
	Guerbet	8	15	23
	Boehringer Ingelheim	0	15	15
	Esperion Therapeutics Inc	5	33	38
	Clearside Biomedical Inc	2	20	22
	Actavis Deutschland GmbH Co KG	1	29	30
Cerebral venous and dural sinus thrombosis	Boehringer Ingelheim	1	7	8

(*Contd.*)

(*Contd.*)

Disease focus	Firm/primary sponsor	No. of trial hospitals		
		Public	Private + charity	Total
	Actelion pharmaceuticals	0	5	5
Hypertension	InnoPharma Inc	0	1	1
	InnoPharma Inc	0	1	1
	United Therapeutics	0	11	11
Rheumatoid arthritis	Hetero Biopharma	3	11	14
	Lupin	1	23	24
	Novo Nordisk	4	17	21
Type 2 diabetes	Novo Nordisk	2	10	12
	Novo Nordisk	3	10	13
	Amylin LLC	1	8	9

Source: Clinical trial registry, India, compiled.

Table 1A.3 Ongoing clinical trials by research institutes (Indian and foreign) by disease focus by type of hospital

Institute/ primary sponsor	Source of monetory support	Disease focus	No. of trial hospitals		
			Public	Private + charity	Total
Composite Interceptice Med-Science, Mazumdar Shaw Centre for Translational Research, Bengaluru	Mazumdar Shaw Centre for Translational Research, Bengaluru	Alcoholic liver disease	1	1	2
Medical Research Council Clinical Trials Unit, London	Sir Dorabji Tata Trust, Mumbai	Cancer	2	11	13

(*Contd.*)

(*Contd.*)

Institute/ primary sponsor	Source of monetory support	Disease focus	No. of trial hospitals		
			Public	Private + charity	Total
Cancer Institute, Chennai	Cancer Institute, Chennai	Cancer	1	0	1
National Health and Medical Research Council of Australia, Canberra	National Health and Medical Research Council of Australia , The George Institute for Global Health, Sydney	Cardiovascular	4	3	7
Patanjali Research Foundation, Haridwar	Patanjali Research Foundation	Obesity (Yoga)	0	55	55
Population Health Research Institute, Hamilton	Population Health Research Institution, Canada	Patients with diagnosis of hip fracture requiring surgery	4	8	12
The INCLEN Trust International, New Delhi	Grand Challenges Canada MaRS Centre, Canada	Pregnant women and children under two years without any major illness	0	1	1
University College London	University College London	Tuberculosis in children	2	2	4

Source: Clinical trial registry, India, compiled.

Table 1A.4 Ongoing clinical trials by research institutes cum hospitals (Indian and foreign) by disease focus by type of hospital

Institute/primary sponsor	Source of monetory support	Disease focus	No. of trial hospitals		
			Public	Private + charity	Total
Frontier Lifeline Pvt. Ltd, Chennai	Frontier Lifeline Pvt. Ltd, Chennai	Cardiovascular	0	1	1
Population Health Research Institute, Hamilton	McMaster University, Hamilton	Cardiovascular	1	8	9
Cancer Institute WIA, Chennai	Department of Science and Technology, GOI	Cancer	1	0	1
Tata Medical Centre	Tata Medical Centre	Cancer	0	1	1
ESI Medical College and Hospital, Faridabad	ESI Medical College and Hospital, Faridabad	Microalbuminuria	1	0	1
Department of Anaesthesiology, All India Institute of Medical Sciences, New Delhi	Institute of Medical Sciences, New Delhi	Musculoskeletal	1	0	1

Source: Clinical Trial Registry, India, compiled.

Table 1A.5 Ongoing clinical trials by government funding agencies (Indian and foreign) by disease focus by type of hospital

Institute/ primary sponsor	Source of monetory support	Disease focus	No. of trial hospitals		
			Public	Private + charity	Total
National Institute of Neurological Disorders and Stroke, US	University of California San Francisco	Epilepsy	1	1	2
Indian Council of Medical Research, India	Indian Council of Medical Research	Cardiovascular	3	15	18
National Cancer Grid, India	Department of Atomic Energy, Government of India	Cancer	1	2	3

Source: Clinical trial registry, India, compiled.

2

The Disease Focus of Health Research and Development

The previous chapter illustrated that innovation is a process of *co-production* in which several institutions and interest groups involve actively. This process of knowledge production essentially is not value neutral. What is, hence, important to understand is the nature of the institutions which are involved in the co-production of innovation and their priorities. This is important in medical innovations given the mutually conflicting priorities of public health and industrial interests. As is well known, research and development (R&D), especially in the pharmaceutical sector, in its initial period was supported by government institutions, public laboratories and government grants. However, with the new patent regime the private players have started participating increasingly in drug, vaccine and medical technology development. Studies have shown that the pharmaceutical industry is one of the sectors that have high R&D spending levels (Dhar and Gopakumar 2006, Abrol et al. 2011). Studies also showed that availability of medicines and medical technology products in the market has increased significantly in India with the expansion of domestic and multinational private companies, which benefited from a facilitating industrial policy environment (Joseph 2016). However, most of the R&D activities in India remain merely a small part of the large global value chain emphasising on contract manufacturing and contract research. The focus of research in the industry, therefore, has been predominantly guided by the consideration of the Western markets (the United States and the European Union), leaving less focus on neglected tropical diseases and population (see Viergever 2013). Studies showed that only 10 per cent of domestic firms' investment on R&D is spent on the needs of developing countries (Rowden 2013). It is, hence, not clear whether the change in the policy design, though it has increased research activity, has taken care of the public health needs of the country.

This chapter attempts to understand the disease focus of health R&D in India. It specifically examines the drugs, vaccines, medical devices and diagnostic technology R&D of private and public sector firms/institutions in India. We have extracted the data on drugs approved for marketing in India from 2001 to 2017 from the Central Drugs Standard Control Organisation (CDSCO), Government of India, to understand the therapeutic focus of drugs R&D. Further, the chapter documents vaccine development in the biopharmaceutical sector in India by surveying major biopharmaceutical firms operating in India to understand the trajectory of the disease focus of the industry. The chapter also discusses the new drug development scenario in India by examining the new chemical entities (NCEs) being developed in both the pharmaceutical and biopharmaceutical sectors. Finally, the chapter discusses the disease focus of medical technology innovations in India.

R&D and disease focus

Studies have shown that the recent increase in R&D in India was set off by contract research by multinational companies (MNCs), collaborative research projects and out-licensing and in-licensing taking advantage of the low-cost manufacturing opportunities as well as the competitive edge of India in drug manufacturing (Joseph 2016). As already discussed in the previous chapter, R&D activities of Indian pharmaceutical firms are largely centred around developing non-infringing processes and new formulations of existing drugs. The development of NCEs constitutes only a minor share of the R&D investments due to the higher likelihood of failures at various stages. However, drug development continues to be an important activity of many of the big pharmaceutical and biopharmaceutical firms due to challenges and opportunities of the new intellectual property rights (IPR) regime. Figure 2.1 illustrates that R&D in the pharmaceutical sector in India is driven majorly by the private firms. Drug development has been a very low priority for public sector pharmaceutical companies. The CMIE Prowess data show that 14 private firms, which include Sun Pharmaceuticals, Cipla, Lupin, Dr Reddy's, Aurobindo Pharma, Cadila, Abbott, Torrent Pharma, Intas Pharmaceuticals, Biocon, Emami, Wockhardt, Glenmark and Ipca Laboratories, have recorded the highest spending on R&D as a percentage of sales. The R&D focus of the biomedical sector has also expanded gradually. As Figure 2.2 shows, R&D spending as a percentage of sales is more than 10 per cent in private biopharmaceutical firms as of 2016 in India. It also shows that much of the R&D activities in the medical biotechnology sector are undertaken in the private sector.

Figure 2.1   R&D as percentage of sale of Indian pharmaceutical sector, 2000–2016

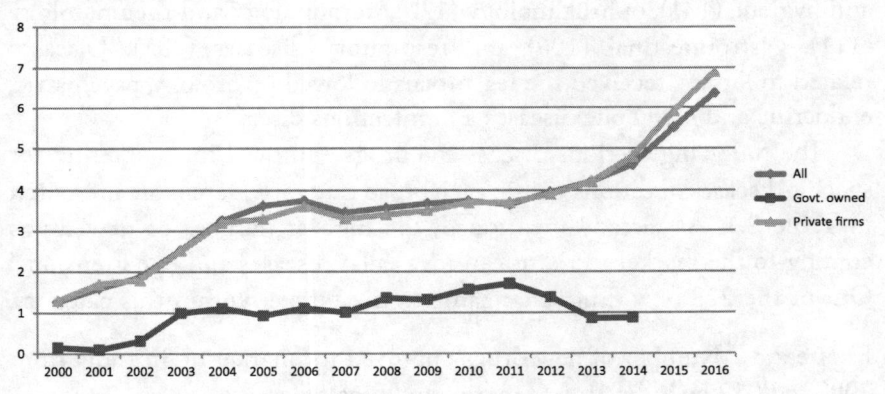

Source: George et al. (2018).

Figure 2.2   R&D as percentage of sale of Indian biopharmaceutical sector, 2000–2016

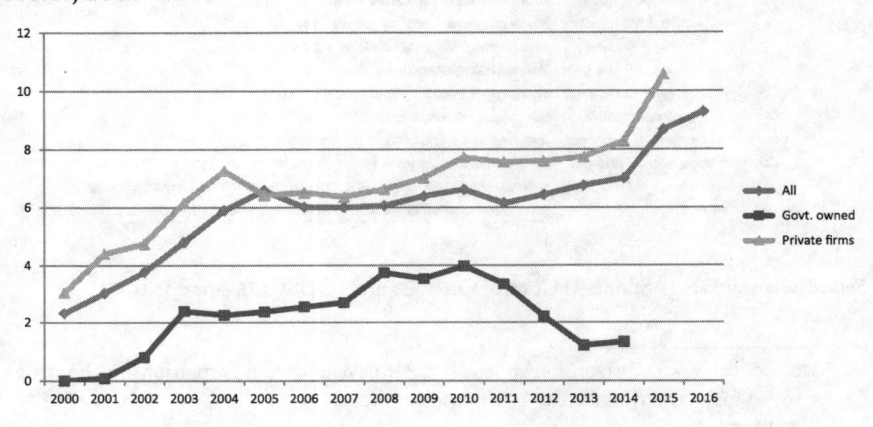

Source: George et al. (2018).

Disease focus of R&D in branded generics and biosimilars

The data from CDSCO on generics and biosimilars developed show that out of 1,635 new drugs approved for marketing between 2000 and 2017, 87 per cent were for non-communicable diseases (NCDs) whereas only 6 per cent of the new drugs that came to the market were for communicable diseases (see Figure 2.3).[1] Within NCDs, the highest number of new drugs came to the market for cardiovascular diseases and hypertension together (228), followed by neurological diseases (220), cancer (153), dermatology and hygiene (131), ophthalmology (120), immunology and rheumatology (111), gastrointestinal (106) and respiratory diseases (105). Diseases related to kidney received the least focus followed by urology, psychiatric, endocrine and metabolic diseases and infectious diseases.

The following sections discuss the drugs approved for marketing for specific disease conditions within each broad category. Details are presented in Table 2.1. As already mentioned, the highest number of new drugs coming to the market were for cardiovascular diseases and hypertension.[2] Out of the 228 new drugs that came to the market within this category,

Figure 2.3   Number of new drugs approved for marketing in India from 2000 to 2017 by indication (generics and biosimilars)

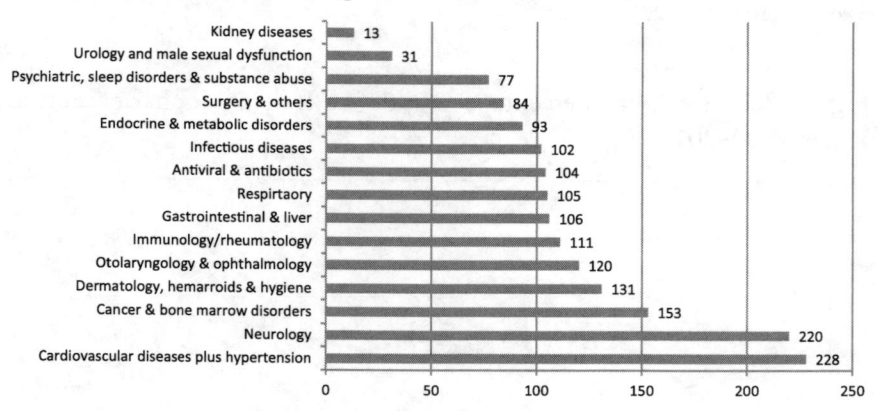

Source: Central Drugs Standard Control Organisation (CDSCO), compiled.

---

[1]   Also see Table 2A.1 given in Appendix 2A for year-wise information on the drugs approved for marketing for the 14 disease conditions.

[2]   See Table 3A.2 for year-wise drugs approved for marketing for various disease conditions in this category.

Table 2.1 Number of new drugs approved for marketing between 2000 and 2017 across disease conditions – 1

Condition	Number	Condition	Number
Cardio vascular		**Gastrointestinal and liver**	
Antihypertensive	103	Antiulcer	60
Heart diseases/ cholestrol	92	Gastritis	6
Vasodilator	2	Irritable bowel syndrome	18
Antithrombotics	18	Liver/gall bladder	14
Aggregation inhibitor	7	Prokinetic agent	2
Chronic iron overload due to blood transfusion	6	Hepatitis B	6
Total	228	Total	106
Neurological diseases		**Endocrinology and metabolic disorders**	
Antiepileptic/ seizure disorder	46	Anti-diabetic	52
Parkinson's disease	12	Hormonal therapy	11
Peripheral/ diabetic neuropathy	26	Hyperprolactinemia	3
Multiple sclerosis	7	Contraceptive	9
Alzheimer's dementia	15	Hyperthyroidism	3
Migraine	11	Pancreatitis	2
Analgesic	88	Obesity	4
Brain damage/ stimulant	15	Osteoporosis	7
Total	220	Total	91
Dermatology and hygiene		**Otolaryngology and ophthalmology**	
Vitiligo/psoriasis	55	Anti-glaucoma	14
Acne vulgaris, reduction of unwanted facial hair in women	19	Ophthalmic	63
Antifungal	25	Ear diseases	5

(*Contd.*)

(*Contd.*)

Condition	Number	Condition	Number
Cardio vascular		*Gastrointestinal and liver*	
Hygiene/wound healing/burns	32	Anti-allergic	38
Total	131	Total	120
Immunology and rheumatology		*Infectious diseases*	
Anti-inflammatory	42	HIV	51
Anti-spasmodic	20	Anti-diarrhoeal	23
Osteo-rheumatoid arthritis	46	Anti-malaria	19
Immunosuppressant	3	Parasites	4
Total	111	Tuberculosis	2
		Kala-azar	2
		Leprosy	1
		Total	102

Source: CDSCO, compiled.

103 were for treating hypertension, followed by drugs used for treating cholesterol (92). Out of the 220 new drugs that came to the market for treating neurological diseases between 2000 and 2017, 88 were analgesics, 46 were anti-epileptic, 26 were for treating diabetic neuropathy, 15 each for Alzheimer's and brain damage, 12 for Parkinson's diseases and 11 for migraine.

Out of the 1,635 new drugs that came to the market between 2000 and 2017, 153 were for treating various forms of cancer and bone marrow disorders. We do not have data on sub-category specific drugs approved for marketing for cancer treatments, but as evident from the data, there was an added focus on developing drugs for cancer treatments in India, which is one of the leading causes of mortality and morbidity within NCDs in India. The fourth priority in drug development was for dermatology and hygiene-related drugs. As many as 131 new drugs were approved for marketing in this category between 2000 and 2017. Out of these drugs, the highest was for treating vitiligo and psoriasis (55), followed by products for wound healing and burns (32), antifungal drugs (25) and for cosmetic treatment (18).

The next highest focus was on treatment of eyes and related conditions. Out of the 1,635 new drugs that came to the market, 120 were for otolaryngology and ophthalmology. As is evident from Table 2.1, out of 120 new drugs, more than 50 per cent (63) were for ophthalmic treatment. While 38 new drugs came for the treatment of allergy-related problems, 14 were for the treatment of glucoma and 5 were for ear diseases. Drugs for treating problems related to immunology and rheumatology received the highest attention after otolaryngology and ophthalmology. Within this segment, the highest number of drugs coming to the market was for osteoporosis and rheumatoid arthritis (46), followed by anti-inflammatory (46) and anti-spasmodic (20) drugs. Out of the 1,635 new drugs that came to the market between 2000 and 2017, 93 drugs were for treating endocrine and metabolic disorders. Within this, 52 new drugs were for treating diabetics. Nearly 106 new drugs came to the market for the treatment of diseases associated with gastrointestinal problems and liver problems. Out of these, the highest number of drugs came to the market for treating ulcer (60), followed by irritable bowel syndrome (18), liver and gall bladder (14), gastritis (6) and hepatitis B (6). Pulmonary diseases and antibiotic/antiviral received the highest focus in drug development after gastrointestinal and liver-related diseases. Out of a total of 104 new drugs that came to the market, 65 were for pulmonary diseases and 40 were for treating asthma and related problems. Similarly, out of the 104 new drugs that came to the market, 94 were antibiotic and 10 were antiviral.

Nearly 84 new drugs that came to the market between 2000 and 2017 were for use during surgery and associated problems (see Table 2.2). Within this segment, the highest number of drugs were for treating surgery and post-partum bleeding (46), followed by supplement/nutritional deficiency (related to excessive bleeding) and diagnostics. Next focus was on drugs for treating psychiatric, sleep disorder and substance use. As Table 2.2 shows, 77 new drugs came to the market in this segment. Within this, the highest number of new drugs were for the treatment of schizophrenia and panic disorder (37) followed by depression (22). A total of 44 new drugs were approved for marketing between 2000 and 2017 for the treatment of urological problems, kidney diseases and sexual dysfunction. Out of these, 13 were for treating kidney diseases, 12 for BPH (benign prostatic hyperplasia, or enlarged prostrate), 11 for male erectile dysfunction and 8 for the treatment of overactive urinary bladder.

Table 2.2   Number of new drugs approved for marketing between 2000 and 2017 across disease conditions – 2

Condition	Number	Condition	Number
Surgery and related issues		*Psychiatric, sleep disorders and substance abuse*	
Sweetening agent	3	Schizophrenia/ panic disorder	37
Diagnostic/ contrast medium	11	Antidepressant	22
Weight gain	2	Sleeping disorder	7
Nutritional deficiency supplement	22	Smoking cessation adjunct	4
Surgery, post-partum bleeding	46	Opioid drug dependence	4
Total	84	Alcohol dependency	2
		Sedative-hypnotic	1
Kidney and sexual dysfunction		Total	77
Kidney	13		
Enlarged prostrate (BPH)	12		
Male erectile dysfunction	11		
Overactive bladder	8		
Total	44		

Source: CDSCO, compiled.

Disease focus of therapeutic and vaccine R&D of biopharmaceuticals in India

We have examined the product focus of major biopharmaceutical companies, which include Indian private companies, Indian and international MNCs and enterprises in the public sector, to understand the products that they developed and those which are in the pipeline and its focus. We have compiled information on product specification and disease focus from the annual reports and websites of these firms. These firms were categorised based on their preventive and therapeutic focus (see Table 2A.2 in Appendix 2A). The domain focus of the biopharmaceutical industry in India in general includes the development of vaccines, bio-therapeutics, diagnostic and regenerative medicine. While most of these companies focus on product development, some of the small companies function as contract research organisations (CROs) of MNCs. A short webnographic account of the product and R&D focus of 27 biopharmaceutical firms is presented in Appendix 2A.

R&D pipeline of major India biopharmaceuticals

Tables 2.4 and 2.5 provide details on vaccines and bio-therapeutics that are in the pipeline of the biopharmaceutical firms examined here. It should be mentioned that the ongoing biopharmaceutical research in India focuses on preventive care in a major way. Out of the 42 companies mentioned in Table 2A.2, 20 have exclusive focus on preventive care, 13 have exclusive focus on therapeutic care and 9 companies focus on both preventive and therapeutic care. The disease focus of vaccine development of Indian biopharmaceutical companies include typhoid, Japanese encephalitis, chikungunya, malaria PvR (Plasmodium vivax Reticulocyte) II, acellular pertussis, tetanus, meningitis, DTwP–HBV (diphtheria and tetanus toxoids and whole-cell pertussis vaccine–hepatitis B virus) combination, haemophilus influenza type B, influenza, malaria, dengue, hapatitis A, rabies, Zika, polio, therapeutic vaccine for pancreatic cancer and oral cancer vaccines (see Table 2.3). In short, vaccine R&D in India focuses on the neglected diseases.

The focus of therapeutic R&D of the biopharmaceuticals, on the other hand, was on NCDs For instance, the therapeutic pipelines of the biopharmaceutical firms reviewed here are mainly for treating diseases/conditions like cancer, inflammation, immunology, retinal angiogenesis/liver fibrosis, obesity, mental health, psoriasis, diabetes, cardiovascular diseases, chronic obstructive pulmonary disease, inflammatory bowel disease, osteoporosis and rheumatoid arthritis (see Table 2.4). The R&D focus of a few of them was on medical diagnostic technologies for NCDs.

Table 2.3 Vaccine R&D pipelines of selected biopharmaceutical firms in India

Biopharmaceutical firm	*Vaccine R&D pipelines*
Sanofi Pasteur India	Dengue fever, enterotoxigenic *Escherichia coli* (ETEC) infections, tuberculosis, rabies, influenza
Serum Institute of India	Rotavirus vaccine for diarrhoea, dtap vaccine for pertussis, vaccine African meningitis, pneumococcal polysaccharide conjugate vaccine, human monoclonal antibody for rabies, HPV vaccine for cervical cancer
Panacea Biotech	pneumococcal conjugate CRM vaccine, chimeric recombinant tetravalent for dengue, Sabin IPV vaccine, viral vaccine for Japanese encephalitis
Bharat Biotech International Limited	Zika, chikungunya, *S. paratyphi*, non-typhoidal Salmonella (NTS) conjugates, human papilloma virus, acellular pertussis, malaria PvRII, Sabin IPV, lysostaphin topical, lysostaphin IV
Indian Immunologicals Limited	Marker vaccine for infectious bovine rhinotracheitis, multicomponent Clostridial vaccine, hepatitis A vaccine, chikungunya vaccine, Japanese encephalitis vaccine, pneumococcal conjugate vaccine, typhoid conjugate vaccine, measles rubella vaccine, dengue vaccine, rabies therapeutic monoclonal antibodies
GlaxoSmithKline India	Vaccines for Ebola, human immunodeficiency virus (HIV), malaria, HIV and tuberculosis
Biological E	Liquid hexavalent vaccine, pneumococcal conjugate vaccine, typhoid conjugate vaccine, paratyphoid vaccine, inactivated polio vaccine
Zydus Cadila Healthcare	Influenza, typhoid, DPT-HIB (diphtheria, tetanus, pertussis and haemophilus influenza type B), hepatitis A, B and E, Japanese encephalitis, HPV, measles-mumps-rubella-varicella, leishmaniasis, haemorrhagic Congo fever, Ebola, malaria

(*Contd.*)

(*Contd.*)

Biopharmaceutical firm	Vaccine R&D pipelines
Bhat Biotech	Detection of malaria, HIV and syphilis and detection of Angelman's, Phelan McDermid syndrome and other genetic disorders
Tergene Biotech	Multivalent pneumococcal vaccine and meningococcal vaccine
Gennova Biopharmaceuticals	Recombinant human papilloma virus (HPV) vaccine
Shantha Biotechnics	Shan 5, hexavalent vaccine (pentavalent + polio), rotavirus, typhoid conjugate, hapatitis A, HPV
Virchow Biotech	novel mucosal vaccine for HPV

Source: Compiled from websites of respective firm.

Table 2.4 Therapeutic R&D pipelines of selected biopharmaceutical firms in India

Biopharmaceutical firm	Therapeutic R&D pipelines
Sanofi Pasteur India	Immuno-inflammation, oncology, rare diseases, rare blood disorders, multiple sclerosis and neurology, diabetes, cardiovascular disease
Reliance Life Sciences	Human adult stem cells such as mesenchymal stem cells, haematopoietic stem cells, live skin substitute, liver cirrhosis, chronic kidney disease, type 1 diabetes mellitus, ischemic limb disease, graft versus host disease
Concord Biotech	Anti-bacterials, oncology
Shreya Life Sciences	Anti-bacterials, anti-diabetics, anti-malarials, anti-hypertensives, nutritionals, enzymes, anti-inflammatory, haematinics, anti-allergics, anti-tubercular
NovoNordisk India	Type 1 and 2 diabetes, obesity, haemophilia, growth disorders
Eli Lilly and Company India Private Limited	Cancer, diabetes, rheumatoid arthritis, Alzheimer's disease and osteoporosis

(*Contd.*)

Biopharmaceutical firm	*Therapeutic R&D pipelines*
GlaxoSmithKline India	Ovarian cancer, multiple myeloma, biliary tract cancer, head and neck squamous cell carcinoma, endometrial cancer, solid tumours and haematological malignancies, HIV, bacterial infection, tuberculosis, hepatitis b, visceral leishmaniasis; rheumatoid arthritis, systemic lupus erythematosus, hypereosinophilic syndrome, ulcerative colitis, Sjogren's syndrome, systemic sclerosis, pain in osteoarthritis, asthma, nasal polyposis, COPD, activated PI3K delta syndrome; anaemia associated with chronic renal disease, postpartum hemorrhage, primary biliary cholangitis, duchenne muscular dystrophy
Pfizer India	Depression, HIV, erectile dysfunction, hypertension, bacterial and fungal infections, cancer, arthritis, osteoporosis
Novartis India	Cancer, cardiovascular diseases, autoimmunity, transplantation and inflammatory diseases, musculoskeletal diseases, ophthalmology and respiratory diseases
Zydus Cadila Healthcare	Oncology, nephrology, inflammation, fertility, infectious diseases, osteoporosis
Virchow Biotech	Wound care and haemostasis, opthalmology, orthopaedics, gastroenterology and probiotics
Intas Pharmaceutical Limited	Cancer, bipolar disorder, hormones
Lupin Limited	Oncology, immunology, metabolic disorders
Biocon Ltd.	Breast cancer, colorectal cancer, chronic plaque psoriasis, chemo-induced neutropenia, stem cell transplantation, auto-immune disorders, diabetes, inflammation
Wockhardt	Recombinant protein therapeutics, anti-infectants, antibiotics
IMGENEX India Private Limited	Biosimilar antibodies for the treatment of breast cancer, arthritis, colorectal cancer, psoriasis and lung cancer

(*Contd.*)

Biopharmaceutical firm	Therapeutic R&D pipelines
Advinus Therapeutics	Inflammation, immunology, cancer, retinal angiogenesis/liver fibrosis, obesity, psoriasis, leishmaniasis, diabetes, chronic obstructive pulmonary disease, inflammatory bowel disease, rheumatoid arthritis
Cellworks	Immunology, oncology, anti-infectives
Clonz Biotech	Ranibizumab, recombinant humanised anti-VEGF mAb fragment
Indian Immunologicals	Monoclonal antibody technologies, recombinant mAb and fragments
Jupiter Bioscience	Cancer agents
Navya Life Sciences	r blood protein, r peptide hormone, r ESA, r enzyme, r 3G clot buster, r mAb AI disorders, biomaterial for wound management
Orchids	OCID, inflammation
Oxygen Heathcare Research	Novel h3 and other gpc receptor ligands
Serum Institute of India	Recombinant products, recombinant granulocyte colony stimulating factor, interferon alpha, recombinant erythropoietin
Stempeutics Research	Allogeneic mesenchymal stem cells
Transgene Biotek	Oncology, immunology

Source: Compiled from websites of respective firms.

The innovation policy of India aims to facilitate biomedical start-ups in a major way to foster academia–industry collaboration and promote innovations in health. As we have already discussed in the previous chapter, start-up companies that focus on customer relationship management, clinical trials, biosimilars, NCEs, diagnostic technologies and other health support services have come up in India. We examined the disease focus of some of the major biopharmaceutical start-ups in India. The details are presented in Table 2.5. Most of these start-ups were into development of diagnostic technologies or therapeutics. The disease focus of the start-ups examined was predominantly on NCDs including cancer, cardiovascular diseases and gastroenteritis. Some of them also focused on hormone therapy, stem cell therapy, tissue engineering, regenerative medicine, genetic and molecular testing, precision medicine, fertility, ophthalmology and body care. A few of them focused on the diagnostics of multi-drug-resistant (MDR) tuberculosis, malaria, hepatitis B and HIV.

Table 2.5 Research focus of selected biopharmaceutical start-ups in India

Name of the start-up	Focus area	End product/ pipeline	Use
Stempeutics	Stem cells for therapy, medical device to isolate stem	Stempeucel Stempeucare Stempeutron	Treatment of critical limb ischemia (CLI), osteoarthritis (OA) and diabetic foot ulcer (DFU) Rejuvenation of ageing skin, hair fall control and hair growth, under eye cream Extraction of mesenchymal stem cells, endothelial progenitor cells, other tissue-building cells
Navya Biologicals	Low-cost biologics	YeXtreme	Homing therapies for stem cellars In-vitro fertilisation (IVF)
LeadInvent	Advance formulations and smart patient selection		
Axio Biosolutions	Biopolymer platform based products for wound care	Axiostat, Maxiocel, Ask+	Sterile, haemostatic dressing intended to control moderate to severe bleeding within minutes of application

(Contd.)

Name of the start-up	Focus area	End product/ pipeline	Use
Achira Labs	Technology platform for immunodiagnostics	ACIX 100	Low resource environments for developing specific tests
Forus Health	Diagnostics systems	3Nethra classic, 3 NethraNeo, 3 Nethra Flora	Advanced medical devices for ophthalmic health
Mitra Biotech	Oncology treatment	CANscript	Personalised cancer treatment.
Pandorum Technologies	Tissue engineering, Regenerative medicine		Human liver organoids Bio-engineered corneas
Cardiac Design Labs	Diagnostics systems	MIRCaM Padma	Cardiac monitoring and diagnosis Single lead diagnostic and monitoring ambulatory electrocardiogram (ECG) device
Yaathum Biotech	Diagnostics systems	Quantitative polymerase chain reaction (PCR), or qPCR, assays	Identification of full range of drug resistant tuberculosis (MDR and XDR [extensively drug resistent]-TB) in single test
Purius Nanosystems	Diagnostics systems		Point-of-care testing devices for single tests for tuberculosis bacilli, malaria, hepatitis B virus or panel tests for HIV
Theramyt Novobiologics	Therapeutic monoclonal antibodies		Oncology, rheumatoid arthritis, diabetes and metabolic disorders

(*Contd.*)

(*Contd.*)

Name of the start-up	Focus area	End product/ pipeline	Use
Tricog	Cloud-based ECG device	Tricog Insta ECG	Remote diagnosis of heart abnormalities
Sattva Medtech	Diagnostics systems	Fetal Life	ECG-based device for monitoring fetal heart rate.
Swagene	Diagnostics systems	DNA extraction kits	Personalised genetic and molecular testing diagnostics

Source: Compiled from the websites and annual reports of respective start-ups.

Disease focus of new chemical entity research in India

Differding (2017) has compiled an exhaustive list of NCEs developed by Indian pharmaceutical and biopharmaceutical companies and which were at various stages of development until 2016. His list shows that the therapeutic focus of the NCEs in the pipeline has also been predominantly on NCDs. We have relied on the data provided by Differding (2017) to supplement our discussion on the therapeutic focus of drug development in India. The data compiled from Differding (2017) until 2016 are presented in Figure 2.4. It details the compounds that were at different stages of development. It should be mentioned that out of these only three compounds have reached up to phase 3 level of development and only one has been launched so far by the Indian pharmaceuticals (saroglitazar developed by Zydus Cadila for the treatment of type 2 diabetes). Differding's data show that out of the 227 NCEs in the pipeline, the therapeutic focus of nearly 84 per cent was on NCDs. Within NCDs, the highest was for endocrine and metabolic disorders (50) and oncology (50), followed by immunology (26), neurology (21) and pulmonary (21). Anticancer drugs were an important priority for both branded generics and NCE developers. The research focus on NCEs was more for those therapeutic indications of NCDs that have fewer medicines available in the market. For instance, while the new drugs that came to the market for endocrine and metabolic disorders were nearly 5 per cent of the total, their share in the total NCEs in the pipeline was almost 22 per cent.

Figure 2.4 Development of NCEs at different stages by indication

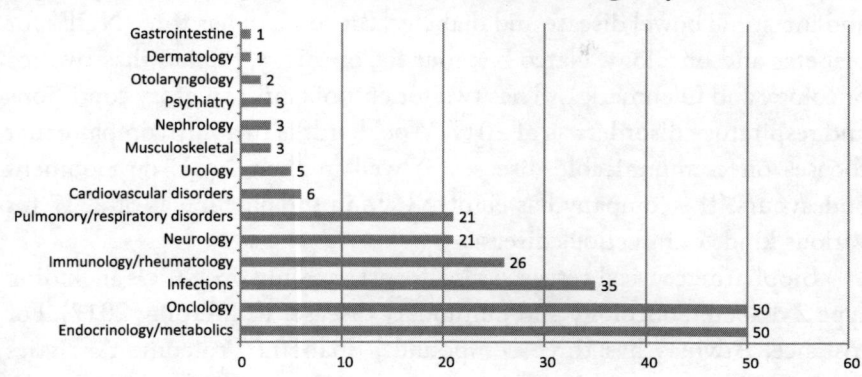

Similarly, while the number of cardiovascular drugs was the highest among the new drugs made available to the market, it constituted only 2 per cent of the NCEs in the pipeline. In short, we can infer that the R&D focus of NCEs is determined largely based on the space available in the market for new drugs in treating diseases like diabetes, cancer, infectious diseases, and so on.

We have further compiled the latest data on therapeutic areas of the major pharmaceutical and biopharmaceutical companies in India from their websites on R&D activities for developing NCEs. It shows a similar trend in the preponderance of NCDs. For instance, Zydus Cadila Healthcare Ltd, which spends nearly 9 per cent of the total sales income on R&D (as of 2017), has six NCEs in the pipeline for therapeutic conditions including dyslipidemia, diabetes, chronic kidney disorder and oncology. Suven Life Sciences, which spends nearly 12 per cent of their sales revenues on R&D, has ten NCEs in the pipeline for disease conditions and indications including Alzheimer's disease, dementias, depressive disorders, pain, nervous system disorders, obesity and metabolic disorders as of 2017. Lupin spends 9 per cent of its sales revenue on R&D and has three NCEs in the pipeline for cognitive deficits, primary hyper-parathyroidism and rheumatoid arthritis. Sun Pharma, another major pharmaceutical company in India, which spends nearly 8 per cent of its sales revenue on R&D, has two NCEs in the pipeline, one each for psoriasis and leukaemia. Torrent Life Sciences Ltd has four NCEs in the pipeline for indications including cardiometabolic risks, kidney failure and intestinal bowel disease and diabetes. Biocon Ltd has three NCEs for diabetes and oncology, Natco has four for oncology, Jubilant has two for oncology and Glenmark Ltd has two for chronic inflammatory conditions and respiratory disorders as of 2017. Wockhardt is the only company that focuses on communicable diseases as well in their NCE development endeavours. The company has eight NCEs in the pipeline as of 2017 for various kinds of infectious diseases.

Biopharmaceutical research also focuses mainly on NCDs including type 2 diabetes, oncology and pulmonary diseases (Differding 2017). For instance, Advinas has three compounds, Shantani Proteome Analytics has two, Connexios Life Sciences has two and Krish Biotech and Kareus Therapeutics have one each in the pipeline for type 2 diabetes. Anthem Biosciences has three compounds, Advinus has two, Invictus Oncology has two and Aurigene, GVK Bio, Rhizen Pharmaceuticals and Sphaera Pharma have one each in the pipeline for oncology. Rhizen Pharmaceuticals has two compounds in the pipeline for pulmonary fibrosis. Among infectious diseases, bacterial infections and MDR tuberculosis have been the research focus of four biopharmaceutical firms. Vitas Pharma has two NCEs in the pipeline for gram-positive infections (mainly skin infections), Vyome Biosciences has two and Aurigene has one for bacterial infection and Sphaera Pharma has one NCE in the pipeline for MDR tuberculosis.

The data on clinical trial experiments that are registered in India provide further information on the disease focus of R&D in India (see Figure 2.5). We have aggregated the number of clinical trial experiments registered by Indian firms, MNCs, Indian and foreign research institutes, contract research firms, Indian and foreign research institutes–cum-hospitals and Indian and foreign government funding agencies in India until March 2019 from the clinical trial registry of India. It shows that the highest number of clinical trial registration in India was for cancer (42), followed by cardiovascular diseases (23), diabetes (16), skin, beauty and body care (13), allergy and asthma (9) and hypertension (7). As illustrated by the data on the disease focus of branded generics and NCEs, infectious diseases continue to receive lower priority in product development in India.

Figure 2.5　Number of registered medical trails in India by disease focus until March 2019

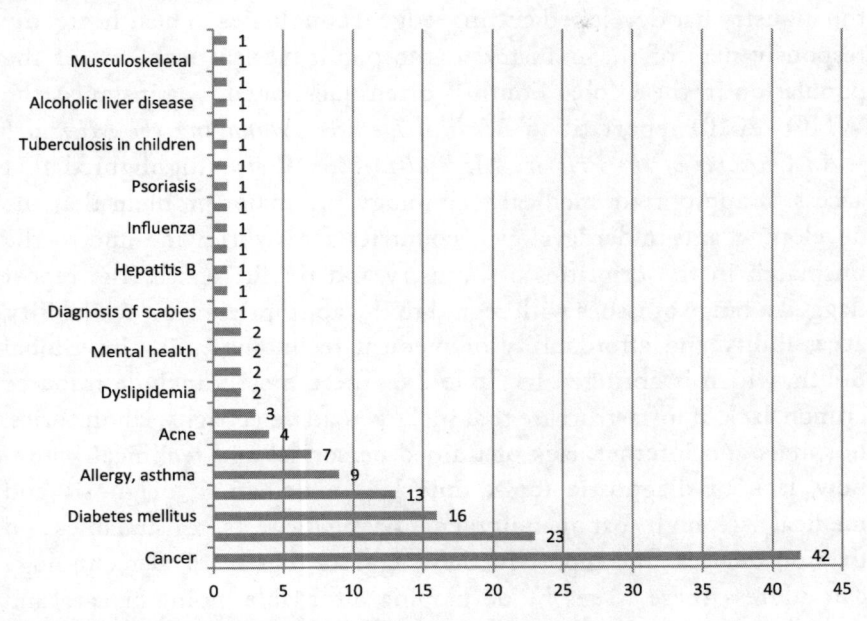

Source: Clinical Trial Registry, India, ICMR, compiled.

Although there are several vaccine and therapeutic compounds in the pipeline, most of them are in the initial stages of development. As already discussed, the success rate of Indian pharmaceutical and biopharmaceutical firms in developing NCEs is very low. For instance, Differding (2017) noted that Indian companies together have only 80 active compounds in the pipeline. He highlighted that out of the 214 compounds that entered pre-clinical development stage, only 82 compounds have gone to phase 1, 34 compounds to phase 2, 4 compounds to phase 3 and only 1 compound was approved and launched (Differding 2017: 806).

Disease focus of medical device/technology R&D in India

Medical technology is another important sector that plays a major role in medical innovations. Industry reports show that in-vitro diagnostic devices, orthopaedic devices, cardiovascular devices, diagnostic imaging, management information system, wound management, diabetes care, ophthalmic devices and care, dental care and nephrology are the areas where global medical technology R&D is mostly concentrated.[3] While the industry has developed cutting-edge technologies in healthcare, the responsiveness of the industry to the public health problems of the population in the Global South is often questioned. For instance, the WHO (2010) report titled *Medical Devices: Managing the Mismatch – An Outcome of the Priority Medical Devices Project* highlighted that access to appropriate medical technology is a major problem that the developing and underdeveloped countries face worldwide due to the mismatch in the priorities of industry and public health. The report flagged a range of issues with regard to the appropriateness, availability, accessibility and affordability of medical technologies in the Global South, which is abridged in Table 2.6. These mostly include resource crunch, lack of infrastructure that include roads, electricity, laboratories, hospitals and internet, lack of trained personnel and technical know-how, lack of diagnostic tools, time lag in detection, diagnosis and medical care, high cost of equipment, diagnostic tests, consumables and fixation devices. The report further suggests that medical technology can address these issues by developing affordable, point of care and appropriate technologies that are epidemiologically, economically, locally and culturally sensitive and responsive.

It is important to examine the disease focus of medical technology research in India in the backdrop of the issues flagged by the WHO report for developing countries. The major actors in the medical technology landscape of India include 'government research laboratories, academic institutions, industrial units in the private sector and international collaborative programs with multi-disciplinary Indian institutions' (WHO 2020: S5). Since there is no systematic data on the companies that develop medical technologies in India, we have relied on the information provided by some of the major firms and start-ups that specialise in medical technology development. Further, published reports of the medical device industry association and academic publications (for instance, Jaroslawski and Saberwal 2013) were used. The review is abridged in Table 2.7.

Table 2.6 Medical technology requirement by disease/conditions in the Global South

Specification/disease	Issues	Medical technology requirement for lower income regions
Laboratory diagnostic tools	Point-of-care diagnostic testing, lack of consumables, lack of good quality, easy-to-use point-of-care for infectious diseases	Development of simple, affordable and reliable sensitivity tests for bacterial and viral antigens, Development of simple, affordable test kits for other high-burden diseases Development of a universally accepted standardised automated laboratory testing system
Telemedicine and labour-saving technologies	Lower physical accessibility to health services, economic and technological viability of telemedicine	Remote patient monitoring, videoconferencing, telemedicine (including tele-diagnostics, tele-health, e-health, and point-of-care systems) Remote home-care technologies, remote communications systems
Safe injections	Reuse of syringes and needles, needle stick injury	Development of needle-free technologies, engineered syringes that prevent reuse and needle stick injuries biodegradable needles
Perinatal conditions	Inadequate care during pregnancy and delivery, lack of essential care upon birth, unavailability of appropriate resuscitation equipment and trained staff	Low false-positive rate electronic foetal monitoring, easy to use and robust ventilators, development of low cost transportable incubators

(Contd.)

Specification/disease	Issues	*Medical technology requirement for lower income regions*
Lower respiratory tract infections	Issues of maintenance of pulse oximeters	Easy use pulse oximeter Affordable diagnostic tests to identify antibiotic resistance
Unipolar depressive disorders	Lack of affordable technologies for diagnosis	Deep brain stimulation, web-based cognitive–behavioural therapy, vagus nerve stimulation, transcranial magnetic stimulation, magnetic seizure therapy and transcranial direct-current stimulation
Ischaemic heart disease	Lack of diagnostic tools like electrocardiographs and cardiac biomarkers	Single channel electrocardiography with interpretation Affordable and robustly designed cardiopulmonary, development of affordable, robust, and appropriately-designed emergency equipment, resuscitation equipment, including affordable defibrillators
Cerebrovascular disease (stroke)	Less availability of magnetic resonance imaging and computer tomographic scanners	Appropriate assistive products to help restore functional capacity for people disabled by stroke
HIV/AIDS	Problems with early detection	Simple diagnostic tests for early diagnosis of HIV infection in newborn infants and young children, affordable and easy-to-operate CD4 and viral load technologies

(*Contd.*)

Specification/disease	Issues	Medical technology requirement for lower income regions
Road traffic accidents	Lag time between accident, timely stabilisation and medical care	Easy-to-use ultrasound devices for diagnosis of internal, especially intra-abdominal bleeding, imaging techniques to diagnose bone trauma in a healthcare facility,
Tuberculosis	Early detection, detection of MDR, XDR and tuberculosis with HIV, time lag in traditional bacterial culture	Development of rapid, cost-effective and affordable tests for case finding, and guiding therapies
Malaria	Non-availability of microbiology laboratories in endemic areas. Treatment based on clinical symptoms leading to medical misuse and overuse	Diagnostic tests that allow differentiation between febrile illness due to malaria and that due to other causes Development of rapid diagnostic tests that have greater stability at tropical conditions (humidity and high temperatures),
Chronic obstructive pulmonary disease	Spirometers are unaffordable in low-resource areas. They are also highly sensitive to extreme temperature changes and humidity	Appropriate portable, affordable spirometry equipment to enable accurate diagnosis and prognosis in hot and humid low resource settings Low cost metered dose inhaler, nebulisers designed to function on solar batteries or cells easy-to-use ventilators with built-in compressors and oxygen tank options

(*Contd.*)

Specification/disease	Issues	Medical technology requirement for lower income regions
Cataract	Low investment on expanding available technologies	Phacoemulsification equipment, injectable liquid intraocular lens (IOL), prevention technologies
Hearing loss	Available equipments for early diagnosis of hearing loss are expensive	Practical, robust, affordable and widely applicable equipment for screening and diagnosing hearing impairment in low-resource settings Development of longer lasting and more adjustable hearing aids Development of appropriately designed and affordable hearing aids and cochlear implants for use in different age groups and contexts
Diabetes mellitus	High cost of disposable syringes and insulin, problems with procurement and delivery of equipment and medicine	Safe disposal of auto-disable low-cost syringes, Development of orthotic devices to avoid foot amputation, affordable BGSM meters that are better adapted to hot, humid climates and designed for use in low-resource settings Development of reliable, robust and affordable HbA1C monitoring kits glucose meters that use multiple languages and measurement systems, affordable screening test for diabetic retinopathy

Specification/disease	Issues	Medical technology requirement for lower income regions
Cancer	Low access to expensive early detection technologies	Effective automated methods that require less-specialised physicians for early detection, affordable radiotherapy equipment Development of a reliable and low-cost oestrogen receptor assay development of robust, Affordable ultrasound equipment for the diagnosis and staging of breast cancer
Osteoarthritis	Poor access to available diagnostic tools in developing world, cost of fixation devices	Develop fracture fixation devices made with affordable material, appropriate to specific contexts

Source: Compiled from WHO (2010).

Table 2.7   Product and disease focus of selected medical device and technology firms in India

Institution/firm	Type	Products	Disease focus
Sree Chitra Tirunal Institute for Medical Science and Technology, Trivandrum	Public	Prosthetic heart valves, blood bags	Cardiovascular
Jai Prakash Narayan Apex Trauma Center (JPNATC), AIIMS	Public	Clinical record integration platform	Cancer

(*Contd.*)

Institution/firm	Type	Products	Disease focus
Mahatma Gandhi Institute of Medical Sciences (MGIMS), Wardha	Public	Medical linear accelerator	Cancer
PGIMER, Chandigarh	Public	Closed loop anesthesia delivery system	General
MeitY	Public	Microwave hospital disinfectant system	General
CSIO, Chandigarh	Public	Pulse oximeter	General
CEERI Pilani	Public	Microwave (MW) pulse magnetron	General
SAMEER, Mumbai	Public	Multileaf collimators	Cancer (radiation therapy)
C-DAC, Mohali	Public	Automated traction unit	Physiotherapy
Reliance	Private	Cytogenetics and molecular genetics	chromosomal abnormalities
		Flow cytometry based diagnostics	HIV
		Anatomic pathology and pytopathology testing	Cancer
		DNA, RNA based diagnostics services	Hepatitis panel, human immunodeficiency virus, herpes simplex, cytomegalovirus, Epstein–Barr virus, parvovirus, BK virus, dengue and chikungunya
Xcyton	Private	HIV detection kit	HIV

(*Contd.*)

Institution/firm	Type	Products	Disease focus
		PCR-based IVD (in vitro diagnostics) kits	Rapid diagnosis of infectious diseases
Bigtec	Private	Micro-PCR device and reagents	Rapid, point-of-care in vitro diagnosis of infectious diseases
GEH	Private	Portable ECG machine	Cardiovascular
ReaMetrix		Dry-Tri	HIV management
Embrace	Private	Portable and safe infant warmer	Child health
Achira	Private	Fabric chips for device-free, point-of-care in vitro diagnosis	Infectious diseases
3M	Private	Several products	Hand hygiene, dental products, health information system, medical device and optical component, patient monitoring, skin and wound care, surgical solutions, vascular access
India Medtronic	Private	Several products	Advanced surgical technology, cardiovascular, diabetes, digestive and gastroenterology, ENT, neurological, dental, renal care, spinal, urology and tumours

(*Contd.*)

(*Contd.*)

Institution/firm	Type	Products	Disease focus
Johnson and Johnson	Private	Orthopaedic	Joint reconstruction, fixation products, spinal care solutions, sports medicine devices, biomaterials
		Surgery	Ethicon – minimally invasive procedures, biosurgery, wound disclosure, breast aesthetics, ENT
		Interventional solution	Cardiovascular, neurovascular, sight
Zimmer India	Private	Replacement solutions and orthopaedic products	Knee, hip, shoulder and elbow replacement products; trauma products, sports medicine, surgical solutions, spine solutions, dental products
BPL Healthcare India	Private	Resting ECG, Stress test system, diagnostic X-rays, foetal monitoring, phototherapy, ventilators, infusion pumps, incubators, oxygen concentrators etc.	Cardiovascular, maternity, general, surgical
GE healthcare	Private	CT scanning machines that consume less power	General
Skanray Technologies	Private	Lightweight affordable X-ray imaging system	General
Philips Healthcare	Private	Live image guidance technology	General

(*Contd.*)

Institution/firm	Type	Products	Disease focus
Cura Healthcare	Private	Digital radiology system which consumes less power	General
Wipro Technologies	Private	Cardiac implant monitoring system, remote patient monitoring system, home dialysis system	Cardiovascular, diabetic and home care
HD Medical Services	Private	Stethoscope with integrated ECG	Cardiovascular
Siemens India	Private	Angiography, CT scanners, magnetic resonance imaging, mammography, molecular imaging, radiography system, robotic X-rays, utrasound scanners, laboratory diagnostics, point of care testing	Cardiovascular, cancer, urology, diabetes
Boston Scientific India Private Limited	Private	Access device – dilatation and sheath, balloons: dilation and extraction, band ligator, atherectomy systems, accessories, baskets, clips, urethral catheters, CRT-D, CTO system, deep brain stimulation system, defibrillators, pacemakers, imaging system, spinal cord stimulator system, stents, needles etc.	Urology, gastroenterology, cardiology, pulmonology, neurological

Source: Compiled from various sources.

As is clear from the product focus of the firms given in Table 2.7, the medical device and technology products manufactured in India are majorly consumables and implants, patient aid and support services, diagnostic imaging and instruments and appliances. The disease focus of these firms/institutions across public and private sectors has predominantly been on NCDs. The focus of the multinational medical technology firms operating from India is largely on advanced technology development for the diagnosis and management of NCDs like cardiovascular diseases, diabetes, cancer, urinary diseases, respiratory diseases, orthopaedic diseases and neurological conditions. Most of the products developed by the MNCs are also high-end technologies, which can be afforded by the richer sections of society.

Public institutions that are devoted to medical device and technology development, on the other hand, focus on affordable technologies for the detection and management of both NCDs and infectious diseases (see Table 2.7). The NCD focus of public institutions was mostly on cardiovascular diseases, cancer, ENT (ear, nose and throat) problems, respiratory diseases, dental problems and orthopaedics. The products such as heart valves, blood bags, oximeter, pulse magnetron and collimators developed by public institutions are indeed welcome additions to the group of appropriate, responsive and affordable medical technology innovations. Besides, a few private companies have focused on the burden of infectious diseases, especially for the early and rapid detection of HIV, tuberculosis and malaria as well as maternity and neonatal care. Similarly, medical technology start-ups have tended to focus on developing technologies that could adapt to the existing resource and infrastructure constraints of the Indian health system. For instance, products like lightweight heart rate monitors, low-cost ventilators for newborn babies, devices for easy measuring of haemoglobin that could be used by anybody, imaging systems that use less power, android-based remote cardiac monitoring systems, to list a few, are some of the examples of appropriate and locally responsive technologies.

It should also be mentioned that medical device and technology companies in the private sector have started investing in *customised* products for India, which, as the Confederation of Indian Industry

(CII) claims, are 'affordable and attending to the infrastructure shortages' of the country. These include computed tomography (CT) scanning machines that consume less power developed by GE Healthcare, lightweight affordable X-ray imaging system developed by Skanray Technologies, live image guidance technology developed by Philips Healthcare to help doctors with diagnosis in small cities, digital radiology system which consumes less power developed by Cura healthcare, low-cost cardiovascular devices developed by Meril Life and affordable coronary stents developed by Sahajanand Medical Technologies (CII n.d.).

However, the appropriateness of such technologies to local constraints and needs is not yet known. For instance, the WHO (2010) study showed that even low-cost technology like X-rays, ECG, and so on, are not always viable in several regions of the developing world due to the lack of trained staff, electricity shortage, power outages, voltage fluctuations and poor maintenance. Similarly, although remote diagnostic technologies enabled by information technology have attracted attention in the developing world, infrastructure and shortage of trained staff could fail their purpose. The challenges of early detection of infectious diseases like tuberculosis, malaria, HIV and typhoid in the rural India have not been sufficiently addressed yet. Similarly, early detection of cancer and hearing and vision disabilities continues to be a challenge in rural India. Trauma care in remote places is another area where appropriate technology could add value.

Conclusion

The chapter examined the disease focus of products and R&D pipelines of drugs, vaccines and medical technology in India. Drug development in India, especially branded generics, biosimilars and NCEs in the pipeline, has a dominant focus on NCDs. For instance, out of the 1,635 new drugs approved for marketing between 2000 and 2017, 87 per cent were for NCDs and only 6 per cent of the new drugs that came to market were for communicable diseases. Within NCDs, the highest number of new drugs came to the market for cardiovascular diseases, followed by neurological diseases, cancer, dermatology and hygiene, ophthalmology, immunology and rheumatology, gastrointestinal and respiratory diseases. Diseases related to kidney received the least focus, followed by urology, psychiatric, endocrine and metabolic diseases and infectious diseases. Similarly, out of the 227 NCEs in the pipeline, the therapeutic focus of nearly 84 per cent was on NCDs. Within NCDs, the focus was more on endocrine and metabolic disorders and oncology, followed by immunology, neurology and pulmonary.

Vaccine development, as obvious, has focussed largely on infectious diseases. The disease focus of vaccine development of Indian biopharmaceutical companies mainly include infectious diseases like typhoid, Japanese encephalitis, chikungunya, malaria, pertussis, meningitis, influenza and Hepatitis A, to list a few. However, realising the demand and the market potential, vaccine development in India also focuses on therapeutic vaccine for pancreatic cancer and oral cancer vaccines. Therapeutics in the pipeline are mainly for treating diseases/conditions like inflammation, cancer, retinal angiogenesis/liver fibrosis, obesity, psoriasis, leishmaniasis, diabetes, chronic obstructive pulmonary disease, inflammatory bowel disease and rheumatoid arthritis. Although there are several vaccines and therapeutic compounds in the pipeline, most of them are in the initial stages of development.

The disease focus of the medical technology sector has also been predominantly on NCDs. While the MNCs focussed more on developing high-end cutting-edge technologies for the management of NCDs and fixation devices, the institutions in the public sector focussed more on affordable technologies for the early detection of infectious diseases and NCDs. Interestingly, a few of the firms in the private sector, including start-ups, focussed on developing appropriate and affordable technologies (frugal innovations) taking the infrastructure constraints in India into account. However, it should be mentioned that the social divide of medical technology is not adequately addressed in India in general.

Appendix 2A

Table 2A.1   Number of new drugs approved for marketing in India from 2000 to 2017 by indication

Indication	Year																	Total
	2001	2002	2003	2004	2005	2006	2007	2008	2009	2010	2011	2012	2013	2014	2015	2016	2017	
Endocrine and metabolic disorders	3	3	2	1	6	3	11	9	3	2	3	2	0	2	1	1	1	50
Cancer and bone marrow disorders	2	3	3	4	4	7	14	18	10	17	18	9	3	14	6	10	11	153
Infectious diseases	4	3	0	5	16	14	10	17	14	5	6	1	2	3	1	1	0	102
Immunology/ rheumatology	2	5	2	5	1	9	5	25	16	21	10	4	2	0	1	0	3	111
Neurology	3	6	2	13	16	13	21	33	27	34	23	7	5	8	1	2	6	220
Pulmonary	2	2	1	4	6	14	11	20	18	11	7	2	2	4	0	0	1	105
Cardiovascular diseases	4	8	11	9	18	23	28	28	22	32	16	6	6	5	3	4	5	228
Urology and male sexual dysfunction	2	3	1	3	0	3	4	2	2	4	2	1	2	2	0	0	0	31
Kidney diseases	0	0	0	0	3	1	0	2	2	3	1	1	0	0	0	0	0	13

(*Contd.*)

(Contd.)

Indication	2001	2002	2003	2004	2005	2006	2007	2008	2009	2010	2011	2012	2013	2014	2015	2016	2017	Total
										Year								
Psychiatric, sleep disorders and substance abuse	3	5	4	6	2	10	8	8	10	7	5	2	1	2	2	2	0	77
Otolaryngology and ophthalmology	2	5	3	5	13	11	14	13	9	19	15	0	3	2	3	3	0	120
Dermatology, haemarroids and hygiene	2	1	4	5	11	10	14	25	26	13	9	3	2	2	1	3	0	131
Gastrointestinal and liver	5	3	0	9	12	10	10	18	10	13	8	0	1	2	0	1	4	106
Antiviral and antibiotics	5	7	3	5	6	22	15	17	6	9	5	1	2	1	0	0	0	104
Surgery and others	1	2	2	1	4	5	8	11	20	9	10	1	3	0	6	0	1	84
Total	40	56	38	75	118	155	173	246	195	199	138	40	34	47	25	27	32	1635

Source: Central Drugs Standard Control Organisation (CDSCO), estimated.

Table 2A.2 Major biopharmaceutical companies in India and their product focus (as of February 2019)

Companies	Biopharma domains	Preventive/therapeutic care
Serum Institute of India Pvt Ltd	Vaccines	Preventive care
Biocon Ltd	Biotherapeutics	Therapeutic care
Reliance Life Sciences	Biotherapeutics, diagnostics, regenerative medicines	Therapeutic and preventive care (screening tests)
Panacea Biotec Ltd	Vaccines	Preventive care
Bharat Biotech International Ltd	Vaccines, biotherapeutics	Preventive care
Bharat Serums and Vaccines Ltd	Vaccines, biotherapeutics	Preventive care
Indian Immunologicals Ltd	Vaccines	Preventive care
Concord Biotech Ltd	Biotherapeutics	Therapeutic care
Shantha Biotechnics Private Ltd	Vaccines	Preventive care
Haffkine Bio-Pharmaceutical Corporation Ltd	Vaccines	Preventive care
Bharat Immunologicals and Biologicals Corporation Ltd	Vaccines	Preventive care
Biological E Ltd	Vaccines	Preventive care
Cadila Healthcare Ltd	Biotherapeutics and vaccines	Therapeutic and preventive care
Glaxosmithkline Pharmaceuticals Ltd	Vaccines	Preventive care
Syngene International Ltd	Contract research organisation	Contract research and manufacturing services (CRAMS)
Intas Biopharmaceuticals Ltd [merged]	Biotherapeutics	Therapeutic care

(*Contd.*)

Companies	Biopharma domains	Preventive/therapeutic care
Gennova Biopharmaceuticals Ltd	Vaccines, biotherapeutics	Therapeutic and preventive care
Wockhardt Ltd	Vaccines, biotherapeutics	Therapeutic and preventive care
Dr Reddy's Laboratories Ltd	Biotherapeutics	Therapeutic care
Virchow Drugs Ltd	Biotherapeutics	Therapeutic care
Navya Biologicals	Biotherapeutics	Therapeutic care
Novo Nordisk India	Biotherapeutics	Therapeutic care
Shreya Life Sciences	Bio-therapeutics and vaccines	Therapeutic and preventive care
Beacon Diagnostics	Diagnostics	Preventive care
Oncquest Laboratories	Diagnostics	Preventive care
Saamya Biotech	Biotherapeutics	Therapeutic care
Bhat Biotech	Diagnostics	Preventive care (screening tests)
Imgenex	Biotherapeutics	Therapeutic care
Xcyton Diagnostics	Diagnostics	Preventive care
Tergene Biotech	Vaccines, biotherapeutics	Therapeutic and preventive care
Mitra Biotech and Anthem Biosciences	Diagnostics and biotherapeutics	Therapeutic care and preventive care (screening tests)
Clonz Biotech	Biotherapeutics	Therapeutic care
ARA Healthcare	Diagnostics, biotherapeutics	Therapeutic care and preventive care (screening tests)
Advinus Theraupeutics	Biotherapeutics	Therapeutic care
Stempeutics Research	Stem cell therapy, regenerative medicine	
Sanofi Pasteur India	Vaccines	Preventive care
Novartis India	Biotherapeutics	Therapeutic care
Novartis Vaccines	Vaccines	Preventive care

(Contd.)

(*Contd.*)

Companies	Biopharma domains	Preventive/therapeutic care
Pfizer	Biotherapeutics	Therapeutic care
Lupin	Biotherapeutics	Therapeutic care
Eli Lilly	Biotherapeutics	Therapeutic care

Source: Compiled from websites of the firms.

Brief webnography of selected biopharmaceutical companies

Sanofi Pasteur India is a subsidiary of Sanofi Pasteur International, the vaccines division of Sanofi Group. The firm has vaccine R&D pipeline against infectious diseases such as dengue fever, hospital-acquired infections (*Clostridium difficile* and enterotoxigenic *Escherichia coli* [ETEC] infections), tuberculosis, rotavirus vaccine or second generation purified vero rabies vaccine (VRVg) and influenza.

Serum Institute of India developed life-saving biologicals for tetanus anti-toxin and anti-snake venom serum, DTaP (diphtheria, tetanus and pertussis) and MMR (measles, mumps and rubella). The vaccines manufactured by Serum Institute include polio, diphtheria, tetanus, pertussis, haemophilus influenzae type b (Hib), BCG, r-hepatitis B, measles, mumps and rubella vaccines. The products that are in the pipeline include rotavirus vaccine for diarrhoea, DTaP vaccine for pertussis, pentavalent meningococcal conjugate vaccine (A, C, Y, W-135, X) for African meningitis, pneumococcal polysaccharide conjugate vaccine, purified vero cell and human monoclonal antibody for rabies and HPV vaccine for cervical cancer.

Reliance Life Sciences focuses on regenerative medicine, clinical research and molecular diagnostics. Within the domain of biopharmaceuticals, it emphasises on plasma proteins, biosimilars that recombinant proteins and monoclonal antibodies, and novel proteins. The domain of regenerative medicine includes stem cell therapies, tissue engineered products, stem cell enriched repository services, assisted reproduction and foetal medicine. Products that the company market in different domains include ReliSeal (fibrin sealants) for wound healing, AlbuRel (albumin) for plasma volume expansion, immunoglobulin, HemoRel for haemophilia A and Pedialb for children for hypovolaemic shock, hypoproteinemia and burns. The company focuses also on degenerative medicines for the treatment of cardiac disorders, neural degeneration, spinal cord injury, metabolic disorders, ophthalmic diseases, chronic and non-healing ulcers, diabetic and venous ulcers, skin pigmentation disorders and bone and cartilage disorders. The firm also focuses on DNA and RNA based diagnostics services, including molecular microbiology services for infectious diseases and detection of viruses for hepatitis panel (A, B, C), human immunodeficiency virus, herpes simplex, cytomegalovirus, Epstein–Barr virus, parvovirus, BK polyomavirus (BKV) virus, dengue and chikungunya. Other diagnostic technologies of the firm include cytogenetics and molecular genetics to detect numerical and structural chromosomal abnormalities, including translocations, amplifications and micro-deletions in peripheral blood cells, bone marrow, products of conception, chorionic villi, amniotic fluid and cord blood; diagnosis and assays for Down's syndrome, chronic myeloid leukemia and acute promyelocytic leukemia; flow cytometry based diagnostics for HIV patients; anatomic pathology and pytopathology testing for gastrointestinal tumours, brain tumours, lung tumours, breast carcinomas, cervical cancer; and predictive oncology detection for breast cancer, cervical cancer, medullary thyroid cancer and human papilloma virus.

Panacea Biotech focuses on organ transplantation and dialysis management, diabetes and cardiovascular management, pain and arthritis management, respiratory and paediatric segment and oncology. The pharmaceutical products produced by the company fall into these categories. The vaccines they market include Easyfive-TT of various packs with different doses that fight diphtheria, tetanus, pertussis, hepatitis B and Polprotec. The R&D pipeline of vaccines of Panacea Biotec includes pneumococcal conjugate CRM vaccine, chimeric recombinant tetravalent for dengue, Sabin IPV vaccine and viral vaccine for Japanese encephalitis. The company has research collaborations with various research institutes, including the Institute for Translational Vaccinology (Intravacc), Netherlands, for in-licensing of know-how for the production of Sabin-based injectable polio vaccine; JSC Binnopharm Inc, Russia; National Institute of Immunology, India, for in-licensing of Japanese encephalitis vaccine; Dr Reddy's Laboratories Limited, India; PT Bio Farma, Indonesia, for manufacturing and marketing of measles vaccine; and with Kremers Urban Inc (UCB Group), USA.

Bharat Biotech International Limited specialises in the manufacturing of vaccines and biotherapeutics. Their R&D efforts have led to the development of patented products like HIMAX vaccine which is theomersal and cesium chloride free Revac-B mcf for hepatitis B. In addition, it has patented biologics like Regen-D for the treatment of diabetic foot ulcers. Till date, the entity has 20 patents to its credit. The firm developed vaccines for several infectious diseases including haemophilus influenzae type b (Hib), poliomyelitis among infants, diphtheria, tetanus, pertussis, hepatitis B, influenza a (H1N1), Japanese encephalitis, typhoid for infants, typhoid, rotavirus gastroenteritis, rabies, diabetic foot ulcers, infantile diarrhoea, HIV-associated and antibiotics-associated diarrhoea, traveller's diarrhoea and diarrhoea caused by Crohn's disease, venous thrombosis, pulmonary and peripheral arterial embolism and unstable angina, to list a major few. The current research of the firm is concentrated on bio-antibiotics, combination probiotics, lysostaphin, recombinant staphylokinase injection, chikungunya vaccine, typhoid conjugate vaccine, oral rotavirus vaccine, malaria vaccine, liquid rabies vaccine and staphylococcus aureus vaccine. The vaccines in the R&D pipeline include vaccines for diarrhoea among infants (rotavirus), typhoid conjugate, chikungunya, malaria PvR II, *Staph. aureus* MRSA (methicillin-resistant *Staphylococcus aureus*), human papilloma virus (HPV), acellular pertussis, tetanus and Japanese encephalitis. The products in biotherapeutics include THR-100, lysostaphin (USFDA) and recombinant human serum albumin.

Bharat Serums and Vaccines Limited specialises in plasma derivatives, monoclonal, hormones, equine anti-toxins and serums, antifungal, anaesthetics, cardiovascular and diagnostic products. The operations in India are specialised in divisions such as gynaecology, assisted reproductive technology, critical care, emergency medicine, neurology, nephrology and haematology and, lastly, urology. The therapeutic/product focus of the firm includes immunoglobin for Rho-D for pregnant women, anovulatory infertility, superovulation, precocious puberty, hypogonadotrophin hypogonadism, cryptorchidism, haemorrhage, hormone responsive cancers, hypogonadotrophic hypogonadism, polycystic ovarian disease and fungal infections and cancer.

Indian Immunologicals Limited (IIL) is one of the major suppliers of vaccines to the states and the central government for the Universal Immunisation Programme run by the Ministry of Health and Family

Welfare. It concentrates on the paediatric and rabies vaccine segments. It is the first entity to launch Abhayrab, purified vero cell rabies vaccine. The vaccines manufactured by IIL include AbhayRab, Abhay-Tox and Abhay RIG for rabies, Abhay-Tag for diphtheria, tetanus and pertussis, and Elovac-B for hepatitis B. The company has undertaken R&D initiatives in collaboration with national and international institutions in the domain of vaccines that include Indian Veterinary Research Institute, Izatnagar, India; Centre for Disease Control (CDC), USA; Indian Institute of Sciences (IIS), Bangalore, India; National Institute of Health (NIH), USA; US Army Medical Research Institute of Infectious Diseases, USA; The Global Alliance for Livestock Veterinary Medicines (GALVmed), UK; Centre for Disease Control, Taiwan; and Institute of Animal Health, UK. The product portfolio that IIL intends to produce include porcine cysticercosis vaccine, canine parvovirus vaccine, marker vaccine for infectious bovine rhinotracheitis, multicomponent clostridial vaccine, recombinant foot and mouth disease vaccine, hepatitis A vaccine, chikungunya vaccine, Japanese encephalitis vaccine, pneumococcal conjugate vaccine, typhoid conjugate vaccine, rubella vaccine, rabies therapeutic monoclonal antibodies.

Haffkine Biopharmaceutical Corporation Limited is a Government of Maharashtra government–owned enterprise involved in the development and production of bacterial and viral vaccines for diphtheria, tetanus, whooping cough, plague, poliomyelitis and rabies. In addition, it is involved in the manufacture of anti-serums against tetanus, diphtheria, gas gangrene, snake and scorpion venoms. The antiserums against the snake venoms is approved and exported through WHO and the United Nations Children's Fund (UNICEF) to other countries.

Concord Biotech focuses on antibiotics, immunosuppressants, antifungals, oncology, statins and anti-obesity. It serves global needs by having its presence in North America, Europe, Central and Latin America, Africa, Asia, New Zealand, Asia Pacific as well as CIS (Commonwealth of Independent States) and MENA (Middle East and North Africa) countries. Concord offers CRAMS services in the field of biotechnology, specifically in the areas of fermentation, semi-synthetic and synthetic products. It also provides CRAMS services that include strain improvement, media optimisation, process development, process scale-up, technology transfer at commercial scale and continuous process improvement. The R&D pipeline of the firm includes anti-bacterials including daptomycin, dalbavancin, telavancin, oritavancin and retapamulin and oncology medicines including doxorubicin, epirubicin, eribulin, bleomycin, epothilone b and ridaforolimus.

Shreya Life Sciences, which is a part of the Shreya Group, operates through three strategic business units, namely Amadeus, AkuCare and Biolife. The dominant therapeutic areas include anti-bacterials, anti-diabetics, anti-malarials, anti-hypertensives, nutritionals, enzymes, anti-inflammatory, haematinics, anti-allergics and anti-tubercular. The enterprise has collaborations with Bio Technology General Corporation, USA, to import and market recombinant human insulin, hepatitis B vaccine and growth hormone. In addition, it has global agreement with the National Institute of Oceanography, Government of India, to develop anti-malaria lead molecules. The products of the company involve anti-emetic, anti-osteoporotic, anti-tuberculosis, antibiotics and anti-infectives, anti-malarial, appetite stimulant, cardiac range, diabetic range, GI care, hormones, nutritional, opthalomolgicals, oral rehydration salt, pain management, plasma volume expanders and surgicals. The therapeutics segment of the company is focused, for in-licensing, on cardiology, diabetelogy, gastroenterology, and gynaecology and biotechnology. The segments for out-licensing are diabetology (rDNA human insulin, diabetic specific nutrient, optimal oral hypoglycaemic agents [OHAs]), opthalmology (hynidase), anaemia treatment (iron dextran), vitamins, minerals and amino acids combinations (specialised nutrition products), anti-platelet, cough and cold, and gastroenterology (enzymes/PPIs).

NovoNordisk India specialises in the field of diabetes care. It also focuses on other chronic conditions that include haemophilia care, growth hormone therapy, obesity and hormone replacement therapy (for women). The biopharmaceutical products of the company are within the broad segment of haemophilia and growth hormone therapy. One of the core competencies within biopharmaceutical research of the enterprise is proteins. It also involves in stem cell research for diabetic care in collaboration with the University of Lund's Stem Cell Center and Cellartis (Takara Bio), Gothenburg, Sweden. The company also developed a product using genetic engineering for people with haemophilia. The disease focus of the R&D of the company includes type 1 and 2 diabetes, obesity, haemophilia and growth disorders.

Eli Lilly and Company India Private Limited is a subsidiary of Eli Lilly. Its main focus is on therapeutic segments like diabetes, cancer, osteoporosis, and growth hormone therapy. The products developed are in the area of diabetes, cancer, endocrine and musculoskeletal. The disease focus of its R&D involves cancer, diabetes, rheumatoid arthritis, Alzheimer's disease and osteoporosis.

GlaxoSmithKline (GSK) India is one of the leading biopharmaceutical companies in India with its focus mainly on prescription drugs and vaccines. The company closely works with organisations like Gavi, The Vaccine Alliance and UNICEF for developing vaccines. The pharmaceutical segment of the firm involves in a range of prescription medicines covering areas like diabetes, oncology, cardiovascular disease and respiratory diseases. The disease focus of vaccines of the firm includes hepatitis, rotavirus, meningitis, whooping cough, small pox, pneumococcal disease, diphtheria, chickenpox, cervical cancer and influenza. The therapeutic focus of the drugs manufactured by GSK includes asthma, chronic obstructive pulmonary disease (COPD), stomach ulcers, bacterial infections, depression/various anxiety disorders, HIV/AIDS, metastatic melanoma and renal cell carcinoma. The disease focus of the therapeutic pipeline of the firm includes various kinds of cancers, HIV and infectious diseases, immune-inflammation, respiratory diseases, anaemia associated with chronic renal disease, postpartum haemorrhage, primary biliary cholangitis and Duchenne muscular dystrophy. The vaccines in the pipeline are for Ebola, HIV, malaria, and HIV and tuberculosis.

Pfizer India is a multinational enterprise and one of the leading biopharmaceutical companies in the world and India. The research focus is on depression, HIV, erectile dysfunction, hypertension, bacterial and fungal infections, cancer, arthritis and osteoporosis.

Biological E specialises in the development of vaccines, sera and other biologics, and pharmaceuticals. Being the first Indian private company in the vaccine market, Biological E played a significant role in the Universal Immunisation Programme. It supplied 60 per cent of the programme's paediatric vaccines to the Government of India. The disease focus of vaccines that the company developed includes diphtheria and tetanus for adults, Japanese encephalitis, hepatitis B, homophiles influenza, pertussis, poliomyelitis and haemophilus influenzae type B (Hib). The vaccines in the pipeline include liquid hexavalent vaccine for diphtheria, tetanus, whole cell pertussis, inactivated polio, Hib and hepatitis B by partnering with GSK, pneumococcal conjugate vaccine, typhoid conjugate vaccine with Novartis Vaccine Institute for Global Health (NVGH), Italy, paratyphoid vaccine with NVGH, measles, rubella vaccine, inactivated polio vaccine with Statens Serum Institute, Denmark, inactivated rotavirus vaccine with Centre for Disease Control and Prevention, USA, and meningitis vaccine.

Novartis India focuses on developing generic medicines. The focus of the company in India is on gynaecology, bone and pain, neurosciences, anti-tuberculosis and anti-infectives. It also focuses on developing biosimilars. The R&D focus of the company is largely on developing biosimilars for cancer, cardiovascular diseases, autoimmunity, transplantation and inflammatory diseases, musculoskeletal diseases, ophthalmology and respiratory diseases.

Dr Reddy's Laboratories focuses on developing therapeutics in the areas of oncology, gastroenterology, pain management, cardiovascular, diabetes and dermatology. The biosimilars developed by the company are for treating anaemia due to chronic kidney disease and cancer chemotherapy; neutropenia caused by chemotherapy and radiation; non-Hodgkin's lymphoma; chronic lymphocytic leukaemia; and rheumatoid arthritis.

Zydus Cadila Healthcare is a global company with its base in India. Cardiovascular, gastrointestinal, women's healthcare, respiratory, dermatology, pain management and anti-infectives are the major therapeutic focus of the company. The biosimilar pipeline products are in the areas of oncology, nephrology, inflammation, fertility, infectious diseases and osteoporosis. Vaccine R&D focuses on influenza, typhoid, DPT-Hib, hepatitis A, B and E, Japanese encephalitis, HPV, measles–mumps–rubella–varicella, leishmaniasis, haemorrhagic Congo fever, Ebola and malaria. The disease and intervention focus of the NCE pipeline of the company in India includes type 2 diabetes, diabetic dyslipidemia, hypertriglyceridemia lipodystrophy NASH (non-alcoholic steatohepatitis)-biopsy and NASH-MRI PDFF (magnetic resonance imaging–estimated proton density fat fraction).

Virchow Biotech established in 2001 focuses on high-value bio-generics. The company has commercialised the biogenerics of recombinant platelet derived growth factor for wound healing and recombinant parathyroid hormone for osteoporosis. The company has developed biogenerics (Healace and Octreotide) for treating diabetic ulcers and osteoporosis. The therapeutic segments it emphasises are advanced wound care, surgical haemostasis, ophthalmology, orthopaedics and oncology. The therapeutic areas of products in the pipeline include wound care and haemostasis, ophthalmology, orthopaedics, gastroenterology and probiotics.

Intas Pharmaceutical Limited specialises in cardiovascular system, diabetology, gynaecology, infertility, respiratory care, gastroenterology and pain management. The company also focuses on biologics for oncology (cancer), rheumatology, auto-immune, nephrology, ophthalmology and plasma derived product based therapies. The focus of NCE development of the company is on cancer and neurogenerative diseases.

Lupin Limited is involved in developing biosimilars that address therapeutic areas like oncology, inflammation, anti-virals, arthritis, endocrinology, diabetes, ophthalmology and women's health. The company has commercialised two biosimilars for oncology. The therapeutic areas of NCEs of the company are oncology, immunology and metabolic disorders.

Biocon Limited focuses on both therapeutics and regenerative medicines. It involves in the production of biosimilars for diabetes, oncology, immunology and chronic plaque psoriasis. The therapeutic focuses of the biosimilar pipeline of the company are breast cancer, colorectal cancer, chronic plaque psoriasis, chemo-induced neutropenia, stem cell transplantation, auto-immune disorders, diabetes and inflammation.

Wockhardt specialises in therapeutic areas such as anti-infectives, cardiology, dermatology, diabetelogy, neurology, pain management and respiratory. Wockhardt sells vaccines for flu, typhoid, hepatitis A and B and erythropoietin hormone under the brand names of Wepox Cartridge and Wepox PFS. The focus of NCE development of the company is on anti-infective and antibiotics.

Bhat Biotech specialises in the development, manufacture and marketing of diagnostics and biotech-based products. It provides diagnostic services for pregnancy, HIV, hepatitis, malaria, dengue, chikungunya, swine flu (H1N1), syphilis, tuberculosis, cardiac markers, dry chemistry, bio-chemistry, haematology and immunology and ELISAs (enzyme linked immunosorbent assays) used in the analysis of body fluids in humans. The products recently launched by the enterprise include fourth-generation HIV ELISA, molecular diagnostics, and DNAmp and dengue combination. It also provides contract research services. The R&D

pipeline of the company includes production of antigens in animal and *E. coli* cells for the detection of malaria, HIV and syphilis and detection of Angelman's, Phelan McDermid syndrome and other genetic disorders.

IMGENEX India Private Limited is a biopharmaceutical company that provides custom services pertaining to antibody development, recombinant protein production and stable cell line development. IMGENEX is involved in R&D areas like osteoporosis, cancer and stem cells and inflammatory diseases. It collaborates with the Institute of Life Sciences (ILS), Bhubaneswar, for developing a therapy for osteoporosis funded by the Department of Biotechnology, Government of India. It is also involved in the development of plant medicine for cancer in collaboration with the Regional Plant Resource Centre (RPRC), Bhubaneswar. The R&D focus of the company is more on biosimilar antibodies for the treatment of breast cancer, arthritis, colorectal cancer, psoriasis and lung cancer.

Tergene Biotech is a biotechnology company involved in developing bio-conjugates, antibody drug conjugates and vaccines. It is involved in the production of biologics with the main focus on bacterial pneumonia. It has developed technologies for manufacturing vaccines for acellular pertussis, haemophilus influenzae type B (Hib), typhoid, streptokinase and terinase. The technologies that are in the pipeline include multivalent pneumococcal vaccine and meningococcal vaccine.

Stempeutics Research is a life science company that produces therapeutics based on adult stem cells. The first product it produced was Stempeucel, developed for treating critical limb ischemia due to Buerger's disease. The second product is Stempeucare, a skin care cosmetic product. The product in the pipeline is Stempeutron – to isolate clinical grade SVF (stromal vascular fraction) from adipose tissue.

3

Drug Development and Responsiveness
to Disease Burden

The Indian pharmaceutical industry has played an important role in the development of generic medicines (Farmer 2001). However, whether those who are heavily dependent on the public sector benefit from this advancement made by the industry is a critical question for several reasons. First, as is well known, the bulk of these generic drugs are exported to international markets and are inaccessible in India (Swain et al. 2014). Second, the market is dominated by branded generics, which are usually priced higher than their corresponding generics (Mathew 2015). The quality of essential generic medicines that are available in the public sector has been also under question (Bate et al. 2009). The prospect of drug development in India assumes paramount significance for public health in this context. This chapter discusses in detail whether drug and vaccine development in India is responsive to the disease burden of the population, epidemiological changes and accessibility of services. To begin with, we present the data on disease burden in the country from 2000 to 2015 and juxtapose the therapeutic focus of the drugs approved for marketing, the new chemical entities (NCEs) in the pipeline and vaccines. The data on disease-specific mortality are collected from the mortality database of health statistics and information systems of the World Health Organization (WHO) for the years 2000, 2005, 2010 and 2015. These data are further disaggregated across four age groups. Data on morbidity are extracted from the National Sample Survey Organisation (NSSO) 71st round on *health in India* (2014). Data on drugs approved for marketing are compiled from the Central Drugs Standard Control Organisation (CDSCO), Government of India.

Causes of deaths in India: a detailed analysis

We have extracted the data of causes of deaths for the years 2000, 2005, 2010 and 2015. As Table 3.1 shows, non-communicable diseases (NCDs) constituted the highest cause of deaths in all these years as compared to communicable diseases (CDs). Furthermore, there is a steady increase in deaths due to NCDs along with a decline in mortality due to CDs in general in the line of the trend of epidemiological transition. For instance, the share of NCDs in total deaths increased to nearly 61 per cent in 2015 from 46 per cent in 2000. Similarly, share of NCDs was reduced to nearly 21 per cent in 2015 from 30 per cent in 2000. The share of injuries and accidents in the causes of death also marginally increased during this period. Table 3.1 presents the causes of death for males and females. As the table shows, the trend of dominance of NCDs was true for both males and females. However, the burden of CDs was found to be more on females than males.

We have further disaggregated the data on causes of death across the age groups of 0–4, 5–14, 15–29, 30–49, 50–59, 60–69 and 70-plus for male and female. Data for the age group 0–4 are presented in Table 3.2. It shows that communicable, maternal, perinatal and nutritional conditions were the reasons for deaths of as much as 84 per cent of males and females in

Figure 3.1 Causes of death, India (all ages)

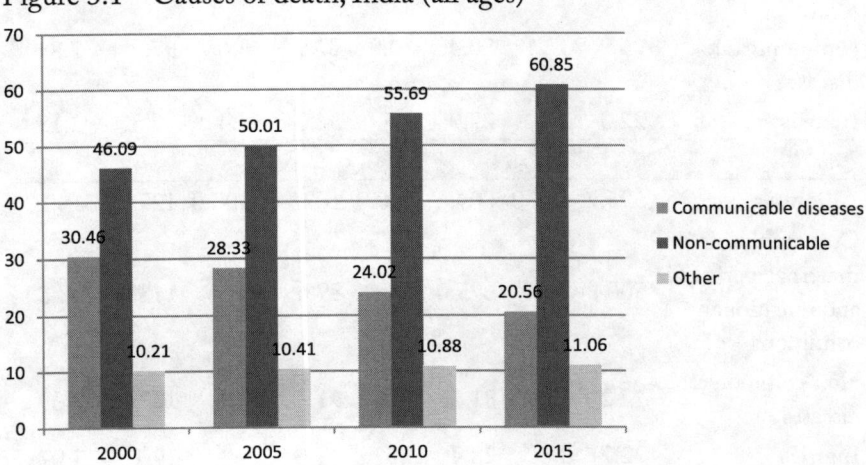

Source: WHO data repository, India.

Table 3.1 Gender-wise distribution of causes of death

Causes of death	2015		2010		2005		2000	
	Male	Female	Male	Female	Male	Female	Male	Female
Communicable diseases	19.5	21.8	22.8	25.4	26.9	30	28.6	32.5
Non-communicable	61.2	60.5	56.4	54.9	51.1	48.8	47.6	44.3
Injuries	19.3	17.7	20.8	19.7	22	21.2	23.8	23.2
Total	100	100	100	100	100	100	100	100

Source: WHO health repository, compiled.

Table 3.2 Causes of death, India: 0–4 age group

Cause	2015		2010		2005		2000	
	No ('000)	%	No ('000)	%	No ('000)	%	No ('000)	%
Male								
All causes	620.1	100.0	804.3	100.0	1018.1	100.0	1253.7	100.0
Communicable, maternal, perinatal and nutritional conditions	522.6	84.3	696.0	86.5	893.7	87.8	1116.4	89.04
Non-communicable diseases	75.2	12.1	80.4	10.0	87.9	8.6	97.9	7.81
Injuries	22.3	3.6	27.9	3.5	34.8	3.4	39.5	3.15
Female								
All causes	595.7	100.0	804.6	100.0	1026.4	100.0	1273.9	100.00
Communicable, maternal, perinatal and nutritional conditions	500.8	84.1	695.0	86.4	899.9	87.7	1131.6	88.83
Non-communicable diseases	72.2	12.1	81.2	10.1	91.3	8.9	103.1	8.09
Injuries	22.7	3.8	28.4	3.5	33.6	3.3	39.1	3.07

Source: WHO health repository, compiled.

the age group of 0–4 in 2015. Although it showed small variations, CDs continued to hold the highest share in the causes of death in this age group in 2010, 2005 and 2000.

Table 3.3 presents the causes of death due to CDs, NCDs and injuries for the age group 5–14. As is evident from the table, CDs continued to be the major cause of death. However, the share of NCDs in the cause of death showed an increase as compared to the 0–4 age group along with a noticeable decrease in the share of CDs for both males and females in 2015, 2010, 2005 and 2000. What is also important to note is that for males in the age group of 5–14, injuries were the major cause of death, which was even greater than due to CDs. The same trend of gradual increase of deaths due to NCDs and decrease due to CDs was true for the age group of 15–29 in general (see Table 3.4). However, deaths due to NCDs were

Table 3.3   Causes of death, India: 5–14 age group

Cause	2015		2010		2005		2000	
	No. ('00)	%	No. ('00)	%	No. ('00)	%	No. ('00)	%
Male								
All causes	103.2	100	123.4	100	149.0	100	174.2	100
Communicable, maternal, perinatal and nutritional conditions	39.2	38.0	52.3	42.4	71.5	48.0	88.1	50.54
Non-communicable diseases	22.6	21.9	24.8	20.1	26.8	18.0	29.2	16.75
Injuries	41.5	40.2	46.2	37.5	50.8	34.1	57.0	32.71
Female								
All causes	95.8	100	122.9	100	158.5	100	187.7	100
Communicable, maternal, perinatal and nutritional conditions	45.2	47.2	65.2	53.1	97.8	61.7	125.9	67.09
Non-communicable diseases	23.1	24.1	26.3	21.4	26.6	16.8	26.3	14.00
Injuries	27.4	28.6	31.4	25.6	34.1	21.5	35.5	18.91

Source: WHO health repository, compiled.

Table 3.4   Causes of death, India: 15–29 age group

Cause	2015		2010		2005		2000	
	No. ('00)	%	No. ('00)	%	No. ('00)	%	No. ('00)	%
Male								
All causes	297.8	100	317.2	100	316.6	100	308.4	100
Communicable, maternal, perinatal and nutritional conditions	57.4	19.3	69.8	22.0	82.9	26.2	80.3	26.05
Non-communicable diseases	83.0	27.9	87.6	27.6	85.3	26.9	85.9	27.86
Injuries	157.4	52.8	159.8	50.4	148.4	46.9	142.1	46.09
Female								
All causes	246.9	100	293.0	100	327.7	100	334.1	100
Communicable, maternal, perinatal and nutritional conditions	78.1	31.7	102.9	35.1	133.1	40.6	140.9	42.16
Non-communicable diseases	73.1	29.6	82.3	28.1	83.6	25.5	82.6	24.72
Injuries	95.7	38.7	107.8	36.8	111.0	33.9	110.6	33.11

Source: WHO health repository, compiled.

more than due to CDs for males in this age group in all four years, which may be noted as an early sign of epidemiological transition, whereas the trend of dominance of CDs in causes of death, although showing a decline, continued for females. What is also important to note is that injuries were the leading cause of deaths in this age group for both males and females.

The signs of epidemiological transition are somewhat clearly visible when we look at the causes of deaths in the age group of 30–49. As is evident from Table 3.5, the leading causes of deaths for males and females were NCDs. We could also see a gradual increase in this trend from 2000 until 2015. By 2015, nearly 55 per cent of the total deaths among males and 58 per cent among females in this age group were due to NCDs. The share of injuries in deaths showed a decrease for males and females in this age group for all four years. Table 3.6 shows the deaths by NCDs, CDs and injuries in the age group of 50–59 for the years 2000, 2005, 2010 and 2015. As is clear from the table, deaths due to CDs have reduced substantially in this age group for males and females. On the other hand, NCDs accounted for as much as 77 per cent of the total deaths of males and 76 per cent of females in this age group. Deaths due to injuries also have come down substantially in this age group.

Table 3.5   Causes of death, India: 30–49 age group

Cause	2015		2010		2005		2000	
	No. ('00)	%	No. ('00)	%	No. ('00)	%	No. ('00)	%
Male								
All causes	796.2	100	764.2	100	712.6	100	663.6	100
Communicable, maternal, perinatal and nutritional conditions	167.8	21.1	190.4	24.9	210.9	29.6	187.7	28.29
Non-communicable diseases	429.5	53.9	394.1	51.6	344.9	48.4	326.9	49.26
Injuries	198.9	25.0	179.7	23.5	156.7	22.0	148.9	22.45
Female								
All causes	422.9	100	440.0	100	444.4	100	426.1	100
Communicable, maternal, perinatal and nutritional conditions	105.2	24.9	130.7	29.7	154.5	34.8	149.0	34.97
Non-communicable diseases	248.7	58.8	242.6	55.1	226.8	51.0	215.3	50.53
Injuries	68.9	16.3	66.7	15.2	63.1	14.2	61.8	14.50

Source: WHO health repository, compiled.

Table 3.6   Causes of death, India: 50–59 age group

Cause	2015		2010		2005		2000	
	No. ('00)	%	No. ('00)	%	No. ('00)	%	No. ('00)	%
Male								
All causes	722.0	100	682.4	100	597.9	100	529.5	100
Communicable, maternal, perinatal and nutritional conditions	115.1	15.9	123.2	18.1	127.3	21.3	118.2	22.33
Non-communicable diseases	531.8	73.7	490.0	71.8	411.4	68.8	359.7	67.93
Injuries	75.1	10.4	69.2	10.1	59.2	9.9	51.6	9.74
Female								
All causes	435.0	100	429.7	100	401.6	100	360.4	100
Communicable, maternal, perinatal and nutritional conditions	69.5	16.0	76.8	17.9	83.3	20.7	76.8	14.51
Non-communicable diseases	330.6	76.0	320.7	74.6	290.8	72.4	260.4	49.18
Injuries	34.9	8.0	32.2	7.5	27.5	6.8	23.2	4.38

Source: WHO health repository, compiled.

A similar trend of dominance of NCDs in deaths was visible in the age group of 60–69 and 70-plus. As is clear from Table 3.7, the causes of death of 78 per cent of males and 76 per cent of females were NCDs in 2015. Similarly, 76 per cent of male and 72 per cent of female deaths in the age group of 70-plus were from NCDs (see Table 3.8). However, it should also be noted that the share of CDs in the cause of death has marginally increased in the 70-plus group as compared to the age group of 60–69.

Table 3.7   Causes of death, India: 60–69 age group

Cause	2015		2010		2005		2000	
	No. ('00)	%	No. ('00)	%	No. ('00)	%	No. ('00)	%
Male								
All causes	997.7	100	852.5	100	811.1	100	781.3	100
Communicable, maternal, perinatal and nutritional conditions	151.9	15.2	142.9	16.8	155.1	19.1	154.6	19.79
Non-communicable diseases	781.0	78.3	656.1	77.0	606.6	74.8	580.2	74.26
Injuries	64.8	6.5	53.6	6.3	49.4	6.1	46.5	5.95
Female								
All causes	797.9	100	713.5	100	681.9	100	629.3	100
Communicable, maternal, perinatal and nutritional conditions	139.8	17.5	136.1	19.1	146.3	21.5	134.3	21.34
Non-communicable diseases	606.8	76.0	533.5	74.8	495.2	72.6	458.3	72.83
Injuries	51.4	6.4	43.9	6.1	40.4	5.9	36.7	5.83

Source: WHO health repository, compiled.

Table 3.8   Causes of death, India: 70-plus age group

Cause	2015		2010		2005		2000	
	No. ('00)	%	No. ('00)	%	No. ('00)	%	No. ('00)	%
Male								
All causes	1679.4	100	1484.8	100	1314.5	100	1149.7	100
Communicable, maternal, perinatal and nutritional conditions	315.0	18.8	297.5	20.0	285.6	21.7	244.1	21.24

(*Contd.*)

(*Contd.*)

Cause	2015		2010		2005		2000	
	No. ('00)	%	No. ('00)	%	No. ('00)	%	No. ('00)	%
Male								
Non-communicable diseases	1268.4	75.5	1101.9	74.2	950.7	72.3	835.7	72.69
Injuries	96.1	5.7	85.5	5.8	78.2	5.9	69.8	6.07
Female								
All causes	1748.4	100	1557.0	100	1345.5	100	1112.5	100
Communicable, maternal, perinatal and nutritional conditions	377.7	21.6	359.9	23.1	338.4	25.1	266.2	23.93
Non-communicable diseases	1270.6	72.7	1107.6	71.1	925.8	68.8	771.3	69.33
Injuries	100.1	5.7	89.5	5.7	81.3	6.0	75.0	6.74

Source: WHO health repository, compiled.

Disease-specific mortality

We have further examined the disease-specific mortality within CDs and NCDs for four recent points in time. Table 3.9 shows the deaths due to 16 CDs. Nearly 27 per cent of the total deaths across all age groups were due to CDs. As is clear from the table, within CDs, respiratory infections caused the highest deaths, followed by neonatal conditions, tuberculosis and diarrhoeal diseases. Another noticeable trend is the gradual decrease, although slow, in deaths due to the mentioned major CDs between 2000 and 2015. Table 3.10 shows the deaths due to various NCDs. NCDs accounted for nearly 62 per cent of the total deaths across all age groups in 2015. Within NCDs, cardiovascular diseases accounted for nearly 43 per cent of the total deaths in 2015. The second largest cause of death was due to respiratory diseases. Nearly 18 per cent of the total NCD deaths were due to respiratory diseases. It was followed by malignant neoplasm (various forms of cancer), which accounted for 13 per cent of total NCD deaths in 2015 and digestive diseases (9 per cent), diabetes mellitus (5.13 per cent) and genitourinary diseases (5 per cent).

Table 3.9 Deaths due to communicable, maternal, perinatal and nutritional conditions

Disease	2015 ('000)	%	2010 ('000)	%	2005 ('000)	%	2000 ('000)	%
Tuberculosis	470.6	17.52	487.5	15.53	556.5	15.12	577.7	14.39
Sexually transmitted diseases (STDs) excluding HIV	6.5	0.24	11.5	0.37	21.6	0.59	30.4	0.76
HIV/AIDS	67.2	2.50	113.8	3.63	146.9	3.99	80.1	2.00
Diarrhoeal diseases	431.2	16.06	530.6	16.91	667.0	18.12	732.5	18.25
Childhood-cluster diseases	59.0	2.20	96.3	3.07	141.2	3.84	210.5	5.24
Meningitis	40.3	1.50	53.8	1.71	68.1	1.85	82.0	2.04
Encephalitis	39.9	1.49	48.9	1.56	57.4	1.56	63.2	1.57
Hepatitis	78.7	2.93	73.8	2.35	62.2	1.69	55.7	1.39
Parasitic and vector diseases	66.4	2.47	76.9	2.45	83.0	2.26	73.2	1.82
Intestinal nematode infections	0.5	0.02	0.9	0.03	1.5	0.04	2.1	0.05
Leprosy	8.3	0.31	9.2	0.29	10.7	0.29	12.0	0.30
Other infectious diseases	46.8	1.74	54.6	1.74	61.0	1.66	68.3	1.70
Respiratory Infectious	650.0	24.20	697.4	22.22	759.4	20.63	809.9	20.18
Maternal conditions	43.1	1.60	56.7	1.81	77.4	2.10	99.3	2.47
Neonatal conditions	602.6	22.44	755.8	24.08	902.9	24.53	1055.4	26.29
Nutritional deficiencies	74.5	2.77	71.0	2.26	63.5	1.73	62.1	1.55
Total (communicable)	2685.5	100	3138.7	100	3680.2	100	4014.2	100

Source: WHO health repository, compiled.

Table 3.10 Deaths due to non-communicable diseases

Cause of death	2015 ('000)	%	2010 ('000)	%	2005 ('000)	%	2000 ('000)	%
Malignant neoplasms	773.3	13.29	682.9	13.06	601.6	12.93	524.4	12.39
Other neoplasms	14.3	0.25	11.8	0.23	9.0	0.19	6.9	0.16
Diabetes mellitus	298.2	5.13	232.6	4.45	172.8	3.71	129.0	3.05
Endocrine, blood, immune disorders	26.2	0.45	36.6	0.70	52.1	1.12	57.6	1.36
Mental and substance use disorders	27.4	0.47	23.1	0.44	20.4	0.44	17.4	0.41
Neurological conditions	189.9	3.26	168.3	3.22	153.5	3.30	132.4	3.13
Cardiovascular diseases	2474.5	42.54	2247.3	42.98	1958.0	42.07	1730.3	40.88
Respiratory diseases	1038.6	17.86	936.2	17.90	895.9	19.25	919.8	21.73
Digestive diseases	502.9	8.65	460.5	8.81	400.0	8.60	356.1	8.41
Genitourinary diseases	294.6	5.06	260.9	4.99	224.8	4.83	190.5	4.50
Skin diseases	11.2	0.19	11.1	0.21	11.0	0.24	9.7	0.23
Musculoskeletal diseases	46.4	0.80	35.3	0.68	27.4	0.59	20.7	0.49
Congenital anomalies	116.1	2.00	119.0	2.28	127.1	2.73	134.9	3.19
Oral conditions	0.5	0.01	0.4	0.01	0.3	0.01	0.3	0.01
Sudden infant death syndrome	2.4	0.04	2.8	0.05	3.2	0.07	3.0	0.07
Total NCDs	5816.5	100	5228.9	100	4653.8	100	4233.0	100

Source: WHO health repository, compiled.

We have further examined the specific causes of mortality within cardiovascular, respiratory, cancer, digestive, genitourinary, mental and substance use and neurological diseases. As already discussed, cardiovascular diseases were the leading cause of deaths across NCDs and CDs. It accounted for 43 per cent of the total deaths within NCDs and 27 per cent of the total deaths in 2015. Within cardiovascular diseases, nearly 58 per cent of the deaths were due to ischaemic heart disease and 28 per cent were due to stroke (see Table 3.11). Hypertensive and rheumatic heart diseases were other causes of deaths within cardiovascular diseases. Respiratory diseases accounted for 17 per cent of the deaths within NCDs and nearly 11 per cent of the total deaths in 2015. Within respiratory diseases, chronic obstructive pulmonary disease accounted for nearly 86 per cent of the deaths (see Table 3.12). Asthma and other respiratory diseases were the cause of death of the remaining 14 per cent within respiratory diseases.

Table 3.11   Deaths due to cardiovascular diseases

Cardiovascular disease	2015 ('000)	%	2010 ('000)	%	2005 ('000)	%	2000 ('000)	%
Rheumatic heart disease	110.9	4.48	108.5	4.83	94.7	4.77	85.6	4.95
Hypertensive heart disease	160	6.47	147.3	6.55	120.7	6.08	99.3	5.74
Ischaemic heart disease	1446.9	58.47	1276.7	56.81	1062.6	53.53	906.4	52.38
Stroke	694.3	28.06	660	29.37	636.4	32.06	605.8	35.01
Cardiomyopathy, myocarditis, endocarditis	17	0.69	16.2	0.72	14	0.71	11.1	0.64
Other circulatory diseases	45.6	1.84	38.6	1.72	29.7	1.50	22.2	1.28
Total	2474.5	100	2247.3	100	1958	100	1730.3	100

Source: WHO health repository, compiled.

Table 3.12   Deaths due to respiratory diseases

Respiratory disease	2015 ('000)	%	2010 ('000)	%	2005 ('000)	%	2000 ('000)	%
Chronic obstructive pulmonary disease	896.8	86.35	795.6	84.98	730.3	81.52	711.3	77.33
Asthma	110.4	10.63	113.8	12.16	142.8	15.94	187.2	20.35
Other respiratory diseases	31.5	3.03	26.8	2.86	22.7	2.53	21.3	2.32
Total	1038.6	100	936.2	100	895.9	100	919.8	100

Source: WHO health repository, compiled.

Malignant neoplasm (cancer) was the cause of 13 per cent of deaths within NCDs and 8.24 per cent of the total deaths in India in 2015. Within this, mouth and oropharynx cancer was the leading cause of death (12.12 per cent), followed by trachea, bronchus and lung cancer (11 per cent), breast cancer (10 per cent), cervix uteri cancer (9 per cent), stomach cancer (8 per cent), colon and rectum cancer (7 per cent), oesophagus cancer (5.34 per cent) and gallbladder and biliary tract cancer (4.6 per cent). Table 3.13 provides detailed information on the causes of deaths due to various forms of cancers in 2000, 2005, 2010 and 2015. Breast cancer accounted for the largest cause of cancer-related death among females (nearly 21 per cent) followed by cervix uteri cancer (18 per cent), gall bladder and biliary tract cancer (7 per cent) and colon and rectum cancer (see Figure 3.2). Mouth and oropharynx cancer was the largest cause of cancer deaths among males followed by trachea, bronchus and lungs cancer, stomach cancer and oesophagus cancer.

Table 3.13   Deaths due to malignant neoplasms (cancer)

Malignant neoplasms	2015 ('000)	%	2010 ('000)	%	2005 ('000)	%	2000 ('000)	%
Mouth and oropharynx cancers	94.4	12.21	83.1	12.18	70.4	11.70	57.6	10.98
Oesophagus cancer	41.3	5.34	36.8	5.39	32.2	5.35	28.5	5.43

(Contd.)

(Contd.)

Malignant neoplasms	2015 ('000)	%	2010 ('000)	%	2005 ('000)	%	2000 ('000)	%
Stomach cancer	61.4	7.94	56.9	8.34	53.1	8.83	50.7	9.67
Colon and rectum cancers	53.4	6.91	45	6.60	37.2	6.18	29.7	5.66
Liver cancer	28.6	3.70	25.9	3.80	22.8	3.79	18.8	3.59
Pancreas cancer	15.7	2.03	13	1.91	11.4	1.89	10	1.91
Trachea, bronchus, lung cancers	84.9	10.98	70.3	10.30	58.2	9.67	49	9.34
Melanoma and other skin cancers	4.4	0.57	3.5	0.51	2.9	0.48	2.6	0.50
Breast cancer	76.4	9.88	66.2	9.70	57.4	9.54	49.9	9.52
Cervix uteri cancer	68.9	8.91	67.7	9.92	68.9	11.45	64	12.20
Corpus uteri cancer	5	0.65	4.6	0.67	4.6	0.76	4.2	0.80
Ovary cancer	21.7	2.81	18.4	2.70	16	2.66	13.6	2.59
Prostate cancer	13.6	1.76	11.2	1.64	9.2	1.53	7.6	1.45
Testicular cancer	1.5	0.19	1.4	0.21	1.4	0.23	1.6	0.31
Kidney cancer	6.7	0.87	5.4	0.79	4.5	0.75	3.9	0.74
Bladder cancer	10.5	1.36	8.7	1.28	7.6	1.26	6.5	1.24
Brain and nervous system cancers	16.3	2.11	14	2.05	12.3	2.04	10.6	2.02
Gallbladder and biliary tract cancer	35.6	4.60	33.5	4.91	30.7	5.10	26.5	5.05
Larynx cancer	19.1	2.47	16.3	2.39	14.6	2.43	13.5	2.57
Thyroid cancer	3.5	0.45	3.1	0.45	3	0.50	3	0.57
Mesothelioma	0.4	0.05	0.4	0.06	0.4	0.07	0.5	0.10
Lymphomas, multiple myeloma	29.3	3.79	25.3	3.71	22.4	3.72	20.4	3.89
Leukaemia	27.8	3.59	24.9	3.65	22.2	3.69	20.9	3.99
Other malignant neoplasms	53.3	6.89	47.4	6.95	38.3	6.37	31.1	5.93
Total cancer death	773.3	100	682.9	100	601.6	100	524.4	100

Source: WHO health repository, compiled.

Figure 3.2   Gender dimensions of cancer mortality in India, 2015

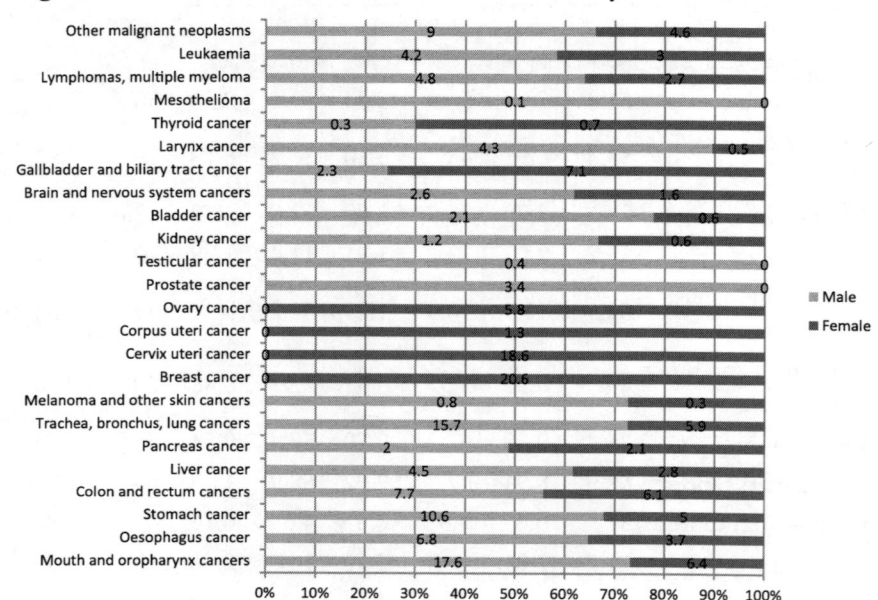

Digestive disorders accounted for 9 per cent of deaths due to NCDs and 5.26 per cent of the total deaths across all categories of diseases and age groups in 2015. Within digestive disorders, cirrhosis accounted for nearly 52 per cent of the deaths (see Table 3.14). Paralytic ileus and intestinal obstruction (14 per cent) and peptic ulcer disease (11.47 per cent) were the other major causes of deaths within this group of diseases. Genitourinary diseases accounted for 5 per cent of deaths within NCDs and 3 per cent of the total deaths in 2015. Table 3.15 provides information on the deaths due to various genitourinary and kidney diseases. As evident from the table, nearly 88 per cent of the deaths within genitourinary diseases were due to kidney-related diseases. Other urinary diseases accounted for nearly 11 per cent of the deaths in this category in 2015. Neurological conditions accounted for 3.3 per cent of the NCD deaths and nearly 2 per cent of the total deaths across all categories and age groups in 2015. Within various neurological conditions, Alzheimer's disease and other dementias caused 67 per cent of the deaths (see Table 3.16). The second largest leading cause of death from this group of diseases was epilepsy (15.6 per cent), followed by other neurological conditions (12.8 per cent).

Table 3.14   Deaths due to digestive diseases

Digestive disease	2015 ('000)	%	2010 ('000)	%	2005 ('000)	%	2000 ('000)	%
Peptic ulcer disease	57.7	11.47	62.6	13.59	79	19.75	97.8	27.46
Cirrhosis of the liver	259.7	51.64	235.5	51.14	197.9	49.48	171.9	48.27
Appendicitis	14.8	2.94	13.8	3.00	10.5	2.63	6.6	1.85
Gastritis and duodenitis	8.6	1.71	7.8	1.69	6.6	1.65	5.8	1.63
Paralytic ileus and intestinal obstruction	69.3	13.78	61.4	13.33	49	12.25	36.7	10.31
Inflammatory bowel disease	7.1	1.41	6.1	1.32	4.6	1.15	3.1	0.87
Gallbladder and biliary diseases	14.1	2.80	12.4	2.69	9.2	2.30	6.2	1.74
Pancreatitis	28.5	5.67	23.1	5.02	14.6	3.65	7.5	2.11
Other digestive diseases	43.1	8.57	37.6	8.17	28.7	7.18	20.6	5.78
Total	502.9	100	460.5	100	400	100	356.1	100

Source: WHO health repository, compiled.

Table 3.15   Deaths due to genitourinary diseases

Genitourinary disease	2015 ('000)	%	2010 ('000)	%	2005 ('000)	%	2000 ('000)	%
Kidney diseases	257.9	87.54	221.5	84.90	180	80.07	143.4	75.28
Urolithiasis	3.3	1.12	3.8	1.46	5.6	2.49	7	3.67
Other urinary diseases	32.2	10.93	34.1	13.07	37.4	16.64	38.2	20.05
Gynaecological diseases	1.2	0.41	1.5	0.57	1.8	0.80	1.9	1.00
Total	294.6	100	260.9	100	224.8	100	190.5	100

Source: WHO health repository, compiled.

Table 3.16   Deaths due to neurological conditions

Neurological condition	2015 ('000)	%	2010 ('000)	%	2005 ('000)	%	2000 ('000)	%
Alzheimer disease and other dementias	126.7	66.72	96.9	57.58	72.7	47.36	49.7	37.54
Parkinson disease	4.2	2.21	3.8	2.26	3.6	2.35	3.2	2.42
Epilepsy	29.7	15.64	37.9	22.52	47.5	30.94	51.7	39.05
Multiple sclerosis	5	2.63	5.3	3.15	5.9	3.84	5.9	4.46
Other neurological conditions	24.3	12.80	24.4	14.5	23.8	15.50	21.9	16.54
Total	189.9	100	168.3	100	153.5	100	132.4	100

Source: WHO health repository, compiled.

Morbidity burden of diseases

The trajectories and patterns of epidemiological transition in India, which show an overall increase in the incidence of NCDs and decrease in CDs, are well discussed. As the studies have already showed, the epidemiological transition has a complex character and the disease burden vary across region and population. Paul and Singh (2017), for instance, estimated the morbidity burden and its changing patterns in India using three rounds of NSSO data for the years 1996, 2004 and 2014. They underscored the growing double burden of diseases in India with the growth of infectious diseases along with NCDs. We have examined the self-reported morbidity data of NSSO survey 71st round on *social consumption* for 23 diseases along with accidents and injuries. The data refer to reported morbidity and the perception of illness of the respondents, and the reporting of the same can vary across socio-economic and educational markers. Hence, the data do not provide a complete picture of morbidity; however, they are indicative of the general disease morbidity distribution across the population. As is clear from Figure 3.3, morbidity due to NCDs was noticeably higher than due to infectious diseases in all age groups except 0–14, where infectious diseases account for substantial morbidity burden. This is in line with the mortality burden as well, as we discussed earlier in the chapter.

However, state-wise data showed some variations in the morbidity pattern. As Paul and Singh (2017) have already revealed, there have been noticeable variations in the pattern of disease morbidity across the states (see Figure 3.4). For instance, while the prevalence of NCDs was more than that of infectious diseases as a whole in India, some states including Arunachal Pradesh, Assam, Bihar, Delhi, Haryana, Manipur, Odisha, Tripura, Uttar Pradesh and Uttarakhand reported infectious diseases more than NCDs. There were states that showed a major transition towards NCDs as well. For instance, NCDs accounted for more than 80 per cent of the disease morbidity in Kerala and between 60 and 80 per cent in Tamil Nadu, Karnataka, Himachal Pradesh, Jharkhand, Punjab and Andhra Pradesh. NCDs accounted for 50–60 per cent of the disease morbidity in the states of Goa, Gujarat, Jammu and Kashmir, Madhya Pradesh, Maharashtra, Rajasthan, Sikkim and West Bengal.

Figure 3.3 Percentage distribution of reported morbidity across age groups, India, 2014

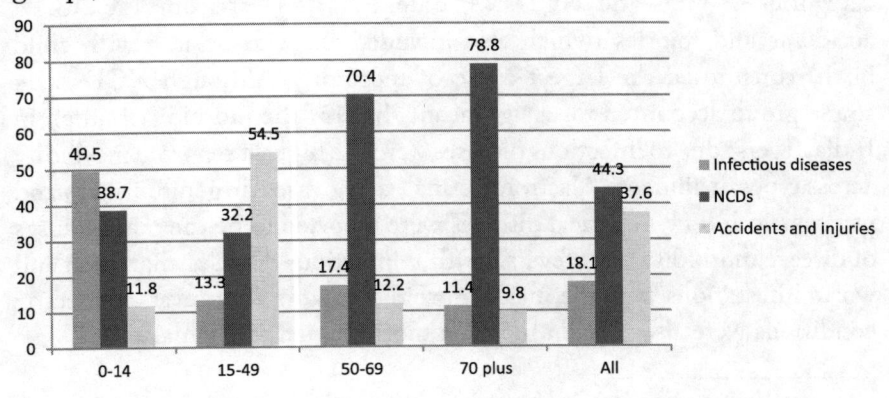

Source: NSSO 71st round, estimated.

Figure 3.4 Self-reported disease prevalence across selected Indian states, 2014 (per '000 population)

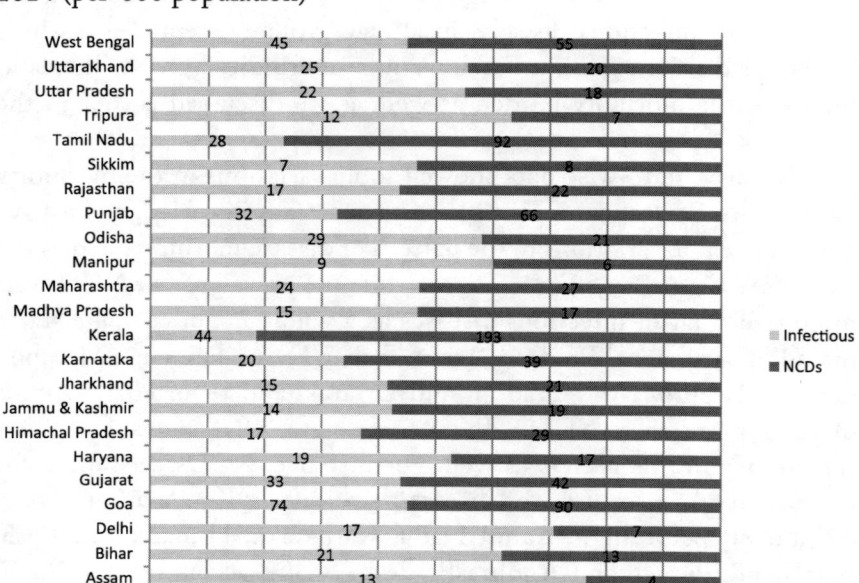

Source: Compiled from Paul and Singh (2017) based on NSSO 71st round (2014).

The morbidity picture changes when we look at each disease in the categories of CDs and NCDs separately. As is clear from Table 3.17, accidents and injuries (which also included those associated with child birth) constituted the largest cause of morbidity. Although NCDs as a single group accounted for a significant share of the morbidity burden in India, fevers[1] due to infectious diseases were the highest reported morbidity across types of ailments. Gastrointestinal, cardiovascular, genitourinary and psychiatric and neurological diseases were reported to be the major causes of disease morbidity after fevers. Within infectious diseases, diarrhoea and worm infestations were the major morbidity factors after fevers. Obstetric conditions were also a major reported morbidity among females.

---

[1] Fevers in this category included fever with loss of consciousness or altered consciousness, fever with rash/eruptive lesions, fever due to diphtheria, whooping cough, malaria, typhoid and fevers of unknown origin and all specific fevers that do not have a confirmed diagnosis.

Table 3.17 Percentage distribution of reported morbidity in India by gender and sector

	Rural			Urban			Rural + Urban		
	Male	Female	Total	Male	Female	Total	Male	Female	Total
Fever	19.0	9.3	12.7	17.1	11.2	13.5	18.3	9.9	13.0
Tuberculosis	1.8	0.6	1.1	1.6	0.4	0.9	1.7	0.6	1.0
Filariasis	0.1	0.0	0.1	0.1	0.0	0.0	0.1	0.0	0.1
Tetanus	0.0	0.0	0.0	0.0	0.0	0.0	0.0	0.0	0.0
HIV/AIDS	0.2	0.2	0.2	0.0	0.0	0.0	0.1	0.1	0.1
Other STDs	0.0		0.0	0.0	0.0	0.0	0.0	0.0	0.0
Jaundice	2.3	0.7	1.3	3.0	0.9	1.7	2.6	0.7	1.4
Diarrhoea	3.4	1.8	2.3	3.3	2.2	2.6	3.3	1.9	2.4
Worm infestation	0.3	0.1	0.1	0.1	0.1	0.1	0.2	0.1	0.1
Cancer	1.8	1.4	1.6	2.4	1.7	2.0	2.0	1.5	1.7
Blood diseases	1.7	1.4	1.5	1.2	1.3	1.3	1.5	1.4	1.4
Diabetes	1.4	0.9	1.1	2.2	2.1	2.1	1.7	1.3	1.4
Thyroid and other metabolic and nutritional	0.6	0.5	0.6	0.4	0.5	0.4	0.5	0.5	0.5
Psychiatric and neurological	5.9	3.0	4.1	7.3	3.5	5.0	6.4	3.2	4.4
Eye related	4.3	2.9	3.4	3.3	3.1	3.2	3.9	3.0	3.3
Ear	0.4	0.2	0.3	0.6	0.3	0.4	0.5	0.3	0.3
Cardiovascular	9.0	3.7	5.6	12.1	6.5	8.6	10.1	4.6	6.6
Respiratory	5.5	2.6	3.6	5.5	3.1	4.0	5.5	2.8	3.7
Gastrointestinal	10.5	6.2	7.7	10.8	6.9	8.4	10.6	6.4	7.9
Skin related	0.9	0.4	0.6	0.8	0.8	0.8	0.9	0.5	0.7
Musculoskeletal	4.5	2.9	3.5	4.2	2.9	3.4	4.4	2.9	3.4
Genitourinary	6.0	3.6	4.5	5.9	5.6	5.7	6.0	4.3	4.9
Obstetric	1.3	6.0	4.3	1.1	4.5	3.2	1.2	5.5	3.9
Injuries and accidents	19.3	51.5	40.1	16.8	42.4	32.5	18.4	48.6	37.6
Total	100	100	100	100	100	100	100	100	100

Source: NSSO 71st round data, estimated.

Responsiveness of therapeutic drug development to disease burden[2]

The changing mortality and morbidity pattern of India showed a complex picture of epidemiological transition in India. What is generally agreeable is that there is an overall transition from infectious diseases to NCDs. The burden of diseases measured in terms of years of life lost (YLL) was more due to NCDs, especially due to Ischaemic heart disease (ICMR, PHFI and IHME 2017). Dandona et al. (2017) estimated that NCDs have been accountable for nearly 55 per cent of the disease burden as against 33 per cent due to CDs. They also highlighted the regional variations of epidemiological transition in India (Table 3.18). In short, the level and pace of this transition vary across age groups, state, regions within states, social groups and economic groups.

Table 3.18   Contribution of disease categories to total deaths by age groups in states grouped by epidemiological transition level (ETL), 2016

Disease	*Low ETL states*	*Lower- middle ETL states*	*Higher- middle ETL states*	*High ETL states*	*All India*
Communicable, maternal and nutritional diseases	**34.7**	**26.0**	**20.9**	**15.9**	**27.5**
HIV/AIDS and tuberculosis	6.4	6.9	4.2	3.4	5.4
Diarrhoea, lower respiratory, and other common infectious diseases	19.8	12.4	11.7	9.7	15.5
Neglected tropical diseases and malaria	1.1	0.9	0.6	0.4	0.8

(Contd.)

---

2   Some of our arguments in this section are reproduced from our paper titled 'Is Drug Development in India Responsive to Disease Burden? A Public Health Appraisal', published as special article in the *Economic and Political Weekly* 53(30): 50–57.

Disease	Low ETL states	Lower-middle ETL states	Higher-middle ETL states	High ETL states	All India
Maternal disorders	0.7	0.3	0.3	0.2	0.5
Neonatal disorders	4.9	4.1	2.9	1.6	3.8
Nutritional deficiencies	0.7	0.3	0.3	0.2	0.5
Other communicable, maternal, neonatal and nutritional diseases	1.1	0.9	0.8	0.5	0.9
Non-communicable diseases	**55.2**	**63.3**	**67.9**	**72.3**	**61.8**
Neoplasm	7.9	8.4	8.7	9.0	8.3
Cardiovascular diseases	21.9	28.9	34.1	37.4	28.1
Chronic respiratory diseases	12.2	11.8	10.0	7.4	10.9
Cirrhosis and other chronic liver diseases	1.8	2.1	2.7	1.8	2.1
Digestive diseases	2.6	1.8	1.7	1.5	2.2
Neurological disorders	1.8	2.3	2.2	2.9	2.1
Mental and substance use disorders	0.4	0.4	0.4	0.4	0.4
Diabetes urogenital, blood and endocrine diseases	5.2	6.4	7.0	11.0	6.5

(*Contd.*)

Disease	Low ETL states	Lower-middle ETL states	Higher-middle ETL states	High ETL states	All India
Musculoskeletal disorders	0.1	0.1	0.1	0.1	0.1
Other non-communicable disease	1.3	1.2	0.9	0.8	1.1
Injuries	**10.1**	**10.7**	**11.2**	**11.9**	**10.7**
Transport injuries	2.9	2.9	2.9	3.2	2.9
Unintentional injuries	5.0	4.9	4.8	5.2	4.9
Self-harm and interpersonal violence	2.3	2.8	3.5	3.4	2.8

Source: Dandona et al. (2017: 8–9).

Does drug development in India takes into account the public health priorities emanating from this varied nature of epidemiological transition across population and region? If we juxtapose the disease burden and the therapeutic focus of drugs, this question could be answered to some extent. The previous chapter discussed in detail the disease/therapeutic focus of the branded generics/formulations that were approved for marketing recently and the NCEs that are in the pipeline. The disaggregated disease focus of the drugs newly approved for marketing in India is presented in Figures 3.5 and 3.6. As is clear from these figures, the highest number of new drugs approved for marketing between 2001 and 2017 was for cancer (153), followed by hypertension (103), antibiotics (94), heart diseases and cholesterol (92), analgesic (88) and pulmonary diseases (65). Diseases for which the least number of new medicines came to the market during this period include leprosy (1), kala-azar (2), tuberculosis (2), worm infestation (4) and gastritis (4). Among CDs, the highest number of new medicines came to market for malaria (18).

Differding (2017) has compiled a detailed list of NCEs that were under various states of development in India until 2016 across their indication and firm, which is discussed in detail in Chapter 2. As per his estimation, drugs/compounds/formulations for the treatment of cancer and metabolic and endocrine diseases received the highest attention in the development of NCEs by the pharmaceutical and biotechnology companies. He highlighted that nearly 35 compounds were under various stages of development until 2016 for infectious diseases. Similarly, he has provided information on the compounds that were abandoned at various stages of development across the disease/therapeutic focus, which highlights the preponderance of NCDs in the therapeutic focus of Indian firms.

Figure 3.5   Number of new drugs approved for ailment/conditions listed as causes of death, 2001–2017

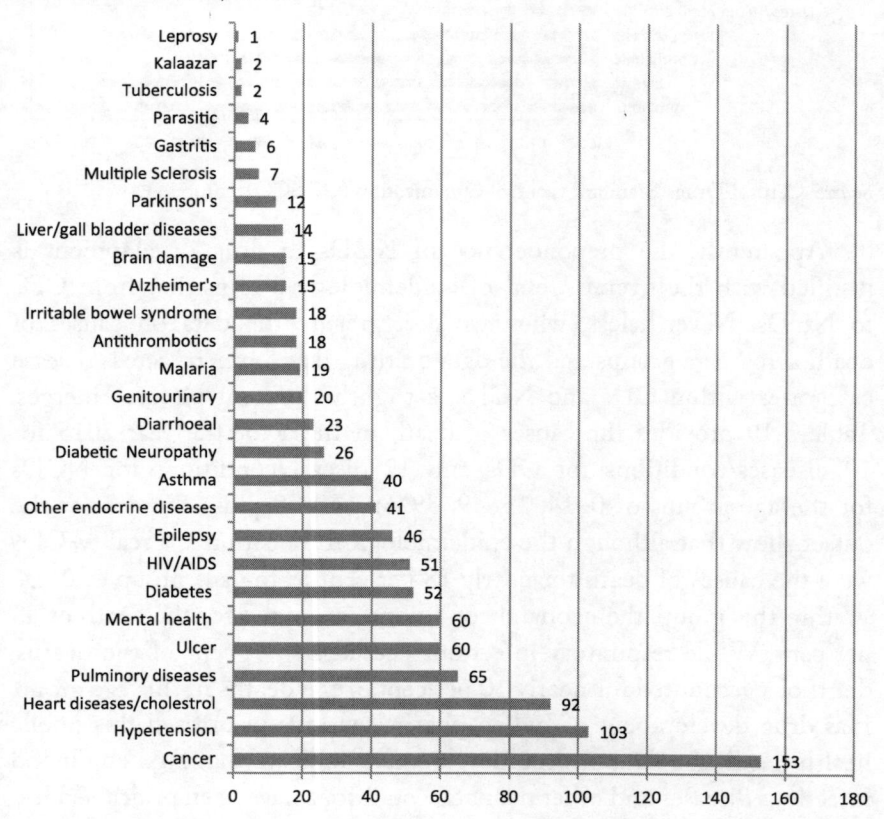

Source: Central Drugs Standard Control Organization (CDSCO), compiled.

Figure 3.6   Number of new drugs approved for other ailment/conditions, 2001–2017

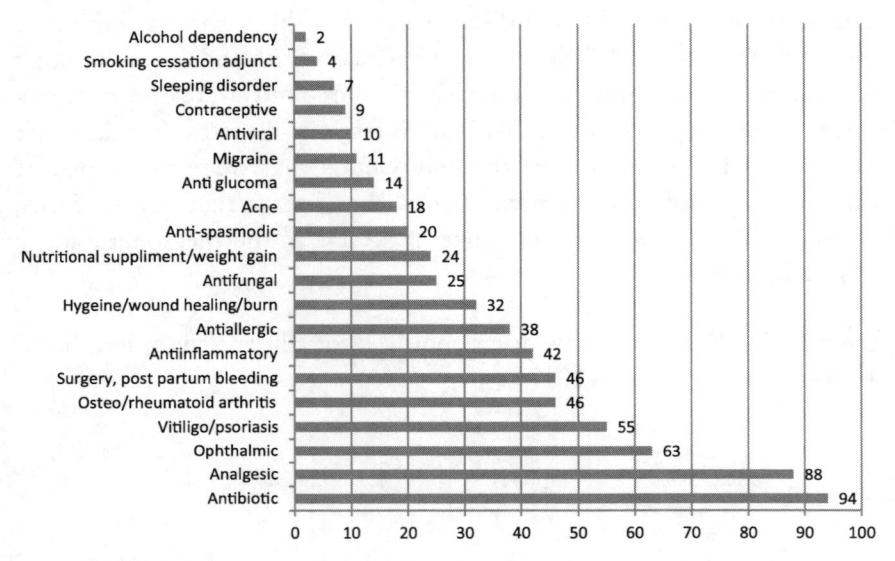

Source: Central Drugs Standard Control Organization (CDSCO), compiled.

Apparently, the preponderance of NCDs in drug development is justified with the overall trend of epidemiological transition from CDs to NCDs. Nevertheless, when we disaggregate the data on causes of death across age groups and the data on drug development across disease categories within CDs and NCDs, a slightly different picture emerges. Table 3.19 provides the causes of death in India for the year 2015 for 10 diseases/conditions for CDs and 12 disease/conditions for NCDs for the age groups of 0–14, 15–49, 59–69 and 70-plus. The data at the outset show that although the epidemiological transition is a reality, CDs were the causes of death for nearly 78 per cent in the age group of 0–14. Within this group, the neonatal conditions accounted for the death of 43 per cent. While respiratory infections caused 14 per cent of the deaths, diarrhoea accounted for nearly 10 per cent of the deaths in this age group. Has drug development of Indian pharmaceuticals prioritised this public health need? The data of drug development indicate that fatal childhood infectious diseases and other neonatal conditions have been prioritised less in the development of generics and biosimilars (see Figures 3.5 and 3.6). For instance, except diarrhoea, for which 23 new drugs came to market between 2000 and 2017, no other major disease causes of deaths in the 0–14 age group figured in the development of new drugs.

Similar to the overall trend, NCDs are the major causes of death in the age group of 15–49, followed by injuries and CDs. The largest single cause of death in this group is cardiovascular diseases (17.4 per cent), which is followed by cancer (11.2 per cent), tuberculosis (9.1 per cent) and digestive diseases (9 per cent). While several new medicines came to the market for cardiovascular diseases, hypertension, cancer and digestive disorders, tuberculosis, which is resurging in several parts of the country in the productive age group of 15–49, did not receive sufficient attention in drug development. Only two new drugs came to market for tuberculosis between 2000 and 2017. It assumes significance in the context of the emergence of the drug-resistant variant of tuberculosis. The leading cause of deaths in the age group of 59–69 is also cardiovascular disease (36 per cent), which is followed by cancer (13 per cent), respiratory diseases (12 per cent), tuberculosis (6 per cent), digestive diseases (6 per cent) and diabetes and endocrine diseases (4 per cent). As is clear from Figure 3.5, except for tuberculosis, the new drugs that came to market in the last 17 years fall in line with the major causes of the disease burden in this age group. When we come to the age group 70-plus, it is found that most of the major causes of deaths except cardiovascular diseases (35 per cent of death in the age group) have not been the priority areas of drug development in India. Interestingly, infectious diseases were prioritised even lower than drugs for cosmetic treatments (acne, weight loss, hair removal, general dermatology), vitiligo, contraceptives, anti-spasmodic, anti-fungal, sleeping disorders and substance de-addiction. This clearly indicates that except for a few NCDs including cardiovascular diseases, hypertension, diabetes and cancer it is mainly the market demand that overrides public health priorities in drug discovery in India. The focus on NCDs has been true in the case of NCEs as well; however, cardiovascular diseases, which are the leading causes of deaths, received less priority. This could be due to the availability of drugs in sufficient numbers for these disease conditions. In short, the R&D of the Indian pharmaceutical and medical-biotechnology industries has focussed less on the diseases burden of children and the elderly (70-plus here) and more on the disease burden of the economically active age group of 15–69, which constitutes its potential customer target group.

Table 3.19 Percentage contribution of causes of death within age groups, India, 2015

Disease/condition	Age group				
	0–14	15–49	50–69	70-plus	All ages
Communicable, maternal, perinatal and nutritional conditions	**78.31**	**23.17**	**16.13**	**20.21**	**28.09**
Tuberculosis	0.98	9.13	6.16	3.32	4.92
HIV/AIDS	0.52	2.88	0.30	0.00	0.70
Diarrhoea	9.65	2.16	3.32	4.62	4.51
Other common infectious diseases	7.00	3.05	1.29	0.79	2.28
Malaria and tropical diseases	1.10	1.48	0.63	0.43	0.79
Other infectious diseases	1.72	0.26	0.31	0.44	0.56
Respiratory infections	13.90	1.16	3.20	9.87	6.80
Maternal conditions	0.00	2.44	0.00	0.00	0.45
Neonatal conditions	42.59	0.00	0.00	0.00	6.30
Nutritional deficiencies	0.84	0.60	0.91	0.73	0.78
Non-communicable diseases	**13.65**	**47.30**	**76.21**	**74.07**	**60.85**
Neoplasms	0.71	11.25	13.08	5.63	8.24
Cardiovascular diseases	0.57	17.48	35.75	32.16	25.89
Respiratory diseases	0.68	2.18	11.66	18.85	10.87
Digestive diseases	1.62	9.07	5.94	4.22	5.26

(*Contd.*)

(*Contd.*)

Disease/condition	Age group				
	0–14	*15–49*	*50–69*	*70-plus*	*All ages*
Neurological conditions	0.84	1.62	1.01	3.49	1.99
Diabetes and endocrine diseases	0.66	1.17	4.00	5.15	3.39
Congenital anomalies	7.89	0.20	0.02	0.01	1.21
Genitourinary diseases	0.44	3.12	3.86	3.48	3.08
Mental and substance use disorders	0.00	0.97	0.23	0.10	0.29
Skin diseases	0.04	0.09	0.11	0.17	0.12
Musculoskeletal diseases	0.01	0.15	0.53	0.81	0.49
Other non-communicable diseases	0.17	0.14	0.08	0.07	0.03
Injuries	**8.04**	**29.53**	**7.66**	**5.72**	**11.06**
Total	100	100	100	100	100

Source: Mortality database of WHO, compiled.

Drug development is also not equitably responding to the morbidity burden of the country. Data on morbidity burden across age groups show that although the disease burden of NCDs is an emerging reality, the burden of fever continues to be noticeable in all age groups (see Table 3.20). It is responsible for as much as 35 per cent of all disease burden in the age group of 0–14 and nearly 13 per cent in the age group of 50–69. Similarly, diseases like jaundice and diarrhoea continue to be majorly responsible in the 0–14 age group. As is clear from Figures 3.5 and 3.6, the focus on these diseases has been negligible in drug development except for three new compounds (NCEs) that are being developed for the treatment of malaria. On the other hand, new branded generics that came to the market and NCEs focussed relatively better on the morbidity burden due to NCDs.

Table 3.20 Percentage distribution of reported morbidity across age groups

Disease/condition	0–14	15–49	50–69	70-plus	All age
Fever	35.12	9.59	12.56	7.00	12.96
Tuberculosis	0.97	0.85	1.25	1.44	0.99
Filariasis	0.00	0.03	0.16	0.04	0.05
Tetanus	0.11	0.03	0.01		0.04
HIV/AIDS		0.23	0.01		0.14
Other STDs	0.06	0.01	0.01		0.02
Jaundice	4.21	1.16	0.85	0.48	1.40
Diarrhoeas	8.44	1.28	2.43	2.35	2.43
Worm infestation	0.57	0.07	0.09	0.06	0.13
Cancer	0.75	1.03	4.00	2.59	1.71
Blood diseases	2.31	1.21	1.54	1.42	1.42
Diabetes	0.33	0.54	3.64	4.27	1.43
Thyroid and other metabolic and nutritional	1.02	0.40	0.57	0.46	0.51
Psychiatric and neurological	5.34	2.80	6.24	9.99	4.35
Eye related	1.29	0.83	10.13	8.18	3.31
Ear	0.66	0.30	0.32	0.09	0.33
Cardiovascular	1.57	3.16	14.68	19.69	6.57
Respiratory	7.34	1.50	6.01	9.90	3.74
Gastrointestinal	6.84	7.48	9.99	7.88	7.94
Skin related	1.17	0.52	0.67	1.04	0.67
Musculoskeletal	1.96	2.44	6.56	5.44	3.44
Genitourinary	2.31	4.66	5.95	7.86	4.90
Obstetric	5.82	5.36	0.11		3.95
Injuries and accidents	11.82	54.50	12.23	9.81	37.58
Total	100	100	100	100	100

Source: NSSO 71st round data, estimated.

Implications of lower focus on infectious diseases

While drugs are already available for several infectious diseases in the market, the data on new drug development show that the industry has not taken the emerging threats of infectious diseases into account adequately. We have recently seen the resurgence and emergence of several infectious diseases in different regions of India in a major way (John et al. 2011; Dikid et al. 2013). For instance, studies have reported the outbreak of cholera in many Indian states (Ramamurthy and Sharma 2014; Gupta et al. 2016; Mathews et al. 2018). Similarly, reports and studies have revealed the resurgence of tuberculosis (Phillips 2013), the emergence of multi-drug-resistant tuberculosis (Sharma and Mohan 2004) and the increasing co-morbidity of tuberculosis with human immunodeficiency virus (HIV) and diabetes (Bishnu et al. 2013; Bishwajit et al. 2014, Trinh et al. 2015) in India. Several parts of India have also witnessed the persistence, resurgence and outbreak of diphtheria (Murhekar and Bitragunta 2011; Parande et al. 2014; Sangal et al. 2017). Studies also reported the outbreak of dengue (Dar et al. 1999; Cecilia 2014; Mutheneni et al. 2017) and the changing epidemiology of dengue in India (Bhatia et al. 2013). Several Indian states have also witnessed the outbreak of chikungunya epidemics (Mavalankar et al. 2007), increasing the financial burden and the morbidity and mortality burden associated with chikungunya (Mavalankar et al. 2008; Krishnamoorthy et al. 2009). The persistence of malaria (Kumar et al. 2007) and avian influenza (Tosh et al. 2007; Fischer et al. 2014) is also reported from many Indian states. Similarly, several places in India have also witnessed outbreaks of Japanese encephalitis (Parida et al. 2006; Wang and Liang 2015), leptospirosis (Sethi et al. 2010), NIPAH virus (Chatterjee 2018) and Zika virus (Bhardwaj et al. 2017; WHO 2018).

The Integrated Disease Surveillance Programme of the Ministry of Health and Family Welfare, India, provided the data of district-wise outbreak of CDs in India. As per their data, there were 1850 outbreaks of acute diarrhoeal diseases, 1,100 outbreaks of measles, 960 outbreaks of chickenpox, 580 outbreaks of dengue, 25 outbreaks of chikungunya and 170 outbreaks of malaria in India between 2015 and 2018 (see Figure 3.7). The data provided by the Ministry of Health and Family Welfare showed that the cases of dengue, for instance, have increased to 151,561 in 2017 from 28,292 in 2010. Similarly, the data show that the cases of chikungunya

Figure 3.7   Disease-wise number of outbreaks of infectious diseases reported in India between 2015 and 2018

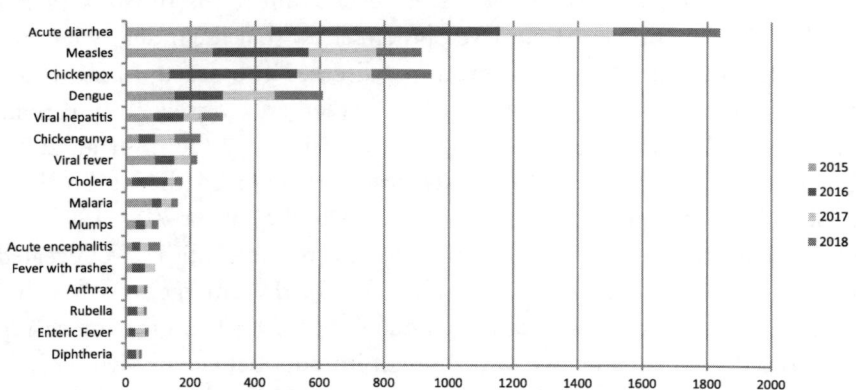

Source: Weekly outbreak report of Integrated Disease Surveillance Programme, GOI.

in India have increased to 58,690 in 2017 (until October) from 20,402 in 2011. The reported cases of malaria increased to 1,090,724 in 2016 from 881,730 in 2010. Malaria continues to be a serious problem in the tribal-dominated regions of central and northeast India. The data also show that the number of deaths due to Japanese encephalitis in India was 962 out of the 12,439 cases reported in 2016, which shows the potential burden of the disease. Also, the data show that once-controlled diseases like kala-azar have started resurging in some states including Jharkhand, Bihar and West Bengal with a high possibility of spreading to other parts of the country. As per the data provided by the Directorate of General Health Services, the incidence of tuberculosis is as high as 211 per 100,000 population in 2016. The Indian pharmaceutical and biopharmaceutical industries appear to have neglected this present and future infectious diseases burden of India, which is expected to be higher for children and elderly from poor and marginalised sections and regions in the country.

Responsiveness of vaccine development to the infectious disease burden

The biopharmaceutical sector in India, however, provides a different picture on the preventive focus. Although the therapeutic focus on CDs and their associated conditions was negligible in drug development, the biopharmaceutical companies have a relatively better focus on the development of vaccines of several CDs. As discussed in the previous chapter, most of the major biopharmaceutical firms have invested in bacterial vaccines, viral vaccines and recombinant and combination vaccines (see Table 2.3). Out of the 42 companies mentioned in the previous chapter, 20 have exclusive focus on preventive care. The vaccines that are in the pipeline of these companies together cover diseases such as typhoid, Japanese encephalitis, chikungunya, malaria PvR II, acellular pertussis, tetanus, meningitis, DTwP-HBV combination, haemophilus influenza type b, influenza, malaria, dengue and hepatitis A. Some of the companies have R&D focus on therapeutic vaccine for pancreatic cancer and oral cancer vaccines.

Conclusion

The chapter examined the mortality data and disease burden in India, followed by the disease focus of the branded generics, NCEs and vaccines developed or being developed in India. The data on the causes of deaths showed that, in line with the overall epidemiological transition, NCDs accounted for as much as 61 per cent of the total deaths while CDs accounted for 28 per cent of the total deaths. The age-wise distribution of causes of deaths showed that CDs were the major cause of deaths for the age group 0–14, injuries for 15–29 and NCDs were the major cause of death from 29 onwards. Within CDs, as evident from the age-wise distribution of causes of death, infancy and childhood-related diseases of neonatal conditions, respiratory infection and diarrhoea together formed the major causes of deaths. Diseases like tuberculosis were a major cause of CD-related deaths in all age groups. Within NCDs, cardiovascular disease was the major cause of deaths in all age groups, followed by respiratory diseases, cancer, digestive diseases and genitourinary and kidney diseases. While cardiovascular diseases accounted for nearly 42 per cent of deaths due to NCDs across all age groups, these diseases accounted for nearly 26 per cent of all deaths. Within the various age groups, cardiovascular diseases were the causes of deaths of nearly 36 per cent in the age group of 50–69, 32 per cent in the age group of 70-plus and 17.5 per cent in the age group of 15–49.

The data presented in the chapter clearly showed that the therapeutic focus of drugs has predominantly been on NCDs, which corresponds to the overall disease burden of the country. However, there were some discrepancies. The industry has focussed less on the major disease burden of children and the elderly (70-plus here) and more on the age group of 15–69. Drugs for infectious diseases, several of which are resurging, are prioritised even lower than those for cosmetic treatments (acne, weight loss, hair removal, general dermatology), vitiligo, contraceptives, anti-spasmodic, anti-fungal, sleeping disorders and substance de-addiction. Except diarrhoea, for which 23 new drugs came to the market between 2000 and 2017, no other major disease causes of deaths in the 0–14 age group figured in the development of new drugs. Similarly, while several new medicines came to the market for cardiovascular diseases, hypertension, cancer and digestive disorders, only two new drugs came to the market between 2000 and 2017 for the treatment of tuberculosis, which is resurging in several parts of the country in the productive age group of 15–49. The prioritisation of the areas of R&D in India, hence, appears to be based solely on market viability wherein less-profitable products, technology and target population are less likely to receive attention.

Vaccine development, especially in the biopharmaceutical sector, on the other hand, has a focus on preventive care. As illustrated in the previous chapter, the focus of vaccine development of Indian biopharmaceutical companies has been on diseases such as typhoid, Japanese encephalitis, chikungunya, malaria PvR II, acellular pertussis, tetanus, meningitis, DTwP–HBV combination, haemophilus influenza type b, influenza, malaria, dengue, hepatitis A, rabies, Zika, polio, therapeutic vaccine for pancreatic cancer and oral cancer vaccines. While these are important R&D initiatives, diseases like acute diarrhoea and respiratory infections, which constitute the highest mortality and morbidity burden among CDs, have not received adequate attention.

In short, the Indian pharmaceutical and biopharmaceutical industries, except the segment of vaccine development, appear to have neglected the present and future infectious disease burden of India, which is expected to be higher for children and the elderly from poor and marginalised sections and regions in the country. While diseases such as HIV, tuberculosis and malaria received some attention worldwide under the public sector and multilateral aid agency funding opportunities, other infectious diseases were not sufficiently addressed even in public funding (West et al. 2017). It should also be noted that there has been a significant reduction in development assistance for health (DAH) in all countries, impying that private capital plays a major role in deciding the research focus of drug and vaccine development, which is not always in line with most of the public health priorities of developing and underdeveloped countries, as the Indian cases discussed in the chapter show.

4

Affordability and the Social Divide

Medical expenditure constitutes a significant component of out-of-pocket health spending in India. Recent research has shown that catastrophic household health expenditure has increased in India (Brinda et al. 2015; Pandey et al. 2018). Studies have found several policy interventions that are responsible for the increase in the cost of medical expenditure. These include structural adjustment policies and the resultant rapid privatisation of healthcare (Ghosh 2011), non-regulation of the private sector (Bonu et al. 2009; Bandameedi et al. 2016), irrational prescription practices of doctors (Bhaskarabhatla and Chatterjee 2017), poor health financial protection (Devadasan et al. 2007; Selvaraj and Karan 2012), market-based pricing policies of drugs (Narula 2015) and, above all, the higher cost of medicine. Development of new branded generics and biosimilars has contributed immensely to the treatment of several infectious and non-communicable diseases in India. However, with the adoption of a market-based pricing policy, it is not clear whether new drugs that are coming to the market are affordable to people. This chapter critically examines the question of affordability due to considerable variations in the prices of newly approved branded generics in the light of the market-based pricing policy of drugs in India. It also offers a discussion on various policy initiatives across the globe on pharmaceutical pricing and its relationship with affordability.

The chapter has used secondary data sources to examine the financial burden of medicines and prices of formulations of drugs. Data on prices of medicines for inpatient and outpatient treatment presented in the chapter are drawn from the nationally representative data of India – *social consumption* – health survey of the National Sample Survey Organisation

(NSSO), Ministry of Statistics and Programme Implementation, Government of India, collected from January to June 2014. Medical expenditure is provided for a reference period of 365 days for inpatient care and 15 days of outpatient care for items including doctor's fee, diagnostic tests, bed charges, cost of medicine and other medical as well as non-medical expenditure. The data on the prices of formulation and brands of selected drugs discussed in the study are obtained from the web portal of Pharma Sahi Dam[1] of the National Pharmaceutical Pricing Authority, Ministry of Chemicals and Fertilizers, Government of India.

Drug price (de)regulation in India

India has taken several policy measures since the 1970s that have reduced the prices of drugs as compared to other major drug manufacturing countries. Among others, the significant ones were the introduction of process patent and drug price control (Selvaraj 2007). The role of process patent in reducing drug prices and its reversal to product patent and the resultant increase in drug prices were well discussed in India (Grace 2004; Chaudhuri et al. 2006) and, hence, we do not discuss it in the chapter. The logic behind the price control and regulation of drugs is that the drug market is supply driven and demand is created or co-produced by the industry with its network of hospitals, practitioners and its knowledge base. The failure of the market in lowering the prices of drugs due to such characteristics was already well illustrated (Gadre and Sardeshpande 2017). Price control has, therefore, been part of India's drug policy. Drug policies, price control and regulation have seen a lot of changes in the country under different regimes. We would like to highlight some of the recent changes that aimed to both regulate and deregulate the price control of drugs in India.

India has seen two major changes in its drug price regulation since the implementation of the Drug Price (Control) Order 1995 and the establishment of the National Pharmaceutical Pricing Authority (NPPA) in 1997, with the objective of ensuring affordability and availability of medicines in India. The first one was the release and revision of the National List of Essential Medicines (NLEM). The list released in 1996

---

[1] See http://nppaimis.nic.in/nppaprice/pharmasahidaamweb.aspx, accessed on 10 October 2020.

was revised in 2003, 2011 and 2014. The NLEM revised in 2011 included 348 essential drugs and further included an additional 108 'life saving drugs' in 2014. As studies have highlighted (Ahmad et al. 2014), this lowered the prices of several medicines for the treatment of cardiovascular diseases, cancer, diabetes and HIV (human immunodeficiency virus). However, this list was further revised and 108 essential drugs, which were under price control, were excluded from NLEM in September 2014, which again led to the escalation of the prices of these drugs. As per the NLEM revised in 2015, 376 drugs are now under price control.

Second was the policy shift to market-based pricing from cost-based pricing. This was essentially a part of the larger process of state withdrawal from regulation in general and restricting its role to market facilitation. One of the important aspects of the market-based pricing policy (MBP) is fixing ceiling price based on the average prices of brands that have a minimum of 1 per cent market share. However, studies have already illustrated that ceiling prices are always the near the prices of top-selling brands, which are generally highly priced (Selvaaj et al. 2012). Many have also argued that unlike other commodity market, where consumers have information and can choose the products, the market-based pricing policies in the drug industry might not lead to competitive pricing due to the very nature of the organisation of the healthcare industry and procurement policies in low and middle income countries (Danzon et al. 2015), regulatory issues (Phadke et al. 2013) and prescription practices (Mazumdar 2015). The market-based pricing for drugs has been criticised for its inability to bring down the prices of drugs of even top-selling brands (see Selvaraj et al. 2012) largely due to the power dynamics in the healthcare industry where care providers are unquestionable authorities and patients are often submissive receivers without proper information and choice. Johnson (2014: 80), based on an extensive literature review on practitioner-induced demand from various parts of the world, noted that treatment decisions and drug prescriptions may not always match the need of the patients and aspects like physician incentives are significant factors of cost of care.

Price regulation of drugs in India has paramount significance in this context since there is no evidence to prove that the shift from cost-based pricing to market-based pricing yielded competitive pricing of drugs. We have attempted to understand this issue a little deeper by examining the share of medicines in inpatient and outpatient healthcare in India.

The financial burden and affordability of medicines in India

As mentioned in the beginning of the chapter, medicines constitute a major part of the out-of-pocket medical expenditure in India. The published report of NSSO (71st round) on *Health in India* (2014) revealed that the cost of medicine constituted nearly 72 per cent of the total outpatient medical expenditure in rural India and 68 per cent in urban India. We have attempted to disaggregate the medical expenditure across outpatient and inpatient care across different systems of medicine in rural and urban areas of Indian states from the unit level data of NSSO 71st round. Unsurprisingly, cost of medicine constituted the highest share in outpatient care in the rural and urban areas of all Indian states (see Table 4.1). Also, households in rural areas spent a little more on medicine than those in urban areas. If we combine both AYUSH (Ayurveda, yoga, naturopathy, Unani, Siddha and homoeopathy) and non-AYUSH (allopathic), the cost of medicine exceeded more than 90 per cent in the rural areas of Himachal Pradesh and Mizoram and the union territories of Lakshadweep and Andaman and Nicobar Islands. While the cost of medicine ranged between 80 and 90 per cent in the rural areas of Rajasthan, Chhattisgarh and Goa, it was between 70 and 80 per cent in the rural areas of 13 Indian states. The states where the cost of medicine was less than the national average included Delhi, Tripura, Meghalaya, Assam, Gujarat and Tamil Nadu. In rural areas, the cost of medicine was the lowest in the union territories of Chandigarh (42 per cent) and Daman and Diu (50 per cent), followed by the states of Gujarat (54.3 per cent) and Tamil Nadu (57.9 per cent). Expenditure on medicine in outpatient care in urban India was a little less than in rural India. However, it constituted more than 80 per cent of the medical expenditure in some states and union territories including Sikkim, Chhattisgarh, Manipur and Chandigarh. The states which reported relatively lower spending on medicine in outpatient care in urban India included Tripura (27.6 per cent), Jharkhand (46.3 per cent), Delhi (52.5 per cent), Assam (52.8 per cent), Uttaranchal (54.5 per cent) and Gujarat (55.4 per cent). Although allopathic medicines dominated the cost of medical expenditure among the different systems of medicines, AYUSH medicines were also a major part of medical expenditure in states like Chhattisgarh (32.8 per cent in rural areas), Himachal Pradesh (20.1 per cent in rural and 23.4 per cent in urban areas), Meghalaya (17.6 per cent in rural areas), Mizoram (15.4 per cent in rural areas) and Kerala (13.1 per cent in rural and 8 per cent in urban areas). Other major items in the outpatient medical expenditure were the consultation fee of doctors and diagnostic tests.

Table 4.1   Percentage distribution of total expenditure by different items of expenditure in outpatient care

State	Doctor's fee		AYUSH medicine expenditure		Non-AYUSH medicine		Diagnostic tests		Other medical expenditure	
	R	U	R	U	R	U	R	U	R	U
J&K	11.2	9.2	0.7	1.4	70.4	65.1	13.0	20.1	4.6	4.2
Himachal Pradesh	2.2	2.0	20.1	23.4	70.8	53.2	4.4	20.7	2.6	0.7
Punjab	9.6	9.5	3.7	2.2	73.1	69.6	12.3	13.5	1.4	5.2
Chandigarh	20.4	10.6	0.0	2.8	42.8	78.5	36.7	7.8	0.1	0.4
Uttaranchal	8.6	23.2	9.9	2.9	60.4	51.6	18.4	15.3	2.7	6.9
Haryana	10.2	15.7	9.6	6.2	62.9	59.6	14.2	14.4	3.2	4.1
Delhi	25.2	21.7	0.0	13.7	66.5	38.8	1.9	17.8	6.4	8.0
Rajasthan	9.8	21.7	3.0	6.7	79.9	60.2	5.6	9.6	1.6	1.8
Uttar Pradesh	12.3	14.4	3.7	3.5	73.3	66.9	7.2	11.4	3.5	3.8
Bihar	11.2	13.4	5.4	4.6	68.5	62.1	10.8	15.9	4.0	3.9
Sikkim	3.1	4.5	0.0	0.4	76.5	87.1	9.2	4.0	11.2	4.1
Arunachal Pradesh	0.7	0.4	11.4	2.2	51.6	67.8	27.1	11.3	9.3	18.3
Nagaland	2.4	12.9	3.1	3.0	76.5	70.8	9.4	11.7	8.6	1.6
Manipur	7.8	6.5	0.0	0.0	74.7	81.9	12.9	6.6	4.6	5.0
Mizoram	4.2	4.8	15.4	1.7	75.4	74.5	3.3	18.3	1.6	0.8
Tripura	9.6	29.4	1.3	0.7	67.5	26.9	20.0	35.0	1.5	8.0
Meghalaya	20.7	25.7	17.6	1.5	44.2	64.0	1.3	4.5	16.2	4.4
Assam	6.7	10.1	3.9	0.7	61.8	52.1	13.5	29.8	14.1	7.4
West Bengal	14.4	14.4	3.1	2.1	69.6	68.5	11.9	11.6	1.1	3.4
Jharkhand	15.2	16.0	1.4	2.0	70.2	44.3	9.3	30.1	3.9	7.6
Odisha	4.6	6.4	7.3	5.6	69.6	73.9	13.9	11.2	4.6	3.0

(Contd.)

(*Contd.*)

State	Doctor's fee		AYUSH medicine expenditure		Non-AYUSH medicine		Diagnostic tests		Other medical expenditure	
	R	U	R	U	R	U	R	U	R	U
Chhattisgarh	8.4	10.5	32.8	13.3	50.6	69.5	4.3	5.5	3.9	1.1
Madhya Pradesh	14.2	14.9	3.7	6.2	65.9	65.5	11.0	11.5	5.2	1.9
Gujarat	26.2	28.2	0.2	0.9	54.1	54.5	8.2	12.3	11.3	4.1
Daman and Diu	14.1	10.4	0.0	0.2	45.8	79.0	18.5	10.1	21.7	0.3
D&N Haveli	20.5	16.4	15.1	17.5	34.9	54.0	29.6	10.0	0.0	2.1
Maharashtra	22.9	22.4	3.2	3.0	61.7	58.2	8.1	10.6	4.0	5.8
Andhra Pradesh	10.6	8.7	1.3	0.8	77.3	77.0	8.3	9.0	2.4	4.5
Karnataka	17.7	16.0	2.0	10.8	64.9	52.8	9.5	10.2	6.0	10.2
Goa	13.5	6.7	0.2	0.2	80.2	77.0	4.5	7.9	1.6	8.2
Lakshadweep	1.0	2.9	45.4	0.0	47.2	72.2	2.9	21.4	3.5	3.5
Kerala	10.6	9.0	13.1	8.0	62.6	66.6	12.2	11.9	1.6	4.4
Tamil Nadu	18.5	15.5	1.6	4.2	56.3	68.1	21.9	10.0	1.7	2.3
Puducherry	23.6	11.8	0.0	10.7	72.9	53.9	3.5	12.7	0.0	10.9
A&N Islands	1.2	44.6	1.9	0.1	96.8	23.6	0.0	6.2	0.0	25.5
Telangana	12.2	13.3	2.6	1.8	67.1	70.7	15.0	8.8	3.0	5.3
All India	13.0	14.8	4.8	4.4	68.0	64.5	10.8	11.9	3.4	4.5

Source: NSSO 71st round, estimated.

Note: R – Rural; U – Urban.

Cost of medicines constitutes an important item in inpatient care as well. The data collected for a reference period of 365 days on inpatient medical expenditure in the NSSO data showed that cost of medicine held the second highest share of medical expenditure in India (see Table 4.2). First was the consultation fee of doctors. As is clear from Table 4.2, medicines accounted for nearly 24 per cent of the total inpatient expenditure in rural India and 20 per cent in urban India. While doctor's fee held the highest share in inpatient expenditure on an average, data show that, in some states, cost of medicines held the highest share. For instance, the data show that cost of medicine had the highest share in inpatient medical expenditure in nearly 10 Indian states and it was

Table 4.2   Percentage distribution of total expenditure by different items of expenditure in inpatient care

	Doctor's fee		Medicine expenditure		Diagnostic tests		Bed charges		Other medical expenses		Transportation		Other non-medical health expenses	
	R	U	R	U	R	U	R	U	R	U	R	U	R	U
J&K	8.7	16.3	36.5	32.0	13.8	11.1	5.5	9.7	11.0	17.4	10.0	5.1	14.5	8.3
Himachal Pradesh	28.2	31.9	25.4	24.8	8.8	9.5	11.5	6.1	9.3	16.8	5.8	5.0	11.1	5.9
Punjab	25.2	23.5	25.9	17.1	10.6	8.6	16.3	20.7	12.8	20.9	3.0	2.9	6.2	6.3
Chandigarh	61.3	25.3	17.8	20.8	6.7	8.5	3.1	3.3	5.8	38.3	1.8	1.1	3.4	2.6
Uttaranchal	18.7	23.1	28.6	19.2	10.8	12.9	14.5	16.3	15.0	18.5	4.6	4.8	7.7	5.2
Haryana	24.5	26.9	26.4	19.9	10.3	9.4	15.1	20.3	12.6	14.6	3.4	2.8	7.6	6.1
Delhi	16.8	32.0	22.2	10.6	9.0	7.7	19.3	22.7	25.7	15.7	2.1	2.9	4.9	8.5
Rajasthan	19.9	32.9	17.4	20.1	8.9	8.2	22.6	15.0	12.1	14.2	6.7	3.0	12.4	6.5
Uttar Pradesh	23.3	18.3	27.5	17.6	8.0	4.6	17.9	19.5	12.3	33.7	3.8	2.2	7.3	4.1
Bihar	22.0	23.4	29.4	25.8	8.6	7.7	12.0	14.2	10.0	14.9	5.5	4.7	12.4	9.3
Sikkim	13.2	16.4	19.7	16.0	9.2	7.9	11.7	15.6	10.0	9.1	10.1	8.5	26.0	26.6
Arunachal Pradesh	16.6	8.6	20.9	30.9	9.3	13.6	14.0	9.4	11.7	13.8	6.9	7.6	20.6	16.1
Nagaland	2.9	5.8	31.7	38.3	6.8	16.6	14.5	14.0	15.1	10.2	10.9	4.0	18.1	11.1
Manipur	4.6	8.4	31.4	26.2	9.2	10.8	15.2	15.0	10.4	13.7	9.6	8.1	19.7	17.6
Mizoram	8.7	20.7	40.0	27.3	5.4	10.4	6.7	10.9	15.4	9.8	7.5	6.1	16.2	14.7
Tripura	11.2	16.4	27.7	30.4	10.6	9.4	19.1	12.9	8.5	7.9	12.9	13.5	10.1	9.6
Meghalaya	24.8	24.2	14.0	16.5	5.7	7.3	16.4	23.3	10.0	17.7	6.7	2.6	22.4	8.5
Assam	21.4	26.2	25.3	15.7	11.7	7.1	6.2	14.6	12.9	17.0	8.3	7.7	14.2	11.7
West Bengal	31.8	41.6	22.0	13.3	12.2	7.6	13.1	12.8	8.7	13.7	5.7	3.1	6.4	7.8

(Contd)

	Doctor's fee		Medicine expenditure		Diagnostic tests		Bed charges		Other medical expenses		Transportation		Other non-medical health expenses	
	R	U	R	U	R	U	R	U	R	U	R	U	R	U
Jharkhand	18.4	22.3	23.7	20.6	6.6	8.6	25.2	17.8	9.1	19.2	5.9	3.9	11.0	7.5
Odisha	18.7	20.2	29.5	29.8	8.8	9.0	17.5	15.8	8.9	9.5	5.9	4.2	10.6	11.5
Chattisgarh	22.2	24.8	18.5	15.9	5.1	5.8	10.5	14.9	30.2	24.2	4.2	3.5	9.2	10.9
Madhya Pradesh	19.4	22.5	23.6	22.2	8.0	8.2	20.9	18.5	10.1	15.0	5.3	3.9	12.6	9.6
Gujarat	32.2	36.4	21.4	19.7	7.8	7.2	15.5	13.9	13.1	15.0	3.5	2.4	6.4	5.3
Daman and Diu	23.5	26.7	18.6	23.1	3.8	3.7	23.1	20.9	21.2	11.4	4.1	8.9	5.7	5.4
D&N Haveli	32.4	62.5	7.7	11.0	3.8	3.9	26.0	9.8	23.5	6.0	2.5	2.7	4.2	4.1
Maharashtra	27.1	31.8	27.0	25.1	8.7	11.0	15.4	17.2	10.8	8.3	4.1	2.0	6.9	4.6
Andhra Pradesh	21.8	30.0	19.1	19.2	9.1	10.8	21.0	17.5	16.1	11.3	4.1	3.0	8.8	8.2
Karnataka	25.2	29.8	29.8	30.5	8.8	8.1	14.0	13.5	9.5	8.9	3.6	2.4	9.2	6.8
Goa	52.7	28.1	15.9	16.3	2.1	2.7	7.7	9.0	16.5	37.3	1.3	1.4	3.9	5.2
Lakshadweep	42.3	28.8	5.7	5.6	3.3	6.8	15.5	13.8	10.7	19.9	3.7	10.6	18.8	14.6
Kerala	26.1	25.0	19.6	20.3	10.9	10.2	17.6	15.1	16.4	19.4	3.0	2.4	6.4	7.7
Tamil Nadu	37.5	34.2	16.6	15.8	6.4	7.8	17.8	17.8	8.7	14.9	4.1	2.4	8.9	7.1
Puducherry	19.0	41.6	18.4	12.2	6.8	5.6	27.4	21.9	14.1	11.5	3.0	2.0	11.3	5.3
A&N Islands	52.2	45.9	0.9	3.5	0.9	5.3	14.0	19.8	29.4	16.0	0.5	2.2	2.1	7.3
Telangana	26.2	30.0	20.8	20.5	10.3	12.0	18.8	15.3	10.2	12.2	4.0	2.3	9.6	7.6
India	25.7	29.3	23.6	20.0	8.9	8.4	17.0	16.7	11.9	16.1	4.3	2.7	8.5	6.8

Source: NSSO 71st round, estimated.

significantly higher than other major costs such as doctor's fee and bed charges in both rural and urban areas of the states of Jammu and Kashmir, Mizoram, Nagaland, Manipur, Tripura and Odisha. Apart from these states, medicine held the highest share in the inpatient medical expenditure in the rural areas of Haryana, Uttar Pradesh, Bihar, Assam, Jharkhand and Madhya Pradesh.

Data across rural and urban areas of various Indian states thus clearly show the preponderance of medicine in the medical expenditure of both inpatient and outpatient care. We have also tried to understand whether there are any changes across expenditure classes[2] (proxy for income groups). Although medicines held the highest share in outpatient treatment in all expenditure classes, it showed interesting variations across class groups in rural and urban areas (see Table 4.3). For instance, while expenditure on medicine was more among the middle and richer class groups than the richest, poorer and the poorest in the rural areas, it was higher among the poorer, richest and the poorest than the middle and richer in urban areas.

Cost of medicine in inpatient care, however, showed steady a declining trend across expenditure classes in rural India with the highest among the poorest, followed by others (see Table 4.4). In urban areas also, the cost due to medicine was reported lower among economically better-off groups than the middle and poor expenditure classes. These differences are not stark enough to lead to any specific inference; however, variations in treatment seeking, place of treatment and access to financial risk protection (insurance) may explain these small differences. It should be noted that the data do not show much variation in cost of medicine as a percentage of medical expenditure across social groups in inpatient and outpatient care (see Figures 4.1 and 4.2). Out of the social groups, Scheduled Tribes (ST) in rural areas have spent marginally less on medicine than other social groups, which is perhaps attributable to their dependence on indigenous and other systems of treatment or less access to allopathic health services.

---

2   Calculated based on the monthly per capita consumer expenditure from the National Sample Survey data.

Table 4.3 Percentage distribution of total expenditure and its items by monthly per capita expenditure class (MPCE) and sector, outpatient

	Doctor's fee		AYUSH medicine expenditure		Non-AYUSH medicine		Diagnostic tests		Other medical expenditure	
	R	U	R	U	R	U	R	U	R	U
Poorest	12.4	15.7	6.2	3.5	66.6	64.6	11.2	12.1	3.6	4.1
Poorer	13.2	13.9	4.1	7.1	64.7	65.4	13.4	10.1	4.5	3.5
Middle	13.2	16.8	4.0	4.3	72.7	62.4	8.2	11.2	1.9	5.3
Richer	13.2	14.3	5.6	5.1	70.4	63.7	8.2	12.3	2.6	4.7
Richest	13.2	14.8	3.7	3.4	66.4	65.3	12.6	12.1	4.2	4.4
Total	13.0	14.8	4.8	4.4	68.0	64.5	10.8	11.9	3.4	4.5

Source: NSSO 71st round, estimated.
Note: R – Rural; U – Urban.

Figure 4.1 Percentage distribution of total expenditure and its items by social group and sector, outpatient

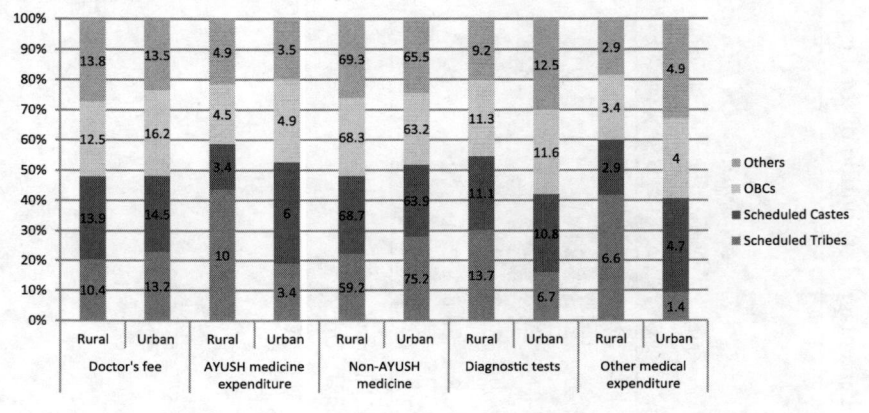

Source: NSSO 71st round, estimated.

Table 4.4 Percentage distribution of total expenditure and its items by MPCE and sector, inpatient

	Doctor's fee		Medicine expenditure		Diagnostic tests		Bed charges		Other medical expenses		Transportation		Other non-medical health expenses	
	R	U	R	U	R	U	R	U	R	U	R	U	R	U
Poorest	24.9	26.6	24.6	21.1	8.9	7.4	15.2	17.7	12.1	16.8	5.0	3.0	9.5	7.3
Poorer	25.0	28.3	24.4	21.3	9.0	8.5	16.9	15.8	10.7	15.9	4.8	2.8	9.1	7.3
Middle	24.1	27.8	24.4	21.8	9.0	9.4	17.0	16.8	11.9	13.8	4.4	3.0	9.2	7.3
Richer	25.9	31.2	23.4	19.4	8.8	7.8	17.2	18.3	11.7	13.3	4.4	2.8	8.5	7.2
Richest	26.8	28.8	23.0	19.8	9.6	8.9	17.1	15.3	13.0	18.4	3.6	2.7	6.8	6.2
Total	25.7	29.3	23.6	20.0	8.9	8.4	17.0	16.7	11.9	16.1	4.3	2.7	8.5	6.8

Source: NSSO 71st round, estimated.
Note: R – Rural; U – Urban.

Figure 4.2 Percentage distribution of total expenditure and its items by social group and sector, inpatient

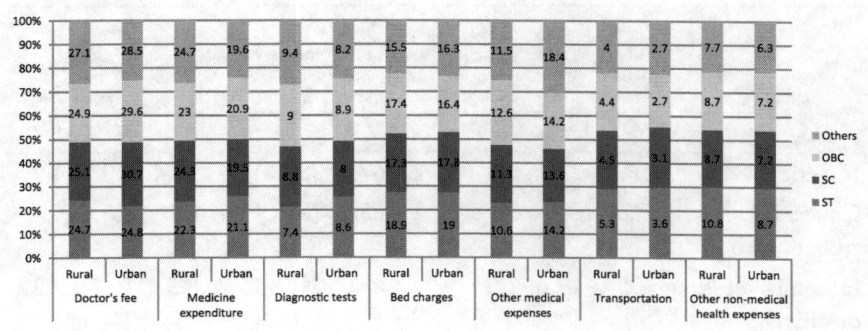

Source: NSSO 71st round, estimated.
Note: R – Rural; U – Urban.

The NSSO data also allow us to estimate the share of the cost of medicine across disease types. As is clear from Tables 4.5 and 4.6, cost of medicines was the highest for cancer treatment both in outpatient and inpatient care. In rural areas, medicines for the treatment of psychiatric and neurological diseases, genitourinary, cardiovascular diseases and respiratory diseases constitute more than 70 per cent of the total medical expenditure. In urban areas, cost of medicines for obstetrics care was the second highest, followed by cardiovascular diseases, diabetes, skin diseases and respiratory diseases. Although doctor's fee constituted the highest share in medical expenditure in inpatient care in general, cost of medicines for cancer, psychiatric and neurological diseases, respiratory diseases, infections and blood diseases in rural India and cancer, diabetes, respiratory diseases, infection and psychiatric and neurological diseases in urban India exceeded doctor's fee.

The NSSO data further show that medicines, especially allopathic medicines, continue to be responsible for the major share of medical expenditure irrespective of economic class, caste and regions in outpatient care and for some states and for some diseases in inpatient care. The data cover both public and private hospitals. What is most important to note is that most of these are out-of-pocket expenditure. As per the published report of the NSSO, a significant proportion of this out-of-pocket expenditure is met by the households from their own savings or by borrowing or with the help of relatives and friends since nearly 86 per cent of the rural and 82 per cent of the urban population were not covered

Table 4.5 Percentage distribution of total expenditure and its items by disease type and sector, outpatient

Disease type	Doctor's fee		AYUSH medicine expenditure		Non-AYUSH medicine		Diagnostic tests		Other medical expenditure	
	R	U	R	U	R	U	R	U	R	U
Infection	16.4	22.1	2.8	3.2	67.3	58.4	10.6	11.4	3.0	4.9
Cancers	5.2	3.8	5.1	6.2	65.0	78.5	15.1	6.1	9.6	5.4
Blood diseases (anaemia/bleeding disorder)	6.1	19.6	1.0	3.9	67.2	59.9	15.7	8.5	10.1	8.2
Endocrine, metabolic and nutritional	13.2	11.1	4.8	2.8	63.4	71.0	16.5	11.6	2.0	3.6
Psychiatric and neurological	11.3	12.1	4.3	5.9	75.3	66.2	6.8	11.6	2.3	4.3
Eye related	15.6	20.0	3.5	3.2	64.1	55.0	10.2	17.5	6.6	4.3
Ear related	7.2	16.9	1.9	17.0	69.7	33.7	16.6	13.3	4.6	19.1
Cardiovascular	10.5	13.1	8.4	1.9	71.7	72.7	6.7	10.0	2.7	2.2
Respiratory	10.3	17.8	5.3	4.2	71.8	69.7	9.7	5.9	2.8	2.4
Gastrointestinal	14.7	16.3	3.2	5.1	64.8	49.2	13.2	23.0	4.1	6.4
Skin related	16.9	12.8	10.5	14.4	67.4	69.2	2.5	2.5	2.7	1.1
Musculoskeletal	10.6	11.9	6.9	9.3	66.9	59.2	11.5	13.0	4.2	6.7
Genitourinary	11.2	9.8	2.4	10.4	72.6	57.0	11.4	19.6	2.5	3.1
Obstetric	19.6	8.6	3.2	0.5	44.5	77.3	28.4	8.9	4.3	4.7
Injuries	16.0	18.5	5.2	3.7	64.5	56.8	9.2	13.1	5.0	7.9
Total	13.0	14.8	4.8	4.4	68.0	64.5	10.8	11.9	3.4	4.5

Source: NSSO 71st round, estimated.
Note: R – Rural; U – Urban.

by any health protection scheme.[3] As Table 4.7 shows, as much as 67 per cent of the households in rural India and 75 per cent in urban India

---

[3]   The newly announced healthcare programme of Ayushman Bharat Yojana is not yet fully rolled out in most of the states (as of March 2019).

Table 4.6 Percentage distribution of total expenditure and its items by disease type and sector, inpatient

	Doctor's fee		Medicine expenditure		Diagnostic tests		Bed charges		Other medical expenses		Transportation		Other non-medical health expenses	
	R	U	R	U	R	U	R	U	R	U	R	U	R	U
Infection	18.7	22.9	25.5	22.7	8.6	10.4	20.5	21.1	11.3	12.0	4.9	2.8	10.4	8.0
Cancers	24.1	25.9	27.3	27.7	10.7	10.6	13.7	13.1	11.3	12.5	3.9	3.0	9.0	7.2
Blood diseases	19.9	25.6	24.6	22.3	11.1	8.8	17.9	18.5	13.4	15.2	4.6	2.7	8.4	6.9
Endocrine, metabolic and nutritional	26.7	21.6	22.0	27.0	9.7	8.9	18.1	19.6	10.1	12.9	4.6	2.8	8.8	7.2
Psychatric and neurological	20.7	29.8	26.2	21.3	11.8	9.5	20.6	18.5	10.8	11.4	3.8	2.7	6.1	6.9
Eye related	36.8	50.8	12.4	7.5	4.8	4.0	11.9	7.4	22.5	15.7	3.8	3.1	7.8	11.5
Ear related	34.7	23.9	20.4	16.1	7.5	11.0	12.0	23.6	11.7	16.2	3.7	2.2	10.0	7.0
Cardiovascular	28.7	29.0	22.7	14.9	9.2	7.3	14.6	11.8	13.8	29.9	4.2	2.3	6.7	4.8
Respiratory	19.5	22.3	25.7	22.3	9.8	9.0	17.7	21.8	11.9	15.0	5.7	2.6	9.6	7.0
Gastrointestinal	24.6	33.2	22.6	21.5	9.5	8.8	17.8	14.5	12.3	13.3	4.2	2.6	9.0	6.1
Musculoskeletal	27.0	32.7	26.2	18.3	9.4	8.1	14.7	16.2	8.7	12.4	4.4	3.5	9.7	8.8
Genitourinary	30.2	34.2	22.7	18.9	9.4	10.0	15.6	14.6	9.4	12.5	4.0	2.9	8.7	6.7
Obstetrics	24.9	29.1	20.4	16.5	7.0	6.8	19.3	22.1	12.9	16.1	6.0	2.9	9.6	6.5
Injuries	30.0	30.5	23.6	20.7	7.6	7.0	15.1	19.4	11.7	13.5	4.1	2.6	7.9	6.2
Skin related	26.7	28.8	22.7	20.7	7.3	7.4	24.6	18.1	7.0	13.4	3.4	3.1	8.3	8.5
Total	25.7	29.3	23.6	20.0	8.9	8.4	17.0	16.7	11.9	16.1	4.3	2.7	8.5	6.8

Source: NSSO 71st round, estimated.
Note: R – Rural; U – Urban.

met the medical expenditure from their own income or savings. While 25 per cent in rural and 18 per cent in urban India met the expenditure by borrowing, nearly 7 per cent in rural and 5 per cent in urban India managed with the contributions of friends and relatives and by selling their physical assets. The share of the poorest and poor households, which were not covered any health insurance scheme, was the highest in both rural and urban areas (Table 4.8). Also private insurance (own purchase) was found to considerably higher among the rich and richest households.

Table 4.7 Percentage distribution of households meeting hospitalisation expenditure by major source of finance in quintile classes of MPCE

Quintile class of UMPCE	Percentage of household reporting as source of finance for meeting the medical expenditure					
	Income/ savings	Borrowings	Sale of physical assets	Contribution from friends/ relatives	Others	All
Rural						
Poorest	65.6	26.8	1.1	5.3	0.5	100
Poorer	67.1	25.8	1.4	4.8	0.5	100
Middle	68.1	25.3	0.6	5.1	0.5	100
Richer	68.8	26.0	0.4	3.8	0.8	100
Richest	68.1	23.1	0.9	6.9	0.7	100
All	67.8	24.9	0.8	5.4	0.7	100
Urban						
Poorest	68.4	21.7	0.4	6.4	2.7	100
Poorer	71.8	21.9	0.4	4.5	1.1	100
Middle	74.1	20.7	0.3	3.9	0.7	100
Richer	74.9	16.1	0.3	6.9	1.6	100
Richest	80.9	13.7	0.4	3.7	1.0	100
All	74.9	18.2	0.4	5.0	1.3	100

Source: NSSO 71st round published report (2014).

In short, nearly 90 per cent of Indian poor and poorest households do not have any form of health protection. The NSSO (2014) report also showed that the government-funded schemes covered only 13 per cent of the population in rural and 12 per cent in urban India. Similarly, the reach of private insurance schemes in both rural and urban India has been extremely poor.

Table 4.8 Percentage distribution of patients by coverage of health expenditure support for each quintile class of usual monthly per capita expenditure (UMPCE)

Quintile class of UMPCE	Percentage of persons having coverage of health expenditure support					
	Not covered	Government funded insurance scheme	Employer (not government) supported health protection	Arranged by household (hh) with insurance company	Others	All
Rural						
Poorest	89.1	10.1	0.7	0.0	0.0	100
Poorer	88.8	10.7	0.4	0.1	0.0	100
Middle	87.4	11.9	0.6	0.1	0.0	100
Richer	83.3	15.9	0.5	0.1	0.1	100
Richest	81.1	17.0	0.8	0.9	0.2	100
All	85.9	13.1	0.6	0.3	0.1	100
Urban						
Poorest	91.4	7.7	0.6	0.0	0.2	100
Poorer	87.5	10.6	1.3	0.5	0.2	100
Middle	84.7	12.9	1.3	1.0	0.1	100
Richer	79.7	13.5	3.3	3.4	0.1	100
Richest	66.6	15.1	5.6	12.4	0.3	100
All	82.0	12.0	2.4	3.5	0.2	100

Source: NSSO 71st round published report (2014).

Price variations of branded drugs

Another important aspect of affordability of medicines is the existing price variations across brands. This is particularly important in the context of the poor regulation of medical practice that provides full freedom to practitioners to decide the treatment, and the non-standardisation of prescription practices of doctors. As already mentioned in the beginning of the chapter, in countries like India, where regulations on medical practices are relatively weak, the branding of generic medicines, market-based pricing policies (Narula 2015), the differences in the prescription practices of doctors (Bandameedi et al. 2016) and irrational prescriptions of medicines by doctors could significantly increase the cost of medical care. As already noted, most people including the poor in India depend on the market for buying medicines due to the non-availability of quality medicines in the public sector. Although India is one of the major manufacturers and exporters of generic medicines, these are predominantly sold under brand names in the domestic market, which, as discussed elsewhere in the chapter, lead to significant price differences for the same product. For instance, Bhargava and Kalantri (2016) found that there was a difference of INR 121 for 10 tablets of 1 milligram (mg) of risperidone, which is commonly used for the treatment of psychosis, between two brands; a difference of INR 64 between the highest and lowest priced generics of 10 units of amlodipine 5 mg tablets used for treating hypertension; a difference of INR 112 for 10 units of glimepiride 2 mg tablets used for the treatment of diabetes and a difference of INR 481 between the highest and lowest priced brands of cisplatin 50 mg injection used for the treatment of cancer. Such differences were also observed for medicines that are under price control for the treatment of diseases like malaria (Ahmad et al. 2014) and antibacterial, antifungal, antacid and antiepileptic medicines (Patel et al. 2005). For instance, Ahmad et al. (2014) found that there was a price variation of 15.5 per cent to 230 per cent between the minimum and maximum costs of branded antimalarials available in the market in rural Tamil Nadu.

We have further examined the price variations of some of the top-selling branded drugs in India and some of the cancer medicines that have recently been approved for marketing in India (until December 2017). Table 4.9 presents the price variation of 10 top-selling brands in India as per the ratings of the *Business Standard* in 2018. As is clear from the table, 5 out of the 10 top-selling brand in India were for the treatment of diabetes. There are significant differences in the prices of the same generics across different brands studied. It varied from as high as 22664 per cent for Glycomet 500 mg tablet for the treatment of diabetes to 7.5 per cent for Galvus Met 50/1000 mg used for the treatment of diabetes. Out of the 10 drugs presented in Table 4.8, 5 are under price control and, surprisingly, the prices of all top-selling brands except Monocef 250 mg injection was higher than the ceiling price fixed by NPPA, pointing to the drawbacks in the actual implementation of price regulation. Moreover, the number of brands that have adhered to the ceiling prices was very low and more than 60 per cent of the brands priced their drugs above the ceiling prices fixed by NPPA.

As already discussed in the previous chapter, the number of new drugs approved for marketing in India was highest for the treatment of cancer. Also, out-of-pocket expenditure was the highest for cancer medicine as compared to any other disease. George et al. (2018) have examined the prices of some of the major cancer drugs that were approved for marketing in India from 2001 to 2017 in order to understand the extent of price variation for the new drugs approved for marketing. They found that the percentage cost variation ranged from 3,058, the highest, for sorafenib 200 mg tablet to 82, the lowest, for bendamustine 100 mg injection. Significant price variations were found for all other generics that were developed and marketed under brand names by big pharmaceutical companies.

We extended this analysis further by including more generics and brands that are under and outside price control. Table 4.10 provides details of selected newly approved cancer drugs approved for marketing between 2001 and 2017 and which are under price control. Out of 24 formulations which are under price control, ceiling prices were available only for 14 since the remaining 10 were brought under price control very recently (in February 2019). Data show that prices of nearly 40 per cent of the branded generics out of the 241 brands of 14 formulations examined here have their prices higher than the ceiling prices fixed by NPPA in India (Table 4.10). The highest number of branded generics that were more than the ceiling price was found for L-asparaginase powder for injection (5,000 kilo unit [ku]), which is used for treating acute lymphoblastlc leukaemia, followed by of the brands of gemcitabine powder for injection (1 gram

Table 4.9   Price variations of 10 top-selling branded generics in India

Formulation/ brand	Unit	Indication	Ceiling price for mentioned unit	Number of brands above ceiling price	Highest price	Lowest	% Variation between highest and lowest	Price of market leader
Mixtard SC 50/50 40 IU injection	10 ml	Diabetes	141.3	18/22	197.78	67.68	192.2	165 (Novo Nordisk India)
Glycomet 500 mg tablet	10	Diabetes	14.1	109/165	280	1.23	22,664.2	15.8 (USV Pvt Ltd)
Spasmo Proxyvon Plus capsule	8	IBS	Not under price control	NA	50.55	NA	NA	50.55 (Wockhardt Ltd)
Lantus 100 IU injection	10 ml	Diabetes	Not under price control	NA	8231	1296	535.1	2983 (Sanofi India)
Galvus Met 50/1,000 mg	10	Diabetes	Not under price control	NA	285.1	265.2	7.5	285.1 (Novartis)
Janumet 50/1000 mg tablet	10	Diabetes	Not under price control	NA	260.6	160	62.9	232.1(MSD Pharmaceuticals)
Augmentin 1,000/200 mg injection	1 packet	bacterial infections	117.87	68/110	284.33	24	1084.7	132 (Glaxosmithkline)

(Contd.)

(*Contd.*)

Formulation/ brand	Unit	Indication	Ceiling price for mentioned unit	Number of brands above ceiling price	Highest price	Lowest	% Variation between highest and lowest	Price of market leader
Monocef 250 mg injection	1 packet	Infections	42.31	53/85	125	13.1	854.2	25.94 (Aristo)
Voveran 50 mg tablet	10	Anti-inflammatory painkiller	17.9	39/81	86.08	3.18	2606.9	22.5 (Novartis)
Pan 20 mg tblet	10	Gastrointestinal conditions	Not under price control	NA	155	22	604.5	94 (Alkem)

Source: NPPA, Government of India.

Table 4.10 Price variations of selected cancer drugs approved for marketing between 2001 and 2017, India (under price control)

Drug name	Indication	NPPA ceiling price per unit (INR)	No. of brands selling above ceiling	Highest price across brands (INR)	% difference of highest from ceiling price	Lowest price across brands (INR)	% variation between highest and lowest
Bortezomib, powder for injection 2 mg	Multiple myeloma (antineoplastics)	11544	9 (16)	13115	13.6	2625	399.6
Capecitabine 500 mg	Breast, colon and rectal cancer	118.62	15 (24)	182	53.4	70.6	157.8
Docetaxel, powder for injection 80 g	Breast cancer, non-small cell lung cancer, prostate cancer, stomach cancer, and head/neck cancer	10682	8 (17)	11566.2	8.3	1290	796.6
Doxorubicin injection 50 mg/ml	Ovarian cancer, breast cancer, Hodgkin's disease, multiple myeloma	763.31	8 (16)	1250	63.8	307.2	306.9
Gefitinib tablet 250 mg	Lung cancer	402	3 (27)	426	6.0	98	334.7

(*Contd.*)

Drug name	Indication	NPPA ceiling price per unit (INR)	No. of brands selling above ceiling	Highest price across brands (INR)	% difference of highest from ceiling price	Lowest price across brands (INR)	% variation between highest and lowest
Gemcitabine powder for injection 1 g	Metastatic bladder cancer, metastatic bladder cancer, non-small cell lung cancer, metastatic epithelial ovarian carcinoma, metastatic breast cancer	4979.45	18 (25)	6825	37.1	2375	187.4
Imatinib tablet 400 mg	Leukaemia, systemic mastocytosis, dermatofibrosarcoma protuberans, gastrointestinal stromal tumour	200	9 (16)	367.5	83.8	74	396.6
Cytarabine 1000 mg injection	Various types of leukaemia	1006	5 (7)	1925	91.4	947	103.3
Temozolomide 250 mg (capsule)	Forms of brain tumours	4399	1 (4)	4485	2.0	4050	10.7
L-asparaginase powder for injection 5000 ku	Acute lymphoblastlc leukaemia	972.6	8 (9)	1510	55.3	970	55.7

Drug name	Indication	NPPA ceiling price per unit (INR)	No. of brands selling above ceiling	Highest price across brands (INR)	% difference of highest from ceiling price	Lowest price across brands (INR)	% variation between highest and lowest
Paclitaxel injection 100 mg	Breast and ovarian cancer	209.47	9 (21)	311	48.5	32	871.9
Bicalutamide tablet 50 mg	Metastatic carcinoma of the prostate	64.3	1 (15)	442.7	588.5	27	1539.6
Letrozole 2.5 mg tablet (femara)	Breast cancer in postmenopausal women	38.27	2 (44)	136	255.4	2.5	5340.0
Exemestane 25 mg	Breast cancer	N/A*	N/A	325	N/A	32	914.1
Erlotinib 150 g	Non-small cell lung cancer, pancreatic cancer	N/A*	N/A	4030	N/A	230	1652
Lenalidomide (25 mg) capsule	Multiple myeloma, myelodysplastic syndromes, mantle cell lymphoma	N/A*	N/A	740	N/A	577	28
Decitabine (50 mg) injection	Chronic myelomonocytic leukaemia	N/A*	N/A	8000	N/A	7428	7.8
Fulvestrant (250 mg) injection	Breast cancer in postmenopausal women	N/A*	N/A	21428	N/A	8440	154

(*Contd.*)

Drug name	Indication	NPPA ceiling price per unit (INR)	No. of brands selling above ceiling	Highest price across brands (INR)	% difference of highest from ceiling price	Lowest price across brands (INR)	% variation between highest and lowest
Bendamustine (100 mg) injection	Chronic lymphocytic leukaemia, a type of non-Hodgkin's lymphoma	N/A*	N/A	11000	N/A	3095	255
Cabazitaxel (60 mg) injection	Metastatic castration-resistant prostate cancer	N/A*	N/A	99999	N/A	19947	401
Everolimus (5 mg) tablet	Breast cancer in postmenopausal women	N/A*	N/A	6015	N/A	1250	381
Pemetrexed (500 mg) injection	Lung cancer	N/A*	N/A	81026	N/A	4500	1,701
Regorafenib (40 mg) tablet	Colon and rectum cancer	N/A*	N/A	2118	N/A	1230	72
Enzalutamid E (40 mg) capsule	Castration-resistant prostate cancer	N/A*	N/A	2997	N/A	982	205

Sources: CDSCO and NPPA, compiled.
Note: *Recently included under price control and ceiling prices were not available.

[g]), a medicine used for different types of cancer treatment, cytarabine 1,000 mg injection, used for treating leukaemia, capecitabine 500 mg and bortezomib powder for injection 2 mg. The increase from the ceiling prices for these medicines ranged from 2 per cent (temozolomide 250 mg) to 589 per cent (bicalutamide tablet 50 mg). Price variations between the highest and lowest priced brands for the same formulation ranged from 8 per cent (decitabine 50 mg) to 1701 per cent (pemetrexed 500 mg injection) for the cancer medicines that are under price control presented in Table 4.6. It should also be noted that temozolomide 250 mg (capsule) and bicalutamide tablet 50 mg have only one brand and letrozole 2.5 mg tablet have only two brands above the respective ceiling prices.

Some of the expensive medicines such as trabectedin (1 mg) injection (price ranges from INR 28,600 to INR 121,485.7) used for treating leiomyosarcoma are outside price control (see Table 4.11). Further, we have found that among the anticancer medicines outside price control, nearly 44 per cent of 55 brands (of eight formulations) examined here priced their medicines above the average unit price. Price variations of medicines that are outside price control are also notably high. For instance, price variation is as high as 4,170 per cent across brands for sorafenib (200 mg) tablet. Similarly, the variation for abiraterone (250 mg) tablet, which is also outside price control, across brands is 1,760 per cent.

The escalating cost of medicine in healthcare and the price variations of branded generics evidently point to the lack of adequate regulation of the pharmaceutical market in India. It is important in this context to critically examine the value of the market-based pricing policy in reducing the prices of drugs. In market-based pricing, the average of the commonly sold drugs is taken to fix the ceiling price.[4] We have illustrated in Table 4.8 that the top-selling brands are also highly priced and the number of highly priced brands is more than that of low-priced brands. Hence, the simple average would always be high. As Selvaaj et al. (2012) already noted, since 'market leaders are often price leaders', the market-based pricing does not reduce the prices of drugs in India. Furthermore, the data on price variations of medicines clearly showed that even if there are attempts to regulate prices of drugs with the introduction of the list of essential

---

[4]   As per the NPPA formula, the ceiling price is the average of prices of all brands of a medicine with more than 1 per cent market share.

Table 4.11 Price variations of selected cancer drugs approved for marketing between 2001 and 2017, India (outside price control)

Drug name	Indication	Average per unit price (INR)	No. of brands selling above average price	Highest price across brands (INR)	Lowest price across brands (INR)	% deviation between highest and lowest
Anastrazole 1 mg	Breast cancer	51.4	4 (8)	59.6	47.7	25
Fasnorm 250 mg Injection	Breast cancer	4146	4 (8)	5115	3573	43
Aprepitant (125 mg) capsule	Supportive drugs for cancer patients to prevent nausea and vomiting	1323	3 (9)	1586	1090	46
Sorafenib (200 mg) tablet	Liver cancer, thyroid cancer, advanced renal cell carcinoma	855	1 (3)	2434	57	4170
Trabectedin (1 mg) injection	Leiomyosarcoma	75043	2 (3)	121485.7	28600	325
Fosaprepitant (150 mg) injection	Supportive drugs for cancer patients to prevent nausea and vomiting	2216	3 (7)	2571	1400	84
Abiraterone (250 mg) tablet	Metastatic high-risk castration-sensitive prostate cancer	697	6 (15)	2790	150	1760
Palonosetron (0.5 mg) tablet	Supportive drugs for cancer patients to prevent nausea and vomiting	15.7	1 (2)	21	10.4	102

Sources: CDSCO and NPPA, compiled.

medicines and price ceiling, several newly approved drugs continue to be outside price control. One could also infer that drugs that are under price control are not effectively monitored since prices of several brands were much above the ceiling prices. Hence, the question of whether open competition and market mechanisms by itself would make the prices competitive and increase affordability is an unsolved one. What is perhaps more important are measures for standardisation of medical practices, mandatory prescription of generics and cost containment in medical care in private hospitals.

Price regulation and drug development: ongoing debates

The debate on drug price regulation in India is caught up in an impasse of public health and industrial priorities. While public health experts and health activists argue for price control and regulation in the light of the failure of market-based pricing, which kept the ceiling prices higher rather than checking price variations, the industry groups argue that price regulation and control would lead to a significant decline in the revenue of the pharmaceutical firms. For them it would also come in the way of addressing public health issues since decline in profits could eventually lower the investments in drug discovery in the future (see Motkuri and Mishra 2018). What is interesting is that the industry groups also articulate the argument for the removal of price control in the language of future public health needs for which innovations that are funded from the current profits are paramount. For instance, as noted by Garthwaite (2018), some of the studies that argued for the unregulated market attempted to empirically prove the correlation between profits and increased spending on development&D (see Acemoglu and Linn 2004; Finkelstein 2004; Dubois et al. 2015).

Even if one agrees with the argument that increased profits of pharmaceutical firms would lead to more research and development (R&D) investments, there is no substantial evidence to prove that innovations that are being carried out in the industry are aimed to take care of the prevailing and emerging public health needs of the developing and underdeveloped countries. Conversely, studies have shown that innovations in R&D of pharmaceutical companies largely prioritise the needs of the population in developed countries and regions, especially with the advancements in biomedical research. For instance, Trouiller et al. (2002), by analysing the

R&D in pharmaceutical companies for more than two decades, showed that the epidemiological priorities and disease burden of the developing world was significantly undermined. Interestingly, the argument that the industry gave for this low focus on the developing world was the high cost of R&D and the higher market risk of investing in such diseases. We have also substantiated elsewhere (George et al. 2018) that drug development in India has not taken care of the disease burden of the marginalised populations, regions and the health needs of children and the elderly.

Value-based pricing and the debate on price reduction in India

We have recently seen a growing literature on value-based pricing (VBP) of originator drugs (those are under patent protection), which is often projected as an engine that could boost R&D and as an alternative to cost-based and market-based pricing for reducing the cost of care (Jayadev and Stiglitz 2008; Danzon et al. 2015; Dang et al. 2016; Basu and Sullivan 2017; McGuire et al. 2008; Kaltenboeck and Bach 2018). VBP is expected to bring a check and control over drugs based on its real value for the patients in terms of efficiency, cost and side effects. Moreover, it is generally believed that VBP can boost R&D in the sector since the price/value of a product is largely determined by its efficiency and performance. Though VBP has been successful in other sectors in the developed countries, it is in a nascent stage in pharmaceutical markets as one of the prerequisites of VBP in healthcare and pharmaceuticals is the presence of an informed and highly evolved market, where there is no significant information asymmetry. Countries like Australia, Sweden, the United States (US) and the United Kingdom (UK) have slowly started to move towards this idea. Unsurprisingly, it has not yet come up in India due to the negligible coverage of health insurance and higher out-of-pocket expenditure on healthcare in general and medicines in particular. However, discussions have already begun about the pros and cons of VBP in India as well, especially in the context of emerging insurance markets and the recently announced (in 2018) ambitious universal health coverage scheme, popularly known as Ayushman Bharat.

It is important to examine the possibilities and limitations of VBP as an alternative approach to cost- and market-based pricing models and in reducing the cost of care as it claims. The essence of VBP in pharmaceuticals is the sharing of risk between the manufacturer of the drugs and the payer, who mostly is an insurance company or the state in countries where there is universal health protection or where state negotiation on prices is in place. In such a system, both the parties agree to 'link payment of drugs to the health outcomes achieved' (see Neumann et al. 2011). Bach and Pearson (2015) defined VBP in drugs as accounting of the benefits and harms for fixing the price of a drug. Irrespective of the various nomenclatures such as risk sharing or performance-based agreements, the central idea of VBP is checking the entry of highly priced 'me too' drugs and ensuring value for the money spent for the patient without significant price escalation.

While VBP appears to be a robust policy initiative to check the prices of prescription and specialised drugs, the success of this model has hitherto been limited to a few cases even in the evolved markets. Neumann et al. (2011), for instance, based on a few case studies of risk sharing conducted in the UK, noted that although risk sharing can be advantageous for both the parties in its conceptual understanding, the success rate is very low and 'the risk of implementing the agreements were higher than expected'. The main challenges they found included 'high transaction costs; the lack of acceptable outcome metrics; difficulties in determining treatment effects; and the absence of suitable data capture systems' (Neumann et al. 2011: 2335). Stanley et al. (2012) analysed six publicly disclosed VBP agreements in the US in 2011 and 2012 and found that in some cases it resulted in improved outcomes and the payers and the patients benefited from the agreements. However, there were concerns raised from manufactures and they required to restrict these agreements to mostly the highly priced and competitive drugs for the treatment of diseases like cancer (see Dang et al. 2016). In short, the experiences from developed countries showed that VBP may not work in favour of the manufacturing firms, payers and patients always due to the heterogeneity of the demand, priorities and expectations of healthcare existing in the market (see Pauly 2017).

Is it possible to adopt VBP in India as an alternative to the existing market-based pricing system now? The answer is, undoubtedly, no. There are several issues ranging from higher out-of-pocket spending on medicines to complex paternalistic doctor–patient relations and non-availability of health personnel and infrastructure facilities in the country. The chapter has already pointed to the increased out-of-pocket spending on health in general and medicines in particular across income groups, social groups and diseases categories. It has also shed light on the lower level of health protection available to people in India and these do not need any further elaboration here.

Another important barrier is the information asymmetry among the manufacturer, practitioner and the patient in the absence of insurance firms or the state to negotiate the agreements of VBP. As already mentioned, the core of VBP is that medical and non-medical risks of drugs are shared between companies and patients or payers (insurance companies) on behalf of the patients. A report by KPMG (2016a) suggests two main conditions that are essential for the patients to benefit from VBP. The doctors should 'choose the right drug for the right patient at the right time' and the patients should be clear about the right medicines for them based on the degree, level and severity of their diseases. Interestingly, the second condition cannot work without the first, which means that the doctor continues to be the centre of care decisions. Even if the patients are aware of the complexities of their disease conditions and the drugs that are suitable to them based on their economic and other preferences, it is extremely difficult to exercise their decision in practitioner-centric care systems. While one can foresee a possibility of such practices working successfully in highly evolved care systems which have a deliberative or informative model of doctor–patient interaction and decision making, it could fail and lead to further escalation of costs in care contexts where doctor–patient interactions are paternalistic and power relations are highly uneven. As we see in countries like India, caregiver–receiver interactions in public health services in India are highly power-ridden and 'paternalistic'. It is the doctor or other medical staff who mediates and controls the doctor–patient interactions by asking questions and prompting the patient to answer and deciding what is good or not good for the patient rather than encouraging the patient to talk, providing necessary information and enabling her/him to decide what is suitable as per the informative model of patient–doctor relationship.

Although the affordability of medicine is a serious problem, the prices of drugs, especially patented drugs for the treatment of diseases like cancer, are relatively low in India as compared to developed countries (Goldstein et al. 2017). The reason for this is the availability of substitutable branded generics, which are relatively lower priced. What is the value of VBP of the branded generics? As per the norms of VBP, one of the important preconditions is that its generic should not be available in the market for a considerable period of time. In other words, the scope of VBP is limited only to originator drugs, which are left with a significant period of patent protection to realise the returns. Hence, VBP of branded generics and biosimulars may not be economically feasible for manufacturers.

The continuing appalling conditions of India's healthcare services in terms of infrastructure and human resource deficiency is another impediment to VBP. As is well known, several rural areas of India, especially its tribal pockets, have serious shortage of healthcare personnel and infrastructure. For instance, George (2016) highlighted that health infrastructure and healthcare personnel are inadequate in tribal areas of states like Chhattisgarh, Jharkhand, Odisha, Uttar Pradesh, Karnataka, Tamil Nadu and Kerala. The possibility of successful implementation of policies like VBP is very distant in such an environment. What perhaps is needed in countries like India is the implementation of price control and regulation and provision of generics so that accessibility to medicines can be improved.

Technological innovation and cost of drugs

Another important debate that surrounds drug prices and R&D is the higher cost of end products due to innovations and technological advancements. Studies have showed that although technological innovations in drugs brought out better outcomes, it led to the increase of cost significantly. Newhouse (1992) showed that a significant part of the rise in medical cost is attributable to technological innovation by drawing attention to the technological innovation happening at that period of time including 'renal dialysis, transplantation, artificial joints, endoscopy, monoclonal antibodies and drugs for mental illness' (Newhouse 1992: 11). Studies later on emphasised on the better health outcomes due to technological advancements in spite of the higher cost. Cutler and McClellan (2001), for instance, illustrated with the cases of depression, cataracts, and breast cancer treatment in the US that the net medical effect of innovation yielded better outcomes although the spending increased considerably. They attempted to value the economic cost due to technological innovation by connecting it to the increase in life expectancy and argued that an increase in medical spending by USD 35,000 between 1950 and 1990 in the US led to an increase in life expectancy by seven years (Cutler and McClellan 2001: 24).

However, the direct relationship between technological innovation and the higher cost of medicines, unlike in other sectors such as telecommunication where it is inversely proportional, has been a puzzle (Gelijns and Rosengerg 1994). The simplistic explanation is the higher cost of newly developed and patented drugs. As is well known, drug development (particularly new chemical entities [NCEs]) is an extremely costly affair and requires cutting-edge technological advancements as well. However, what we see in other sectors is that the cost of the products with high-end technology will be at the higher side only for a certain period of time mainly due to the scaling up of sales and competition from other manufacturers. Patent protection in drugs insulates the new product from imitation and competition from other manufactures. Hence, higher volumes of sales do not lead to lowering of prices of pharmaceutical products as we already discussed in this chapter (see Table 4.9).

Another reason, as already discussed in the chapter, lies in the asymmetrical power relations in medical practice due to its predominantly practitioner-centred approach and the possible physician-induced demand[5] of medical care products. Studies have already demonstrated physician-induced demand in medical care that increased the cost. For instance, Johnson (2014: 80) in a review noted that 'obstetricians do more C-sections in response to declining fertility, cardiac surgeons treat more intensively when their incomes are impacted by fee reductions, and physicians in China prescribe more medication to "un- informed" patients'. This demand is not always induced by the practitioners alone; however, as is well known, it is mediated through a network of manufacturers, promoters, investors, hospitals and insurance companies (Gelijns and Rosengerg 1994).

Innovations are integral to drug discovery. The question, however, is how manufacturers could sustain innovations without increasing the prices of drugs. Jayadev and Stiglitz (2001) suggested that VBP and the public funding of clinical trials could lower both the prices and the cost of pharmaceuticals. We have already discussed the apprehensions with regard to VBP drawing from the experiments in countries like the UK, US and Australia. Public funding of innovation appears to be a robust

---

5 McGuire (2000) defines physician-induced demand as the demand that 'exists when the physician influences a patient's demand for care against the physician's interpretation of the best interests of the patient'.

option. However, one cannot ignore the fact that public funding for research in general and medical innovations in particular has shrunken in several countries, including the developed ones. For instance, studies have showed that funding for innovations in the pharmaceutical and biopharmaceutical sectors is coming predominantly from the private sector, including venture capital (Rottingen et al. 2013). George et al. (2018) noted that the R&D investments in the Indian biopharmaceutical sector also came predominantly from the private sector and public investment in the biopharmaceutical sector was negligible. Venture capital investments are also gradually increasing in global health R&D (West et al. 2017), including India (see KPMG 2016b).

Innovative drugs are also outside the purview of price regulation in many countries largely to help the drug companies realise the cost of innovation. For instance, a recent decision taken by the Government of India (in January 2019) exempts innovative drugs from ceiling prices.[6] It would certainly incentivise the manufacturers for innovation; however, it can also significantly affect accessibility to better healthcare for diseases like cancer and genetic disorders.

The social divide

It is generally considered that innovations in preventive and therapeutic medicines as well as medical diagnostics will transform the healthcare landscape in a major way. Innovations in healthcare are often aimed at developing new products and technologies, improving precisions of the existing drugs and diagnostics, improving quality, reducing side effects, predicting risks and reducing risk. Innovations, however, have also never been value neutral or always fully in tandem with the epidemiological priorities when it comes to its translation to end products. It raised several concerns with regard to affordability, usefulness and the overemphasis on biological determinism and the biomedical model of health. We discuss some of the questions pertaining to the changes that are happening to the

---

[6] As per the Drugs (Prices Control) Amendment Order, 2019, by the Ministry of Chemicals and Fertilisers, a manufacturer producing a new drug patented under the Indian Patent Act, 1970 (39 of 1970), is exempted from price control for a period of five years from the date of commencement of its commercial marketing by the manufacturer in the country.

understanding of health due to the new epistemic paradigms of health research and the possible inequalities that innovations can bring about in society.

Medicalisation, pharmaceuticalisation and social inequality

Biomedical research could bring about advancements in deciphering the risks of a normal healthy body to diseases. Research in the fields of cancer and cardiovascular drugs attest to it. However, it is also true that the pharmaceutical and biopharmaceutical companies have emerged as influential actors in the healthcare sector all over the world. The rise of market economy and the declining role of the state in the neoliberal world have commoditised 'health' (Levinas and Lewontin 1985) and due to this rising power and influence, the companies have been successful in *medicalising* every natural transition in the human body (Rose 2007; Clarke et al. 2009). Studies have already showed that the increasing risk focus of pharmaceutical research can lead to medicalisation of the body by qualifying normal bodily changes such as ageing, menopause, loss of sexual vigour, mood fluctuations, and so on, as 'treatable' pathological conditions and developing medicines for their treatment, as scholars have already argued. For instance, Strasser (2014) highlighted the case of hormone replacement therapy for women of menopausal age to keep their skin flexible and shiny, the case of Viagra, and other individual performance improvement drugs such as adderall for students and professionals.

We have a growing literature on medicalisation, biomedicalisation, geneticisation and pharmaceuticalisation that expands the understanding of the linkage of science and modern capitalism, as well as the subtle and coercive control and the monitoring of bodies and minds by creating and normalising newer notions of health, normalcy and deviance. These concepts are well discussed in the literature of medical sociology and anthropology (see Conrad 2005; Shostak et al. 2008; Clarke et al. 2009; Abraham 2010). These concepts have also significantly helped us to understand how innovations in healthcare products turn people into medical customers. For instance, Bell and Figert (2012) in their review article on pharmaceuticalisation discussed the scholarly works that unravelled the processes through which new medical customers are constructed. For instance, Abraham (2010), as quoted in Bell and Figert

(2012), listed the factors such as 'medicalisation, industry drug promotion and marketing, policy of the state, biomedicalism and consumerism' (Bell and Figert 2012: 779) that work through various formal and informal channels to pharmaceuticalise the population.

What is also important is the possible inequalities and the social divide that innovations in healthcare in general and processes like medicalisation and pharmaceuticalisation in particular bring about. We have already discussed the inequality associated with physical and financial access to the end products of innovations, especially drugs, in the previous chapter. Similarly, the lack of focus on the disease burden of the poor in general and the vulnerable in particular, including the elderly, children, women and ethnic groups, in drug development was also discussed in Chapter 3. Recent studies have also discussed the inequality pertaining to technological innovations in health in terms of information, accessibility and utilisation across social, cultural, regional, population and income groups. Weiss et al. (2018) in their review article discussed the major research studies that dealt with the questions of inequality associated with the use of information and communication technology, therapies, diagnostic equipment and vaccines in different parts of the world. For instance, an article by Baum et al. (2014), which was discussed in Weiss et al. (2018), found that the use of digital technologies for the delivery of common public goods such as employment, education, housing, drinking water and sanitation, which are also the social determinants of health, affected the health outcomes of lower economic and marginalised ethnic groups in Australia. Similarly, studies conducted in the US (Perez et al. 2016) and countries in Europe (Lang and Mertes 2011) found the unequal distribution of the benefits of information-technology-based medical innovations. Slade and Anderson (2001), based on a study on the relationship between per capita income and use/diffusion of technologies conducted in the Organisation for Economic Co-operation and Development (OECD) countries, found that developed countries use/adapt early to new technologies and 'the effects of reimbursement incentives are greater for purchases of diagnostic technologies than for lifesaving technologies'.

Concepts like pharmaceuticalisation help us understand another dimension of inequality associated with medical innovation that largely relates to the uneven distribution of the burden of medicalisation and pharmaceuticalisation. For instance, studies have already discussed how women's bodies are more medicalised than men's bodies by carefully and effectively converting conditions like fertility, infertility, contraception, pregnancy, abortion, delivery, menstruation, breast feeding, child rearing and menopause into medical encounters (see Purdy 2006; Komesaroff 2008; Forsythe 2009; Berer 2010; Gonçalves et al. 2011; Torres 2014). Similarly, the gendered constructions of *feminity* as well as *beauty*, which are essentialised through attributes like appearance, skin colour, attitude and confidence, are also subjected to medicalisation (Rayner et al. 2010). For instance, we have already discussed the focus on women's beauty products in drug development, especially in the areas of managing skin colour, skin wrinkles, hormone therapy, hair growth, and so on. Similarly, with the coming of health and wellness centres, gymnasiums, beauty parlours and career/personality development centres, attributes like confidence, emotions and mannerisms are increasingly considered as psychological conditions that can be managed with drugs. This is an area that needs further research.

Another issue of inequality relates to the sharing of the benefits and burdens of medicalisation/pharmaceuticalisation as part of participating in clinical trial experiments. Clinical trials have been a controversial issue in India due to the casualties associated with it and the lack of agency of the participants of the trial who are normally from poor social and economic background. Studies and reports on clinical trials have already highlighted the issues of poor regulation as well as lack of agency, poor awareness and helplessness of the participants of clinical research in India.[7] For instance, Shah et al. (2010), based on a meta-analysis of a few selected qualitative studies, highlighted that although personal health benefits motivate patients in India to participate in clinical trials, other concerns such as money, other incentives and altruism are also important reasons. Deaths due to clinical trials are common in India. There are no official data available on the deaths due to clinical trials in India; however, civil society groups collect information on deaths through the Right to Information Act (RTI) from the Ministry of Health and Family Welfare. For instance, as per the report released by *Down to Earth* based on the

---

[7] Several national and international newspapers flagged these issues. One of the important reports was by the BBC available at https://www.bbc.com/news/magazine-20136654, accessed on 19 March 2019.

data obtained from the Drugs Controller General of India through RTI, 2,031 people died due to clinical trials in India between 2008 and 2011.[8] Swasthya Adhikar Manch, a civil rights organisation, reported that there were 2,868 deaths between 2005 and 2012 due to clinical trials.[9] Another report published by *The Sunday Guardian* based on the data obtained by Swasthya Adhikar Manch showed that there were 24,117 cases of deaths and 'serious adverse events' due to clinical trials in India between 2005 and 2016.[10] The report also noted that most of the families of the dead persons did not receive any compensation. Another online news platform reported that 1,100 participants died during clinical trials in India between 2015 and 2018.[11]

Clinical trials, evidently, brings several adverse health side effects for the participants along with potential benefits. It is difficult to assess the net value of clinical trials since benefits are commonly shared while sufferings are individual. However, in most of the cases developing countries are at the receiving end of clinical trial since most of the experiments are part of the outsourced, contract research or collaborative research of multinational companies operating from the developed countries, which are predominantly focused on the health of their own population. This, as Bell and Figert (2012) noted, will lead to 'unequal distribution of burden' and benefits of clinical trials where the population in the developed country benefits at the cost of the burden of medical trial of the participants in the developing countries. The data presented on ongoing clinical trials in Chapter 1 (see Figure 1.11 and Table 1A.2) show that clinical trials in India are dominated by the global firms and their disease focus was predominantly on cancer, followed by cardiovascular diseases and hypertension, type 2 diabetes and cosmetic products.

It is also important to emphasise the benefits of clinical trials that could possibly bring out better medicines/technologies for several health problems. The question of who benefits from clinical trials, hence, is also equally important along with the question of who are at the receiving end of clinical trials. The US Food and Drug Administration (FDA) in

---

[8] For details, see Paliwal (2015).

[9] For details, see Bagcchi (2015).

[10] For details, see Ravi (2017).

[11] For details, see Watts (2019).

their report on global participation in clinical trials showed that there are regional, gender and racial differences in the participation of *useful* clinical trials (FDA 2017). Their report showed that 31 per cent of the participants in the clinical trials in 2015 and 2016 were US citizens. Within the US, men participated more than women and whites participated significantly higher (79 per cent) than non-whites. In other parts of the world, participation of men was considerably more than women. Similarly, studies have also showed that participation of the elderly in clinical trials was less in countries like India where clinical trials have been on the rise (see Shenoy and Harugeri 2015). This uneven representation in clinical trials is also indicative of the regional, population and racial disease focus of the pharmaceutical industry. It is already well established that the disease burden of the developing and underdeveloped world, marginalised groups, the elderly and children are less prioritised in drug development (Chaudhuri 2010; Viergever 2013; George et al. 2018).

Conclusion

Striking the right balance between drug development, price control and affordability is a huge public policy challenge in India. It is true that R&D projects of pharmaceutical firms are based on their returns since drug development is an extremely costly project with very low rate of success. However, as already discussed in the chapter, the therapeutic focus of drug development revolves around high-profit products and target groups. Hence, it is difficult to justify the argument of current financial burden of drugs for the future mitigation of disease burden. Moreover, the cost of R&D is often linked to the price of the newly launched product. There are several policy measures initiated by the state in India at various points in time to address the question of medicine affordability, as already discussed in the chapter. However, our analysis shows that such policies have not led to better access. There were also several policy measures by the government to facilitate the industry in terms of uniform value-added tax (VAT) of 4 per cent on medicines, reduction in excise duty, committed biotechnology development parks, financial assistance for start-ups, removal of cap in foreign direct investments, arranging investments, and linking industry and research institutions, to list a few, to promote R&D. It is premature to assess the results of these initiatives.

It is also a challenge to balance the industrial and public health priorities in India. As already discussed elsewhere, the health and drug policies in India continue to be mutually exclusive frameworks pertaining to objectives and functions although there are several overlapping concerns when it comes to the affordability of drugs (George et al. 2018). Drugs and pharmaceuticals in India is under the Ministry of Chemicals and Fertilisers, while in several other countries, drug development is a wing of the health ministry. Therefore, the industrial growth and promotional activities related to foreign direct investments, export promotion and tax incentives of the pharmaceutical and biopharmaceutical sectors are guided by the industrial and export–import policies of India in which the thrust is more on investment promotion as well as industrial and economic growth (George et al. 2018). The prices and affordability of drugs are not a direct concern of the industrial policy. The proliferation of supply-driven health products on the one hand results in varying kinds of social divisions on the other. First of all, it undermines the disease burden of the poor regions and populations. Second, the burden of medicalisation is more on women than men. Third, the benefits of innovation are shared by the economically better-off population while the burden of innovation, by being part of the clinical trials, is often borne by the poor. It is important in this context that that the drug industry has formal obligations to public health concerns. Drug and vaccine development, as well as their pricing, also need to be informed from the present and future public health challenges of the heterogeneous population of the country.

5

The Puzzle of Responsive and Responsible Medical Innovation

Striking the right balance between healthcare priorities and pharmaceutical policies is a critical public health challenge for India given their mutually conflicting nature and interests. On the one hand, the country has an expanding pharmaceutical and biopharmaceutical sector with a strong presence of domestic and multinational private companies. The sector, with significant state facilitation, could effectively position itself as the future engine of economic growth by reorienting itself to the new intellectual property and trade regimes. The dominant discourse now is that 'all publicly funded research should be translated into private entrepreneurial activities because technological innovations contribute to nation's economic growth' (Lehoux et al. 2016b: 115). The most important outcome of this discourse is the domination of the financial logic in all matters pertaining to state facilitation, research and development (R&D), dissemination, trade and market expansion of the industry over population health. On the other hand, India has a huge burden of diseases stemming from a gamut of public health problems, including the uneven distribution of demographic and epidemiological transition, increasing privatisation of healthcare, insufficiently regulated pharmaceutical market, low affordability of life-saving medicines and, most importantly, the escalating out-of-pocket healthcare expenditure coupled with poor financial risk protection. Public health relevance of R&D in healthcare is to be assessed in the context of these conflicting concerns of health and industrial policies in India.

Challenges of responsive medical innovation

What should be the focus and priorities of medical innovations in countries like India? The simple answer should be the diverse epidemiological needs of the country across regions, income groups, age groups and gender. Unsurprisingly, what is strongly emerging from the data of growth, expansion and the disease focus of R&D across the globe in general and India in particular is the mismatch between the priorities of industry and public health. We identified five overriding patterns in the product innovations in the drug, vaccine and medical technology sectors that illustrate these mismatches in India. First is the near-complete dominance of 'me too drugs' (including branded generics and biosimilars) in the R&D in drug development in the pharmaceutical and biopharmaceutical sectors. While development of new chemical entities (NCEs) is a costly business with huge risks of failure, the lower focus on NCEs in R&D would weaken both the industry and the public health preparedness for the emerging disease burden. Second is the poor focus on the infectious diseases and the disease burden of the poor population in general and children and the elderly in particular. We have already discussed the double burden of the communicable and non-communicable diseases (NCDs) and its disproportionate regional and demographic distribution in India. It should be mentioned that there has been an increase in public funding for neglected diseases like tuberculosis, malaria and diarrhoeal diseases in India. For instance, as per the G-Finder report on R&D in neglected diseases,[1] public funding for neglected diseases in India increased by 37 per cent between 2016 and 2017. However, as discussed in Chapter 1, public investments constitute only a very negligible part of the total health R&D in India. Third is the increased focus on NCDs on the one hand and the dominance of certain diseases within NCDs on the other. It is true that NCDs have emerged as a significant cause of mortality and morbidity in many parts of the world, including India. Cardiovascular diseases and diseases of the central nervous system are the major causes of mortality within NCDs. However, oncology medicines and diagnostic technologies received the highest focus within NCD R&D. In other words, there is an increased focus on drugs and diagnostic technologies that have better market returns

---

[1] For details, see https://www.who.int/research-observatory/monitoring/inputs/
   neglected_diseases/en/, accessed on 11 September 2019.

within NCDs. Fourth is the shift of innovations in medical technology towards information-technology-enabled diagnostic services and lack of focus on appropriate and affordable medical device development that is sensitive to the local infrastructure challenges in the country. For instance, as discussed in Chapter 2, several effective technology-based medical equipment for the early detection and management of infectious diseases, NCDs and other health emergencies may not be locally appropriate due to the lack of infrastructure, trained personnel and technical know-how and the high cost of equipment, diagnostic tests, consumables and fixation devices. Fifth is the emerging focus on customised individual medicine/ therapies with the advancements in life sciences, genomics and synthetic biology, which propagates the individualised technological responses to population health. In short, the epistemic base of the present health R&D is predominantly a technological and biomedical response to individual health, and the concerns of market success and viability drive the product focus of R&D in healthcare rather than the public health concerns and concerns for the cost-effectiveness of the innovations for patients.

Actors, priorities and equity issues

There is a growing scholarship that attempts to understand how industrial interests dominate the landscape of medical innovations. Questions are asked on how R&D in healthcare is organised. And who sets the agenda for health R&D? There have seen serious discussion going on about the politics of knowledge production in health R&D and its normalisation across the globe. Strasser (2014) elaborated the processes and institutions through which biomedical knowledge is produced, circulated and consumed, especially in countries like the United States (US) where biomedicine has come up in a big way as both a paradigm of economic growth and *techno-scientific* health management. Strasser (2014) noted that several institutions have directly and indirectly participated in the production, dissemination and legitimisation of the knowledge base of biomedicine and its actual practice. For instance, he noted that the policies pertaining to regulations of pharmaceutical as well as biological research on mandatory laboratory testing in the US and several countries of Europe favoured the big manufacturers since only they have the resources to conduct large-scale laboratory experiments. Simultaneously, policy relaxations were also made to undertake drug safety experiments in the post-marketing phase, which helped the manufacturers to undertake safety trials at the cost of the consumers (Strasser 2014: 26). Similarly, policy measures such as patent protection further helped the industry to expand and consolidate. The active participation of the universities, philanthropies and the biomedical complex in the US in the beginning of the biomedical era significantly catalysed the research. The industry, as Strasser (2014) elaborated, also aligned with specialised hospitals for clinical trials. The present model of biomedical and pharmaceutical innovations, thus, consists of a strong network and collaboration of universities, private funders, philanthropists, research institutes, large manufacturers who have access to the diverse genetic pool across the world for trials, specialised hospitals and a network of practitioners.

Who are the funders of health R&D and what do they fund for? As already discussed in the Introduction and Chapter 1, there is a decline of public investments in health R&D and an increase in the share of the private sector, including venture capital (VC), in many countries. It is estimated that as much as 60 per cent of the funding for health R&D across the globe is from the for-profit private sector (Rottingen et al. 2013). West et al. (2017) showed that a major share of the funding for R&D is coming from the firms from the Western developed countries. As per their estimation, out of the USD 156.7 billion R&D spending in various countries, nearly 60 per cent (USD 93.6 billion) came from the Western world (West et al. 2017: 4). The share of Indian pharmaceuticals in this was nearly 1.2 per cent (see Chapter 1). What is important to note is that although Western pharmaceuticals invested in drug development in developing countries like India through contract research and outsourcing, the focus on the disease burden of the developing world was minimal. For instance, as per the data provided by West et al. (2017), out of the USD 93.6 billion spent by the Western firms in 2016, only 10 per cent of the R&D spending was for drugs and vaccines devoted to the developing world. In other words, R&D in neglected diseases receives very limited funding of the public sector and philanthropies as compared to NCDs. There are mismatches in the prioritisation of R&D of neglected diseases as well since a major part of the funding within neglected diseases is dedicated to vaccine development of HIV/AIDS (human immunodeficiency virus/ acquired immunodeficiency syndrome). The disease burden of tuberculosis and malaria is high in several parts of India. Also, the country has an emerging burden of diseases like dengue, diphtheria, drug-resistant tuberculosis and Japanese encephalitis, to name a few. It should be noted that India does not have an accurate point-of-care test for tuberculosis diagnosis, vaccines for malaria and dengue, and adequate preparedness to identify and control the outbreak of infectious diseases.

The emergence of entrepreneurial biomedicine with enormous state patronage and facilitation is another important development in the health R&D landscape. Governments play a major role in the facilitation of start-up entrepreneurial projects, which are often spill-offs from universities and research institutions and other individual initiatives. Early funding of these start-ups are largely from private VC funds. How do private VC investments influence the disease/product focus of medical innovations? How do investors take the decisions to invest? In other words, how do new investors, especially VC funds, reconfigure the landscape of innovations? Recent research on VC investments in medical innovations showed that technology-based ventures which have strong intellectual property protection strategies and the potential to be transformed as per the market as well as on which venture capitalists can have authority had a better chance to attract investment (Lehoux et al. 2016a). These considerations, evidently, are not of the healthcare sector, but of the speculative financial market. The research focus of those firms, hence, can be guided by the investment logics of the ventures and does not necessarily need to be in line with the public health concerns. Lehoux et al. (2016a), drawing from their study on VC investments in medical innovations in Canada, explained the logic of VC investments in medical innovation as follows:

> ... capital investors do more than just provide resources to technology-based ventures. By choosing which are valuable from a speculative standpoint and by actively intervening on the technology design process, they ultimately contribute to the shaping of new medical technology and, by extension, of healthcare systems. When capital investors' decisions and practices are analysed in light of their interactions with technology developers and the policy environment, the logic at play raises fundamental questions because it largely determines which health technologies make their way into healthcare

systems and which may never come into existence. If innovation policy-makers around the world increasingly endorse this logic, important societal considerations will be left unaddressed. (Lehoux et al. 2016a: 383)

Lehoux et al. (2016b) further examined the nature of medical innovations that received VC funding in Canada. Examining several VC investments in healthcare R&D they demonstrated that innovations that could realise better market outcomes had better chances of receiving investments. For instance, after closely examining the VC funding for three innovations,[2] they found that the level of congruence 'between the mandate of venture capital and health technology-based ventures' was the lowest for the one which had the potential to reduce unnecessary hospital visits of the patients and thereby reduce their health expenditure (Lehoux et al. 2016b: 114). Another important observation that Lehoux et al. (2016b) make is that VC normally funds medical innovations that have completed the initial processes of product development, including regulatory compliance, and have reached a stage of expansion and, according to them, the 'overarching goal of venture capital is not so much to foster the creation of innovation, but to extract economic value from innovative firms and technologies' (Lehoux et al. 2016b: 115). They also found that VC funding can decide and govern the focus and direction of R&D as per their assessment of market risks and return. Their research showed that VC firms do this by holding significant positions in the board of directors of the venture, intervening in staff recruitment and achieving efficiency and negotiating contracts with other firms (Lehoux et al. 2016b: 113). In short, VC investments not only influence the nature of innovations but also design its priorities and target population in a major way.

Data on VC across the globe are indicative of this mismatch between capitalistic interests and societal considerations. For instance, out of USD 3.2 billion of VC investments for global R&D by 2016, only 1.25 per cent (USD 40 million) was dedicated for the neglected diseases (West

---

[2]   They studied the development of (*a*) a heart ablation catheter that can identify cardiac cells causing arrhythmia and neutralise them, (*b*) a labour decision support software that can improve obstetricians' decisions during labour and delivery and (*c*) a home monitoring system that can help clinicians support chronically ill patients from a distance to avoid unnecessary hospital visits. For details, see Lehoux et al. (2016b: 114).

et al. 2017). Some studies have examined the disease focus of the R&D projects that received venture financing in different parts of the developed world. Thomas and Wessel (2015) highlighted that there is an increase in the funding of biologics by VC in the US. They also found that although NCDs dominated in the priorities of VC R&D funding, funding for diseases within NCDs including diabetes, psychiatry, gastrointestinal, respiratory and cardiovascular that accounted for the major part of the disease burden in the US has declined whereas it has increased for rare diseases.[3] Our discussion on VC investments in the healthcare sector in India also highlighted this trend of added focus on NCDs (see Chapter 1). We found that the major shares of VC investments were received by the start-ups that develop medical devices and diagnostic technologies of NCDs and online service aggregating platforms.

Policy mismatches

The mismatch between the drug and healthcare policies stems from the mutually conflicting interests of industrial growth and public health management that we have already discussed (George et al. 2018). The Science, Technology and Innovation (STI) Policy, 2013,[4] of India also reiterates the pronounced focus of economic growth in innovations. Health and drug discovery are prioritised as a critical area along with agriculture, telecommunication, energy, water, environment and climate variability. The STI Policy of India states that 'science, technology and innovation for the people is the new paradigm of the Indian STI enterprise' (p. 3). It further states that the 'national STI system must recognise Indian society as its major stakeholder'. The policy document also talks about concepts like 'affordability' and 'inclusiveness'. The overriding focus of STI, however, is

---

[3] These include 'Epidermolysis Bullosa (EB), Hereditary Inclusion Body Myopathy (HIBM), Friedreich's Ataxia, Primary Hyperoxaluria (PH), Familial Amyloid Polyneuropathy, Spinal Muscular Atrophy, Transthyretin amyloidosis, Hypohidrotic Ectodermal Dysplasia, Pompe disease, Fabry's disease, von Gierke's disease, Leber's Congenital Amaurosis, Muscular Dystrophy (MD), Narcolepsy, Hunter Syndrome, Hurler Syndrome, and Lymphangioleiomyomatosis (LAM)'. For details, see Thomas and Wessel (2015: 36).

[4] For more details, see Science, Technology and Innovation Policy, 2013, available at http://dst.gov.in/sites/default/files/STI%20Policy%202013-English.pdf, accessed on 12 September 2019.

economic growth. The following excerpt from the section on the need for science, technology and innovation policy clearly states this focus:

> Scientific research utilises money to generate knowledge and, by providing solutions, innovation converts knowledge into wealth and/or value. Innovation thus implies S&T based solutions that are successfully deployed in the economy or society.[5]

Further, the policy is eloquent about issues like wealth generation through STI, technology-led growth path, advantage of demographic dividend, the huge talent pool of India, value creation, creating wealth from R&D, competitiveness, enhancing private sector participation, conversion of R&D output to commercial projects and performance-linked rewards and investments.

Studies have also noted that although it is well stated in the policy, the new STI paradigm is not responsive to the societal needs and challenges of innovation (Dhar and Saha 2014). As mentioned in the beginning, the agenda of economic growth has been an overriding concept in the health and innovation policies of India. This is not surprising since the industry groups played a significant role in the STI Policy, 2013. Abrol (2013) illustrated the official recognition by the government of the role of industry groups in the STI Policy as follows:

> Dr. T. Ramasami, Secretary, department of science and technology (DST), Government of India … brought out the real force active behind the scenes in the case of the formulation of the contents of policy mechanisms incorporated in STIP, 2013. The Secretary, DST suggested that the new STIP, 2013 has been formulated through a pro cess of consultations held with more than 4,800 persons mobilised by the national and state-level Chambers of Commerce active in different parts of the country. It is obviously disappointing to learn that the new policy has been formulated in consultation with persons mobilised by those organisations whose paramount interest is the promotion of their business interest. (Abrol 2013: 66).

---

[5]   See Science, Technology and Innovation Policy, 2013, p. 2, available at http://dst.gov.in/sites/default/files/STI%20Policy%202013-English.pdf, accessed on 12 September 2019.

While the STI Policy, apparently, tends to be vocal on the societal benefits of innovations, its epistemic base is firm on innovation-led industrial and economic growth. The questions of societal benefits, responsiveness and responsible innovation would become more relevant when we consider innovations in drug and healthcare since the entire justification of product development in the health sector is made around population health, which is a common public good. As already discussed, it is mostly the market that creates the demand of drugs and health technologies in the present organisation of production. The STI Policy unfortunately does not provide any roadmap to convert drug and health research to societal benefits other than emphasising on improving competitiveness, competence, value realisation and efficiency. It is also questionable how the objective of 'affordability' would be realised in a policy framework that is built on the market logic of competitiveness, efficiency and value generation. In short, the existing policy frameworks in India pertaining to drugs and innovations continue to conflict with the public health priorities. The separation of drug and medical innovations from the frameworks of industrial and economic growth is the significant policy step that India needs to take to achieve the objective of responsiveness, affordability and inclusiveness.

Responsive and responsible innovation: the way ahead

The equity issue of innovations in health has been debated by science and technology scholars, and there is a growing body of knowledge on responsible research and innovation. 'Responsible innovations in health' is a new framework in this domain that has been developed by a group of medical sociologists (see Silva et al. 2018). They suggest five value domains, including population health, health system, economic, organisational and environmental, for responsible innovations in health. The questions of innovation and health relevance, mitigation of ethical, legal and social issues and promotion of health equity are the dimensions in the domain of population health. Inclusiveness of the development processes of innovation in the health system, dynamic solutions to the challenges of the health system and compatibility of the level of care of the innovation with the health system are the dimensions in the domain of the health system. Frugality in terms of bringing value to people using fewer resources is the main part in the economic domain of this framework. The value to users, purchasers and the larger society due to innovation by the organisation is the main theme in the organisational domain. Finally, the environmental domain of the responsible innovation framework asks questions related to the ecological responsibility of the innovation in terms of limiting its negative environmental impacts. The essence of such a framework is societal benefits of research with the collaboration of all stakeholders including the manufactures, buyers and the state machineries.

The pertinent question is whether it is possible in the present organisation of R&D in India, which is dominated by private funding in all stages of product development. It is already well discussed that the R&D focus of Indian firms is either generic drugs or that of the global pharmaceutical giants due to the international division of innovations where India is still at the bottom of the hierarchy. As scholars have already argued (Abrol 2006, Abrol et al. 2011), India does not have an independent R&D agenda and a major part of the R&D initiatives are collaborative projects with foreign firms through various institutional arrangements. While R&D in developing generic brands and biosimilars helped to improve access to medicine in India, the low focus on NCEs and the development of new vaccines and affordable diagnostic technology continues to be a serious public health concern as we have already discussed. As is well known, the development of new drugs, vaccines and diagnostic technologies is a highly expensive and time-consuming endeavour with huge risks of failure. Publicly funded R&D, hence, in the present organisation of medical innovation may not be feasible. What, perhaps, is feasible is the extension/restriction of state facilitation where innovations are in tandem with the public health priorities. Similarly, funding support in key stages of the development of *significant* products where chances of failure could be less. For instance, Jayadev and Stiglitz (2008) noted that public funding in clinical trials can lower the costs and prices of pharmaceuticals.

Regulation with facilitation

The role of the private sector (including Indian private companies, multinational corporations and start-ups) is indeed paramount in medical innovations. Rather, they play the dominant role in the R&D landscape of India. The state has been a major facilitator in the growth of the industry in several ways. For instance, in order to promote both the pharmaceutical and the biopharmaceutical industries, the government has taken steps related to regulation of standards, funds availability, fiscal incentives, human resource development and training as it sees potential growth in this sector.[6] How is it possible to adopt a framework of responsible innovation where the medical innovation landscape is dominated by private capital?

As already discussed, the state has shifted its role from control and regulation to facilitation in the neoliberal regime as a strategy to attract investment and boost economic growth. While the repercussions of this strategy are confined mostly to labour (in terms of informality and flexible labour relations) in other industrial sectors, the lack of regulation can alter the medical innovation agenda in India and subvert the public health priorities of the country in future. The most important step towards responsible innovation is the setting of a research agenda in which the state and other stakeholders of population health could play an important role. The medical innovation agenda should be informed of the present and future disease burden and its diverse distribution in the country. The state, along with facilitation and research promotion, should play an active consultative role in setting and prioritising the health R&D agenda.

The facilitation regime of the state has flexibilised several regulations with regard to procurement, registration, foreign direct investment, taxation and pricing for the promotion of innovation. The cost-based pricing of drugs and vaccines had been instrumental in containing the cost of medicine. However, the shift from cost-based to market-based pricing is one of the reasons that increased the prices of medicine (Selvaraj et al. 2012; George and Balachandran 2019). Although the National Pharmaceutical Pricing Authority (NPPA) fixes ceiling prices, our analysis showed that there are noticeable price variations among top-selling brands for several life-saving drugs. Importantly, most of the highly expensive new cancer drugs that came to the market recently are not under price control. The huge price variations across brands can have both positive and negative implications for affordability for patients, depending upon the doctor–patient interactions and prescription practices. However, medical practice

---

[6] For details on the promotion policies, see 'Pharma Industry Promotion', Department of Pharmaceuticals, Government of India, available at http://pharmaceuticals.gov.in/pharma-industry-promotion, accessed on 15 July 2018.

is also an area that is not sufficiently regulated in India. It is important to note that for most of the diseases, India does not have standard treatment protocols. For diseases like cancer, which has a treatment protocol, there are no mechanisms to update or monitor the same. Similarly, while the Indian state has resorted to an ambitious insurance-based model, the country still has not come up with any measure to contain the cost of medical care in private hospitals. Another important area related to regulation is medicalisation and pharmaceuticalisation. As already discussed in Chapter 2, there are several informal but highly influential and powerful channels that inform, normalise and legitimise the health products that come to the market through direct advertising. We have already showed that a major part of the seed and VC funding in healthcare went to start-ups that aggregate services through online pharmacies, online health and welfare centres, online health information portals, telemedicine and home-based care services, which are outside of stringent regulation or can easily evade state regulations and monitoring by being in the virtual space. Similarly, promotional activities of the firms through informal groups and direct advertisement to patients/customers are also not regulated in India. Studies conducted in other countries have already shown that directly advertising to people through such channels led to medicalisation and pharmaceuticalisation. These also help to normalise and legitimise the choice of certain products and technology that otherwise is carried out under the monitoring of an authorised medical practitioner.

Regulation is often considered as a *bad* word in the neoliberal industrial policy discourses. However, it is already proven that state regulations could work favourably for industries that are into innovations, especially for firm stability. For instance, Edquist and Johnson (1997) noted that regulations 'will provide incentives for innovations, supply information, reduce uncertainty, foster cooperation and make available mechanisms to handle conflicts'(Edquits and Johnson, 1997, as quoted in Lehoux et al. 2016b: 114). This is significant, especially for pharmaceutical and biopharmaceutical innovations, which are produced, circulated and commercialised through a complex chain of funders that include private capital, state, VC, angel funding and collaborators that include international firms, universities, research institutes, hospitals, practitioners and civil society organisations. Most importantly, regulations can encourage original innovations by controlling the highly priced 'me too' innovations that are now rampant in markets like India. If India moves to regimes like 'value-based pricing', which is now picking up in developed countries as a solution to balance the prices, values and quality, regulations will help the industry to realise its desired output by checking the 'me too' technologies. Also, value-based pricing cannot realise better outcomes without state regulation as cases that discussed in Chapter 4 have already illustrated.

Another area where the state could intervene is the promotion of fundamental research in universities and other public-funded research laboratories. At present the Department of Science and Technology (DST) is operating in an entrepreneurial mode since its approaches and programmes are heavily influenced by the agenda of economic growth. The overemphasis on academia–industry collaborations in the programmes of the DST proves it. While it is important to convert knowledge into viable solutions, it is also equally important to produce knowledge that is useful to take care of the health needs of the country. Public funding for fundamental research, hence, should be a major agenda in the innovation policy in India.

Balancing the power in global R&D

The politics of knowledge production and the role of funding institutions in setting the research agenda are well discussed in the social science literature of science and technology. Researches in universities and research institutions are usually funder-driven, and hence the first layer of power division in research is between the funders and the researchers. In most of the cases, researchers have to design their proposals in line with the themes that have already been decided by the funders. Sometimes, even the methodology is pre-decided. Hence, the scope of further negotiations with the funding agencies is often limited for researchers in such situations. Besides, funding calls are usually competitive bidding that further adds to the existing power of the funders to award the projects that are best suited to their themes. The winning of competitive research bidding is often portrayed as a marker of 'success' of the researchers notwithstanding their real passion and preferences. Moreover, the number of research projects and the amount of grant generated by the researchers are also part of their individual assessment for career mobility in universities and research institutes. The areas of focus of the researchers in such settings, unsurprisingly, fall in line with the already dominant themes, which are already set by the funders. In short, there are definite institutional systems through which research agendas are set, circulated and realised.

Second is the unequal power distribution between the researchers of the developed and the developing/underdeveloped world. The involvement of researchers from developing countries in the stages of project formulation is generally low, and they mostly come in the later stage of data collection. Pratt (2019) noted that the participation of researchers in neglected regions in R&D in multi-country and coordinated research projects were more of that of data collectors. Research themes and objectives, in such cases, are likely to be set in accordance with the preferences and priorities of the countries and regions where the principal investigators and funding agencies are located. It is, hence, important to balance the distribution of power in global R&D with the adequate participation of researchers from developing countries and the representation of regional priorities.

Third is the complete absence of users in the entire process of R&D in health. The active engagement of communities, especially of the neglected and marginalised sections, is a key factor for inclusive and responsible innovation. Pratt (2019), drawing from literature on community participation in innovations, noted that 'being female, being poor, having little education, living with a disability and/or belonging to certain ethnic groups means community members are listened to less or not at all in health priority-setting' (p. 347). He further noted that inadequate representations of the needs of marginalised communities in research studies would lead to the production of knowledge that is not relevant for them. This has been found true for India as well. For instance, we found that the disease burden of people from poor regions, the elderly and children were not adequately represented in the pharmaceutical and biopharmaceutical R&D in India (see Chapter 3).

To sum up, India has adequate institutional arrangements in place to facilitate medical innovation. What is lacking is the prioritisation of innovation based on the diverse health and disease burden of the population. To begin with, India needs to adopt a responsible innovation framework in health, which involves responsiveness to diverse health needs, regulation along with facilitation, participation of researchers and engagement of community from neglected regions in all stages of innovation and promotion of fundamental research to take care of the present and future burden of diseases.

References

Abraham, J. (2010). 'Pharmaceuticalization of Society in Context: Theoretical, Empirical and Health Dimensions'. *Sociology* 44(4): 603–622.

Abrol, D. (2006). 'Conditions for the Achievement of Pharmaceutical Innovation for Sustainable Development: Lessons from India'. *World Review of Science, Technology and Sustainable Development* 3(6): 344–361.

———— (2013). 'Where Is India's Innovation Policy Headed?' *Social Scientist* 41(3/4): 65–80.

Abrol, D. and N. Singh (2016). 'Pharmaceutical Innovation and Contribution of In-House R&D of Domestic Firms after TRIPS in India'. Working Paper 189, Institute for Studies in Industrial Development, New Delhi.

Abrol, D., P. Prajapati and N. Singh (2011). 'Globalization of the Indian Pharmaceutical Industry: Implications for Innovation'. *International Journal of Institutions and Economies* 3(2): 327–365.

Acemoglu, D. and J. Linn (2004). 'Market Size in Innovation: Theory and Evidence from the Pharmaceutical Industry'. *The Quarterly Journal of Economics* 119(3): 1049–1090.

Advant, S. J. and J. Jacob (2014). 'The Rise of Biopharmaceutical Outsourcing to Indian CDMOs'. *BioProcess Int* 12(6). Retrieved from https://bioprocessintl.com/upstream-processing/upstream-contract-services/the-rise-of-biopharmaceutical-outsourcing-to-indian-cdmos/ accessed on 10 March 2019.

Ahmad, A., I. Patel, S. Sanyal, R. Balkrishnan and G. Mohanta (2014). 'Availability, Cost and Affordability of Antimalarial Medicines in India'. *International Journal of Pharmaceutical and Clinical Research* 6(1): 7–12.

Aitken, M. (2016). 'Understanding the Pharmaceutical Value Chain'. *Pharmaceuticals Policy and Law*. 18(1–4): 55–66.

Arora, P. (2005). 'Healthcare Biotechnology Firms in India: Evolution, Structure and Growth'. *Current Science* 89(3): 458–464.

Bach, P. B. and S. D. Pearson (2015). 'Payer and Policy Maker Steps to Support Value-based Pricing for Drugs'. *Jama* 314(23): 2503–2504.

Bagcchi, S. (2015). 'Thousands Die in Clinical Trials in India, but Compensation Is Rarely Paid'. *BMJ* 2015;351:h6149. Available at https://www.bmj.com/content/351/bmj.h6149, accessed on 19 March 2019.

Bagchi-Sen, S. and H. Lawton Smith (2008). 'Science, Institutions, and Markets: Developments in the Indian Biotechnology Sector'. *Regional Studies* 42(7): 961–975.

Bandameedi, R., S. Mohammed and H. Soma (2016). 'A Case Study on National List of Essential Medicines (NLEM) in India and WHO EML 2015 – Overview'. *Pharmaceut Reg Affairs* 5(1): 159.

Basu, A. and S. D. Sullivan (2017). 'Toward a Hedonic Value Framework in Healthcare'. *Value in Health* 20(2): 261–265.

Bate, R., R. Tren, L. Mooney, K. Hess, B. Mitra, B. Debroy and A. Attaran (2009). 'Pilot Study of Essential Drug Quality in Two Major Cities in India'. *PLoS One* 4(6): e6003.

Baum, F., L. Newman and K. Biedrzycki (2014). 'Vicious Cycles: Digital Technologies and Determinants of Health in Australia'. *Health Promotion International* 29(2): 349–360.

Bell, S. E. and A. E. Figert (2012). 'Medicalization and Pharmaceuticalization at the Intersections: Looking Backward, Sideways and Forward'. *Social Science and Medicine* 75(5): 775–783.

Berer, M. (2010). 'Cosmetic Surgery, Body Image and Sexuality'. *Reproductive Health Matters* 18(35): 4–10.

Bhardwaj, S., M. D. Gokhale and D. T. Mourya. (2017). 'Zika Virus: Current Concerns in India'. *The Indian Journal of Medical Research* 146(5): 572–575.

Bhargava, A. and S. P. Kalantri (2016). 'The Crisis in Access to Essential Medicines in India: Key Issues Which Call for Action'. Indian Journal of Medical Ethics 10(2): 80–95.

Bhaskarabhatla, A. and C. Chatterjee (2017). 'The Role of Physicians in Prescribing Irrational Fixed-dose Combination Medicines in India'. *Social Science and Medicine* 174(C): 179–187.

Bhatia, R., A. P. Dash and T. Sunyoto (2013). 'Changing Epidemiology of Dengue in South-East Asia'. *WHO South-East Asia Journal of Public Health* 2(1): 23.

Birch, K. and D. Tyfield (2013). 'Theorizing the Bioeconomy: Biovalue, Biocapital, Bioeconomics or ... What'? *Science, Technology, and Human Values* 38(3): 299–327.

Bishnu B., S. Bhaduri, A. M. Kumar, E. S. Click, V. K. Chadha, S. Satyanarayana, et al. (2013). 'What Are the Reasons for Poor Uptake of HIV Testing Among Patients with TB in an Eastern India District'? *PLoS One* 8(3): e55229.

Bishwajit, G., S. Ide and S. Ghosh (2014). 'Social Determinants of Infectious Diseases in South Asia'. *International Scholarly Research Notices*.

Bonu, S., I. Bhushan, M. Rani and I. Anderson (2009). 'Incidence and Correlates of "Catastrophic" Maternal Health Care Expenditure in India'. *Health Policy and Planning* 24(6): 445–456.

Brinda, E. M., P. Kowal, J. Attermann and U. Enemark (2015). 'Health Service Use, Out-of-Pocket Payments and Catastrophic Health Expenditure among Older People in India: The WHO Study on Global AGEing and Adult Health (SAGE)'. *J Epidemiol Community Health* 69(5): 489–494.

Cecilia, D. (2014). 'Current Status of Dengue and Chikungunya in India'. *WHO South-East Asia Journal of Public Health* 3(1): 22.

Chakraborty, C. and G. Agoramoorthy. (2010). 'A Special Report on India's Biotech Scenario: Advancement in Biopharmaceutical and Healthcare Sectors'. *Biotechnology Advances* 28(1): 1–6.

Chatterjee, P. (2018). 'Nipah Virus Outbreak in India'. *The Lancet* 391(10136): 2200.

Chaturvedi, S. (2007). 'Exploring Interlinkages between National and Sectoral Innovation Systems for Rapid Technological Catch-up: Case of Indian Biopharmaceutical Industry'. *Technology Analysis and Strategic Management* 19(5): 643–657.

Chaturvedi, S. and K. R. Srinivas (2014). 'Survey on Biotechnology Capacity in Asia-Pacific: Opportunities for National Initiatives and Regional Cooperation'. Research and Information System for Developing Countries (RIS), New Delhi. Available at https://www.ris.org.in/survey-report-biotechnology-capacity-asia-pacific-opportunities-national-initiatives-and-regional, accessed on 11 March 2019.

Chaudhuri, S. (2010). 'R&D for Development of New Drugs for Neglected Diseases in India'. *International Journal of Technology and Globalisation* 5(1–2): 61–75.

Chaudhuri, S., P. K. Goldberg and P. Gia (2006). 'Estimating the Effects of Global Patent Protection in Pharmaceuticals: A Case Study of Quinolones in India'. *American Economic Review* 96(5): 1477–1514.

Chien, C. V. (2007). 'HIV/AIDS Drugs for Sub-Saharan Africa: How Do Brand and Generic Supply Compare?' *PLoS One*, 2(3): e278. http://doi.org/10.1371/journal.pone.0000278.

Chowdhury, P. R. (2011). *Outsourcing Biopharma R&D to India*. Cambridge UK: Elsevier.

CII (n.d). *Medical Technology Shaping Healthcare for All in India*. Available at https://www.gita.org.in/Attachments/Reports/Medical%20Technology%20%20Shaping%20Healthcare%20For%20All%20In%20India.pdf, accessed on 17 September 2018.

Clarke, A. E., J. Shim, S. Shostak and A. Nelson (2009). 'Biomedicalising Genetic Health, Diseases and Identities'. In Paul Atkinson, Peter Glasner and Margaret Lock (eds), *Handbook of Genetics and Society: Mapping the New Genomic Era*. London and New York: Routledge, 21–40.

Conrad, P. (2005). 'The Shifting Engines of Medicalization'. *Journal of Health and Social Behaviour* 46(1): 3–14.

Cooper, M. E. (2011). *Life as Surplus: Biotechnology and Capitalism in the Neoliberal Era*. Seattle: University of Washington Press.

Cutler, D. M. and M. McClellan (2001). 'Is Technological Change in Medicine Worth It?' *Health Affairs* 20(5): 11–29.

Dandona, L., R. Dandona, A. Kumar, K. Cowling, P. Titus, V. M. Katoch and S. Swaminathan (2017). 'Mapping Health Research Funding in India'. *The National Medical Journal of India* 30(6): 309–316.

Dandona, L., R. Dandona, G. A. Kumar, et al. (2017). 'Nations within a Nation: Variations in Epidemiological Transition across the States of India, 1990–2016 in the Global Burden of Disease Study'. *The Lancet* 390(10111): 2437–2460.

Dang, A., N. Likhar and U. Alok (2016). 'Importance of Economic Evaluation in Health Care: An Indian Perspective'. *Value in Health Regional Issues* 9: 78–83.

Danzon, P. M. (2006). 'Economics of the Pharmaceutical Industry'. *NBER Reporter*, 14–16.

Danzon, P. M., A. W. Mulcahy and A. K. Towse (2015). 'Pharmaceutical Pricing in Emerging Markets: Effects of Income, Competition, and Procurement'. *Health Economics* 24(2): 238–252.

Danzon, P., A. Towse and J. Mestre-Ferrandiz (2015). 'Value-based Differential Pricing: efficient Prices for Drugs in a Global Context'. *Health Economics* 24(3): 294–301.

Dar, L., S. Broor, S. Sengupta, I. Xess and P. Seth (1999). 'The First Major Outbreak of Dengue Hemorrhagic Fever in Delhi, India'. *Emerging Infectious Diseases* 5(4): 589.

Devadasan, N., B. Criel, W. Van Damme, K. Ranson and P. Van der Stuyft (2007). 'Indian Community Health Insurance Schemes Provide Partial Protection against Catastrophic Health Expenditure'. *BMC Health Services Research* 7(1): 43–54.

Dhar, B. and K. M. Gopakumar (2006). 'Post-2005 TRIPS Scenario in Patent Protection in the Pharmaceutical sector: The Case of the Generic Pharmaceutical Industry in India'. Online publication, UNCTAD-ICTSD Regional Research Paper, Geneva. Available at https://unctad.org/en/PublicationsLibrary/ictsd-idrc2006d2_en.pdf, accessed on 24 March 2019.

——— (2011). *Effect of Product Patents on Indian Pharmaceutical Industry*. New Delhi: Center for WTO Studies, Indian Institute of Foreign Trade.

Dhar, B. and S. Saha (2014). *An Assessment of India's Innovation Policies*. New Delhi: Research and Information System for Developing Countries.

Differding, E. (2017). 'The Drug Discovery and Development Industry in India: Two Decades of Proprietary Small-Molecule R&D'. *ChemMedChem* 12(11): 786–818.

Dikid, T., S. K. Jain, A. Sharma, A. Kumar and J. P. Narain (2013). 'Emerging & Re-emerging Infections in India: An Overview'. *The Indian Journal of Medical Research* 138(1): 19–31.

DSIR and IIFT (2005). *Study on Foreign R & D Centres in India*. New Delhi: DSIR-IIFT.

Dubois, P. O. Mouzon, F. Scott-Morton and P. Seabright (2015). 'Market Size and Pharmaceutical Innovation'. *The RAND Journal of Economics* 46(4): 844–871.

Edquist, C. and B. Johnson (1997). Institutions and Organisations in Systems of Innovation'. In C. Edquist (ed.), *Systems of Innovation: Technology, Institutions and Organisation*. London: Pinter, 41–63.

Farmer, P. (2001). 'The Major Infectious Diseases in the World: To Treat or Not to Treat?' *The New England Journal of Medicine* 345(3): 208–210.

FDA (2017). 'Global Participation in Clinical Trials Report, 2015–16'. Available at https://www.fda.gov/downloads/Drugs/InformationOnDrugs/UCM570195.pdf, accessed on 15 March 2019.

FICCI (2005). 'Comprehensiveness of the Indian Pharmaceutical Industry in the New Product Patent Regime'. FICCI Report for National Manufacturing, Competitiveness Council, New Delhi.

Finkelstein, A. (2004). 'Static and Dynamic Effects of Health Policy: Evidence from the Vaccine Industry'. *The Quarterly Journal of Economics* 119(2): 527–564.

Fischer, W. A., M. Gong, S. Bhagwanjee and J. Sevransky (2014). 'Global Burden of Influenza: Contributions from Resource Limited and Low-Income Settings'. *Global Heart* 9(3): 325–336.

Forsythe, S. (2009). 'Social Stigma and the Medicalisation of Infertility'. *Journal of the Manitoba Anthropology Students' Association* 28: 22–36.

Frew, S. E., H. E. Kettler and P. A. Singer (2008). 'The Indian and Chinese Health Biotechnology Industries: Potential Champions of Global Health? *Health Affairs* 27(4): 1029–1041.

Frost and Sullivan (2007). 'Strategic Analysis of Contract Research and Manufacturing Services Market in India'. Available at http://www.frost.com/sublib/display-report.do?id=P5D0-01-00-00-00, accessed on 12 March 2016.

Fuchs, V. R. and H. C. Sox Jr. (2001). 'Physicians' Views of the Relative Importance of Thirty Medical Innovations'. *Health Affairs* 20(5): 30–42.

Gadre, Arun and Nilangi Sardeshpande (2017). 'Cut Practice in Private Healthcare, Commentary'. *Economic and Political Weekly* 52(48): 12–14.

Garthwaite, C. (2018). 'The Economics of Drug Development: Pricing and Innovation in a Changing Market'. NBER Reporter Number 3. Available at https://www.nber.org/reporter/2018number3/garthwaite.html, accessed on 12 February 2019.

Gelijns, A. and N. Rosenberg, N. (1994). 'The Dynamics of Technological Change in Medicine'. Health Affairs 13(3): 28–46.

George, S. (2016). 'Health for Not All: Mapping the Discriminated and Detached Terrains of Health Services in Rural India'. Journal of Health Systems 1(1): 20–26.

George, S., A. B. Chandran, P. O. Nadh and K. H. Apurva (2018). 'Is Drug Development in India Responsive to the Disease Burden?' *Economic and Political Weekly* 53(30): 51–57.

George, S. and A. Balachandran (2019). 'The Economic Burden of Anticancer Medicines for Households in India: Evidence from Data on Expenditure on Medicine and Drug Prices'. Available at https://papers.ssrn.com/sol3/papers.cfm?abstract_id=3449371, accessed on 14 August 2019.

Ghosh, S. (2011). 'Catastrophic Payments and Impoverishment due to Out-of-pocket Health Spending'. *Economic and Political Weekly* 46(47): 63–70.

Goldar, B. (2013). 'R&D Intensity and Exports: A Study of Indian Pharmaceutical Firms'. *Innovation and Development* 3(2): 151–167.

Goldstein, D. A., J. Clark, Y. Tu, J. Zhang et al. (2017). 'A Global Comparison of the Cost of Patented Cancer Drugs in Relation to Global Differences in Wealth'. *Oncotarget* 8(42): 71548.

Gonçalves, H., A. D. Souza, P. A. Tavares, S. H. Cruz and D. P. Béhague (2011). 'Contraceptive Medicalisation, Fear of Infertility and Teenage Pregnancy in Brazil'. *Culture, Health & Sexuality* 13(2): 201–215.

Grace, C. (2004). 'The Effect of Changing Intellectual Property on Pharmaceutical Industry Prospects in India and China'. DFID Health Systems Resource Centre, 1–68. Available at http://www.isc.hbs.edu/resources/courses/moc-course-at-harvard/Documents/pdf/student-projects/India_Biopharmaceutical_Cluster_2009.pdf, accessed on 19 August 2018.

Gupta, S. S., K. Bharati, D. Sur, A. Khera, N. K. Ganguly and G. B. Nair (2016). 'Why Is the Oral Cholera Vaccine Not Considered an Option for Prevention of Cholera in India? Analysis of Possible Reasons'. *The Indian Journal of Medical Research* 143(5): 545.

Hu, H. and C. C. Chung (2015). 'Biopharmaceutical Innovation System in China: System Evolution and Policy Transitions (Pre-1990s–2010s)'. *International Journal of Health Policy and Management* 4(12): 823.

ICMR, PHFI and IHME (2017). *India: Health of the Nation's States the India State-Level Disease Burden Initiative.* New Delhi: Indian Council of Medical Research, Public Health Foundation of India, and Institute for Health Metrics and Evaluation.

ICRA (2011). 'CRAMS India: Overlook and Outlook'. Available at http://www.icra.in/Files/Articles/CRAMS%20Note,%20Overview%20and%20Outlook.pdf, accessed on 12 March 2016.

IFPMA (2017). 'The Pharmaceutical Industry and Global Health: Facts and Figures 2017'. Available at www.ifpma.org/wp-content/uploads/2017/02/IFPMA-Facts-And-Figures-2017.pdf, accessed on 19 August 2018.

Iyer, A., P. Koudal, H. Saranga and S. Seshadri (2009). 'Indian Manufacturing: Strategic and Operational Decisions and Business Performance'. In J. M. Swaminathan (ed.), *Indian Economic Superpower: Fiction or Future?* Singapore: World Scientific, 79–100.

Jarosławski, S. and G. Saberwal (2013). 'Case Studies of Innovative Medical Device Companies from India: Barriers and Enablers to Development'. *BMC Health Services Research* 13(1): 199–207.

Jasanoff, S. (2004). 'The Idiom of Co-operation'. In Sheila Jasanoff (ed.), *States of Knowledge: The Co-Production of Science and Social Order*. London: Routledge, 1–12.

Jayadev, A. and J. Stiglitz (2008). 'Two Ideas to Increase Innovation and Reduce Pharmaceutical Costs and Prices'. *Health Affairs*, 28(1): w165–w168.

John, T. J., L. Dandona, V. P. Sharma and M. Kakkar (2011). 'Continuing Challenge of Infectious Diseases in India'. *The Lancet* 377(9761): 252–269.

Johnson, E. M. (2014). 'Physician-induced Demand'. *Encyclopedia of Health Economics* 3(77): 77–83.

Joseph K. R. (2016). *Pharmaceutical Industry and Public Policy in Post-reform India*. New Delhi: Routledge.

——— (2011). 'The R&D Scenario in Indian Pharmaceutical Industry'. RIS Discussion Paper No. 176, Research and Information System for Developing Countries, New Delhi.

——— (2009). *India's Trade in Drugs and Pharmaceuticals: Emerging Trends, Opportunities and Challenges*. New Delhi: Research and Information System for Developing Countries.

——— (2011). *The R&D Scenario in Indian Pharmaceutical Industry*. New Delhi: Research and Information System for Developing Countries.

——— (2012). 'Policy Reforms in the Indian Pharmaceutical Sector since 1994: Impact on Exports and Imports'. Available at https://papers.ssrn.com/sol3/papers.cfm?abstract_id=2049286, accessed on 14 May 2016.

Joseph, K. R., B. Dhar and A. A. Singh (2019). 'FDI in R&D in India: An Analysis of Recent Trends'. ISID Working Paper, No. 209. Available at http://isid.org.in/wp-content/uploads/2019/08/WP209.pdf, accessed on 16 December 2019.

Kaltenboeck, A. and P. B. Bach (2018). 'Value-based Pricing for Drugs: Theme and Variations'. *Jama* 319(21): 2165–2166.

Kethineni, V. (1991). 'Political Economy of State Intervention in Health Care'. *Economic and Political Weekly* 26(42): 2427–2433.

Komesaroff, P. A. (2008). *Experiments in Love and Death: Medicine, Postmodernism, Microethics and the Body*. Austin, TX: River Grove Books.

Konde, V. (2009). 'Biotechnology Business Models: An Indian Perspective'. *Journal of Commercial Biotechnology* 15(3): 215–226.

Kotwani A. (2009), 'Availability, Price and Affordability of Asthma Medicines in Five Indian States. *International Journal of Tuberculosis and Lung Disease* 13(5): 574–579.

KPMG (2016a). 'Value Based Pricing in Pharmaceuticals: Hype or Hope?' Available at https://assets.kpmg/content/dam/kpmg/xx/pdf/2016/10/value-based-pricing-in-pharmaceuticals.pdf, accessed on 25 February 2019.

——— (2016b). 'Indian Healthcare Start-ups'. Available at https://assets.kpmg.com/content/dam/kpmg/in/pdf/2016/09/FICCI-   Heal.pdf, accessed on 28 January 2018.

Krishnamoorthy, K., K. T. Harichandrakumar, A. K. Kumari and L. K. Das (2009). 'Burden of Chikungunya in India: Estimates of Disability Adjusted Life Years (DALY) Lost in 2006 Epidemic'. *Journal of Vector Borne Diseases* 46(1): 26–36.

Kumar A., N. Valecha, T. Jain and A. P. Dash (2007). 'Burden of Malaria in India: Retrospective and Prospective View'. *American Journal of Tropical Medicine and Hygiene* 77(6): 69–78.

Laal, M. (2012). 'Innovation and Medicine'. *Procedia Technology* 1: 469–473.

Lang, A. and A. Mertes (2011). 'E-health Policy and Deployment Activities in Europe'. *Telemedicine and e-Health* 17(4): 262–268.

Langer, E. (2007). *Advances in Biopharmaceuticals Technology in India*. Rockville, MD: Bioplan Associates.

Lehoux, P., F. A. Miller, G. Daudelin and D. R. Urbach (2016a). 'How Venture Capitalists Decide Which New Medical Technologies Come to Exist'. *Science and Public Policy* 43(3): 375–385.

Lehoux, P., F. A. Miller and G. Daudelin (2016b). 'How Does Venture Capital Operate in Medical Innovation? *BMJ Innovations* 2(3): 111–117.

Levins, R. and R. C. Lewontin (1985). *The Dialectical Biologist*. Cambridge, MA: Harvard University Press.

Lohray, B. B. (2003). 'Medical Biotechnology in India'. In T. K. Ghosh et al. (eds), *Biotechnology in India II* . Berlin, Heidelberg: Springer, 215–281.

Loitongbam, B. S. (2016). 'Impact of TRIPS and RTAs on the Indian Pharmaceutical Product Exports'. Available at https://mpra.ub.uni-muenchen.de/75764/1/MPRA_paper_75764.pdf, accessed on 15 May 2018.

Lu, Y., P. Hernandez, D. Abegunde and T. Edejer (2011), *The World Medicines Situation 2011: Medicine Expenditures*. Geneva: World Health Organization.

MacLean, Sandra J. and D. R. MacLean (2009). 'The Political Economy of Global Health Research'. In S. J. MacLean, S. Brown and P. Fourie (eds), *Health for Some*. London: Palgrave Macmillan UK, 165–182.

Mathew, P. (2015). 'Generic Drugs: Review and Experiences from South India'. *Journal of Family Medicine and Primary Care* 4(3): 319–323.

Mathews, E. B., B. Sunil, N. Prejit, C. Sunanda et al. (2018). 'Occurrence and Antibiotic Susceptibility Testing of Vibrio cholerae from District Wayanad, Kerala, India'. *Proceedings of the National Academy of Sciences, India Section B: Biological Sciences*, 1–6.

Mavalankar, D., P. Shastri and P. Raman (2007). 'Chikungunya Epidemic in India: A Major Public-health Disaster'. *The Lancet Infectious Diseases* 7(5): 306–307.

Mavalankar, D., P. Shastri, T. Bandyopadhyay, J. Parmar and K. V. Ramani (2008). 'Increased Mortality Rate Associated with Chikungunya Epidemic, Ahmedabad, India'. *Emerging Infectious Diseases* 14(3): 412.

Mazumdar, S. (2014). 'The Murky Waters of Medical Practice in India: Ethics, Economics and Politics of Healthcare'. *Economic and Political Weekly* 50(29): 40–45.

McCreath, S. B. and R. Delgoda (2017). *Pharmacognosy: Fundamentals, Applications and Strategies*. London: Academic Press.

McGillivray, J. (2017). '"Pyrates" of the Lyceum: Big Pharma, Patents, and Academic Freedom in Neoliberal Times'. Available at https://yorkspace.library.yorku.ca/xmlui/bitstream/handle/10315/33607/McGillivray_James_C_2017_PhD.pdf?sequence=2&isAllowed=y, accessed date 26 March 2019.

McGuire, A., M. Raikou and P. Kanavos (2008). 'Pricing Pharmaceuticals: Value Based Pricing in What Sense'. *Eurohealth* 14(2): 3–5.

McGuire, T. and M. Pauly (1991). 'Physician Response to Fee Changes with Multiple Payers'. *Journal of Health Economics* 10(4): 385–410.

McGuire, T. G. (2000). 'Physician Agency'. In A. J. Culyer and J. P. Newhouse (eds), *Handbook of Health Economics*. Amsterdam: North-Holland, 461–536.

McMillan, G. S., F. Narin and D. L. Deeds (2000). 'An Analysis of the Critical Role of Public Science in Innovation: The Case of Biotechnology'. *Research Policy* 29(1): 1–8.

Milne, C. P. and K. I. Kaitin (2019). 'Are Regulation and Innovation Priorities Serving Public Health Needs?' *Frontiers in Pharmacology* 10: 144. doi:10.3389/fphar.2019.00144.

Mondal, S. S. and V. Pingali (2017). 'Competition and Intellectual Property Policies in the Indian Pharmaceutical Sector'. *Vikalpa* 42(2): 61–79.

Motkuri, V. and R. N. Mishra (2018). 'Pharmaceuticals Industry and Regulation in India: A Note'. Working Paper No.250, Gujarat Institute of Development Studies, Ahmedabad.

Murhekar, M. and S. Bitragunta (2011). 'Persistence of Diphtheria in India'. *Indian Journal of Community Medicine* 36(2): 164.

Mutheneni, S. R., A. P. Morse, C. Caminade and S. M. Upadhyayula (2017). 'Dengue Burden in India: Recent Trends and Importance of Climatic Parameters'. *Emerging Microbes & Infections* 6(1): 1–10.

Nadh, P. O. (2018). 'Political Economy of Biomedical Technology'. *Economic and Political Weekly* 53(35): 37–43.

Naresh Kumar, C. V. M. and D. V. R. Sai Gopal (2010). 'Reemergence of Chikungunya Virus in Indian Subcontinent'. *Indian Journal of Virology* 21(1): 8–17.

Narula, S. (2015). 'Current Drug Pricing Status in India. *Pharmacoeconomics* 1(1): e101. doi: 10.4172/2472-1042.1000e101. Available at https://www.omicsonline.org/open-access/current-drug-pricing-status-in-india-pe-1000e101.php?aid=62871, accessed on 15 December 2017.

Neumann, P. J., J. D. Chambers, F. Simon and L. M. Meckley (2011). 'Risk-sharing Arrangements That Link Payment for Drugs to Health Outcomes Are Proving Hard to Implement'. *Health Affairs* 30(12): 2329–2337.

Newhouse, J. P. (1992). 'Medical Care Costs: How Much Welfare Loss'? *Journal of Economic Perspectives* 6(3): 3–21.

Otto, R., A. Santagostino and U. Schrader (2014). *Rapid Growth in Biopharma: Challenges and Opportunities*. McKinsey & Company. Available at https://www.mckinsey.com/industries/pharmaceuticals-and-medical-products/our-insights/rapid-growth-in-biopharma#, accessed on 16 December 2017.

Paliwal, A. (2015). 'Drug Trials in India Killed 2,031 Persons'. *Down To Earth*, 4 July. Available at https://www.downtoearth.org.in/news/drug-trials-in-india-killed-2031-persons-38587, accessed on 19 March 2019.

Pandey, A., G. B. Ploubidis, L. Clarke L. and Dandona (2018). 'Trends in Catastrophic Health Expenditure in India: 1993 to 2014'. *Bulletin of the World Health Organization* 96(1): 18–28.

Parande, M. V., A. M. Parande, S. L. Lakkannavar, S. D. Kholkute and S. Roy (2014). 'Diphtheria Outbreak in Rural North Karnataka, India'. *JMM Case Reports* 1(3): e003558.

Parida, M., P. K. Dash and N. K. Tripathi (2006). 'Japanese Encephalitis Outbreak, India, 2005'. *Emerging Infectious Diseases* 12(9): 1427.

Patel, A., V. Thawani and K. Gharpure (2005). *Medicine Pricing, Availability and Affordability: Report of Four Regions, Maharashtra, India*. World Health Organization and Health Action International. Available at http://apps.who.int/medicinedocs/documents/s18025en/s18025en.pdf, accessed on 10 January 2018.

Paul, K. and J. Singh (2017). 'Emerging Trends and Patterns of Self-reported Morbidity in India: Evidence from Three Rounds of National Sample Survey'. *Journal of Health, Population and Nutrition* 36(1): 32–45.

Pauly, M. V. (2017). 'The Questionable Economic Case for Value-Based Drug Pricing in Market Health Systems'. *Value in Health* 20(2): 278–282.

Perez, S. L., R. L. Kravitz, R. A. Bell, M. S. Chan and D. A. Paterniti (2016). 'Characterizing Internet Health Information Seeking Strategies by Socioeconomic Status: A Mixed Methods Approach'. *BMC Medical Informatics and Decision Making* 16(1): 107.

Phadke, A., S. Srinivasan and T. Srikrishna (2013). 'Drug Price Control Order 2013. As Good as a Leaky Bucket'. *Economic and Political Weekly* (29 June): 130.

Phillips, L. (2013). 'Infectious Disease: TB's Revenge'. *Nature* 493(7430): 14–16.

Porter, G. and N. Grills (2016). 'Medication Misuse in India: a Major Public Health Issue in India'. *Journal of Public Health* 38(2): e150–e157.

Pratt, B. (2019). 'Towards Inclusive Priority-setting for Global Health Research Projects: Recommendations for Sharing Power with Communities'. *Health Policy and Planning* 34(5): 346–357.

Purdy, L. (2006). 'Women's Reproductive Autonomy: Medicalisation and Beyond'. *Journal of Medical Ethics*, 32(5): 287–291.

Rajan, K. S. (2006). *Biocapital: The Constitution of Postgenomic Life*. Durham and London: Duke University Press.

———— (2017). *Pharmocracy: Value, Politics, and Knowledge in Global Biomedicine*. Durham and London: Duke University Press.

Ramamurthy, T. and N. C. Sharma (2014). 'Cholera Outbreaks in India'. In G. Nair and Y. Takeda Y (eds), *Cholera Outbreaks: Current Topics in Microbiology and Immunology*, 379. Berlin, Heidelberg: Springer, 49–85.

Ramani, S. V. and A. Maria (2005). 'TRIPS: Its Possible Impact on Biotech Segment of the Indian Pharmaceutical Industry'. *Economic and Political Weekly* 40(7): 675–683.

Ravi, A. (2017). 'Over 24,000 Clinical Trial Deaths and SAEs in India in Ten Years'. *Sunday Guardian Live*, 5 November. Available at https://www.sundayguardianlive.com/news/11550-over-24000-clinical-trial-deaths-and-saes-india-ten-years, accessed on 19 March 2019.

Rayner, J. A., P. Pyett and J. Astbury (2010). 'The Medicalisation of "Tall" Girls: A Discourse Analysis of Medical Literature on the Use of Synthetic Oestrogen to Reduce Female Height'. *Social Science & Medicine* 71(6): 1076–1083.

Rezaie, R., A. M. McGahan, S. E. Frew, A. S. Daar and P. A. Singer (2012). 'Emergence of Biopharmaceutical Innovators in China, India, Brazil, and South Africa as Global Competitors and Collaborators'. *Health Research Policy and Systems* 10(1): 1.

Rezaie, R. and P. A. Singer (2010). 'Global Health or Global Wealth'? *Nature Biotechnology* 28(9): 907–909.

Rose, N. (2007). *The Politics of Life Itself: Biomedicine, Power, and Subjectivity in the Twenty-first Century*. Princeton and Oxford: Princeton University Press.

Rottingen, J. A., S. Regmi, M. Eide, A. J. Young et al. (2013). 'Mapping of Available Health Research and Development Data: What's There, What's Missing, and What Role Is There for a Global Observatory?' *The Lancet* 382(9900): 1286–1307.

Rowden, R. (2013). *The Deadly Ideas of Neoliberalism: How the IMF Has Undermined Public Health and the Fight against AIDS*. London: Zed Books Ltd.

Sangal, L., S. Joshi, S. Anandan, V. Balaji, J. Johnson, A. Satapathy, P. Haldar, et al. (2017). 'Resurgence of Diphtheria in North Kerala, India, 2016: Laboratory Supported Case-Based Surveillance Outcomes', *Frontiers in Public Health* 5(218): 1–8. Available at https://www.ncbi.nlm.nih.gov/pmc/articles/PMC5582196/, accessed on 30 November 2017.

Satyanarayana, K. and S. Srivastava (2007). 'Poverty, Health & Intellectual Property Rights with Special Reference to India'. *Indian Journal of Medical Research* 126(4): 390.

Schuhmacher, A., O. Gassmann and M. Hinder (2016). 'Changing R&D Models in Research-Based Pharmaceutical Companies'. *Journal of Translational Medicine* 14(1): 105. http://doi.org/10.1186/s12967-016-0838-4.

Selvaraj, S. (2007). *How Effective Is India's Drug Price Control Regime?* Boston, MA: Harvard School of Public Health. Available at https://cdn1.sph.harvard.edu/wp-content/uploads/sites/114/2012/10/RP256.pdf, accessed in November 2016.

Selvaraj, S. and A. K. Karan (2012). 'Why Publicly-financed Health Insurance Schemes Are Ineffective in Providing Financial Risk Protection?' *Economic and Political Weekly* 47(11): 60–68.

Selvaraj, S., H. Hasan, M. Chokshi, A. Sengupta, A. Guha, M. Shiva, S. Srinivasan, A. Phadke, K. M. Gopakumar, M. R. Santhosh and L. Menghaney (2012). 'Pharmaceutical Pricing Policy: A Critique'. *Economic and Political Weekly* 47(4): 20–23.

Sethi, S., N. Sharma, N. Kakkar, J. Taneja, S. S. Chatterjee, S. S. Banga and M. Sharma (2010). 'Increasing Trends of Leptospirosis in Northern India: A Clinico-Epidemiological Study'. *Plos Neglected Tropical Diseases* 4(1): e579. Available at http://journals.plos.org/plosntds/article?id=10.1371/journal.pntd.0000579, accessed on 30 November 2017.

Shah, J. Y., A. Phadtare, D. Rajgor, M. Vaghasia, S. Pradhan, H. Zelko and R. Pietrobon (2010). 'What Leads Indians to Participate in Clinical Trials? A Meta-Analysis of Qualitative Studies'. *PLoS One* 5(5): e10730.

Sharma, S. K. and A. Mohan (2004). 'Multidrug-resistant Tuberculosis'. *Indian Journal of Medical Research* 120(4): 354–376.

Shenoy, P. and A. Harugeri (2015). 'Elderly Patients' Participation in Clinical Trials'. *Perspectives in Clinical Research* 6(4): 184–189.

Shostak, S., P. Conrad and A. V. Horwitz (2008). 'Sequencing and Its Consequences: Path Dependence and the Relationships between Genetics and Medicalization'. *American Journal of Sociology* 114(S1): S287–S316.

Silva, H. P., P. Lehoux, F. A. Miller and J. L. Denis (2018). 'Introducing Responsible Innovation in Health: A Policy-Oriented Framework'. *Health Research Policy and Systems* 16(1): 90.

Singer, M. (1992). 'Biomedicine and the Political Economy of Science'. *Medical Anthropology Quarterly* 6(4): 400–404.

Singh, A. and S. Singh (2005). 'The Connection between Academia and Industry'. *Mens Sana Monographs* 3(1):5–35.http://doi.org/10.4103/0973-1229.27876.

Slade, E. P. and G. F. Anderson (2001). 'The Relationship between Per Capita Income and Diffusion of Medical Technologies'. *Health Policy* 58(1): 1–14.

Sriram, M. (2018). 'Health-tech Startup Funding Hits All-time High of $510 Million in 2018'. *Live Mint*, 12 November. Available at https://www.livemint.com/Companies/euHgMPBTiM6GxrTZm9Ly7K/Health-tech-startup-funding-hits-alltime-high-of-510-milli.html, accessed on 10 March 2019.

Stanley, E., P. Keckley and G. Snyder (2012). *Value-Based Pricing for Pharmaceuticals: Implications of the Shift from Volume to Value*. New York: Deloitte Center for Health Solutions.

Stevens, T. and S. Newman (2019). *Biotech Juggernaut: Hope, Hype, and Hidden Agendas of Entrepreneurial Bioscience*. London: Routledge.

Strasser, B. J. (2014). *Biomedicine: Meanings, Assumptions, and Possible Futures*. Geneva: The Swiss Science and Innovation Council. Available at https://www.swir.ch/images/stories/pdf/en/SWIR_1_2014_Biomedicine.pdf, accessed on 12 January 2018.

Swain, S., A. Dey, C. N. Patra and M. E. Bhanoji Rao (2014). 'Pharma Regulations for Generic Drug Products in India and US: Case Studies and Future Prospective'. *Pharmaceutical Regulatory Affairs* 3(2): 119–125.

Thomas, D. and C. Wessel (2015). *Venture Funding of Therapeutic Innovation: A Comprehensive Look at the Decade of Venture Funding of Drug R&D.* Washington DC: Biotechnology Industry Organization (BIO).

Tiwari, R., R. Trika, M. Khokhar, M. Bhardwaj and A. Naosekpam (2017). *Industry–Acadmia R&D Ecosystem in India.* Chandigarh: Publication Bureau, Panjab University. Available at http://cpr.puchd.ac.in/wp-content/uploads/2017/05/Industry-Academia-RD-Ecosystem-in-India.pdf, accessed on 10 May 2018.

Torres, J. M. (2014). 'Medicalizing to Demedicalize: Lactation Consultants and the (De)Medicalization of Breastfeeding'. *Social Science & Medicine* 100: 159–166.

Tosh, C., H. V. Murugkar, S. Nagarajan et al. (2007). 'Outbreak of Avian Influenza Virus H5N1 in India'. *The Veterinary Record* 161(8): 279.

Trinh Q. M., H. L. Nguyen, V. N. Nguyen, T. V. A. Nguyen, V. Sintchenko and B. J. Marais (2015). 'Tuberculosis and HIV Co-infection: Focus on the Asia-Pacific Region'. *International Journal of Infectious Diseases* 32: 170–178.

Tripathi, N., F. Kerketta, P. Chatterjee and V. R. Raman (2016). 'Availability and Access to Essential Medicines in Public Health Facilities in Chhattisgarh, India'. *BMJ Global Health* 1(1): A33.

Trouiller, P., P. Olliaro, E. Torreele, J. Orbinski, R. Laing and N. Ford (2002). 'Drug Development for Neglected Diseases: A Deficient Market and a Public-health Policy Failure'. *The Lancet* 359(9324): 2188–2194.

Viergever, R. F. (2013). 'The Mismatch between the Health Research and Development (R&D) That Is Needed and the R&D That Is Undertaken: An Overview of the Problem, the Causes, and Solutions'. *Global Health Action* 6(1): 22450.

Waldby, C. (2002). 'Stem Cells, Tissue Cultures and the Production of Biovalue'. *Health* 6(3): 305–323.

Wang, H. and G. Liang (2015). 'Epidemiology of Japanese Encephalitis: Past, Present, and Future Prospects'. *Therapeutics and Clinical Risk Management* 11: 435–448. https://doi.org/10.2147/TCRM.S51168.

Watts, K. (2019). 'Clinical Trials: The Human Cost'. *Health Issues India*, 14 February. Available at https://www.healthissuesindia.com/2019/02/14/clinical-trials-human-cost/, accessed on 19 March 2019.

Weiss, D., H. T. Rydland E. Øversveen, M. R. Jensen, S. Solhaug and S. Krokstad (2018). 'Innovative Technologies and Social Inequalities in Health: A Scoping Review of the Literature'. *PloS One* 13(4): e0195447.

West, D. M., J. Villasenor and J. Schneider (2017). 'Private Sector Investment in Global Health R&D: Spending Levels, Barriers, and Opportunities'. Available at https://www.brookings.edu/wp-content/uploads/2017/09/private-sector-investment-in-global-health-rd_final.pdf, accessed on 28 January 2018.

Williams, S. J., P. Martin and J. Gabe (2011). 'The Pharmaceuticalisation of Society? A Framework for Analysis'. *Sociology of Health & Illness* 33(5): 710–725.

World Health Organization (WHO). (2010). *Medical Devices: Managing The Mismatch: An Outcome of the Priority Medical Devices Project.* Geneva: World Health Organization.

——— (2018). *Zika Virus Infection: India.* Available at https://www.who.int/emergencies/diseases/zika/india-november-2018/en/, accessed on 26 February 2019.

Yadav, S. and P. Arokiasamy (2014). 'Understanding Epidemiological Transition in India'. *Global Health Action* 7(1): 23248–23262.

Index